Beatles
For Sale

BEATLES FOR SALE

David Rowley

MAINSTREAM PUBLISHING

EDINBURGH AND LONDON

First published in Great Britain in 2002 by
MAINSTREAM PUBLISHING COMPANY (EDINBURGH) LTD
7 Albany Street
Edinburgh EH1 3UG

ISBN 1 84018 567 8

A catalogue record for this book is available from the British Library

Typeset in Stone
Printed and bound in Great Britain by
MacKays of Chatham

Contents

Acknowledgements

Thanks to Kimie for believing and Maya for inspiration. Thanks to my mother for listening and typing out my early handwritten drafts before I even owned a typewriter. Thanks to Janick for faith early on when no one else had any. Thanks to Una too for sensible insider advice on the publishing world. Thanks to Jonathan who did such a good job in setting up my www.Sgt.peppers.co.uk website. Last but most of all, thanks to the Beatles for the music.

Notes to the text

The release dates of records are for the UK. Where a US release date is shown this indicates that the record was released in the USA days before the UK release date.

For songwriting credits (Lennon) or (McCartney) indicates that as far as is known John or Paul were the sole writers of a song. (Lennon/McCartney) indicates that John was the dominant writer and vice versa.

Introduction

A mind-boggling list of number one singles and albums, a score of firsts in popular music, young, glamorous, radical-but-vindicated and rich beyond our wildest dreams. We love the Beatles' story so much we want it told to us again and again. We have put the Beatles on a pedestal so high that their success and fortune has become mythological. Rather than using it as an inspiration, we immerse ourselves in the Beatles' story to vicariously experience the highs of their career as a palliative for our own less extraordinary lives. Media coverage of the Beatles is happy to rehash Beatles statistics, chat show anecdotes and trivia. We rarely get a convincing explanation of the Beatles' achievements and are fed soft-focus legends rather than hard truth.

In music lessons, school children today are more likely to have class projects on the music of the Beatles than learn how to play 'Greensleeves' on a recorder. Most of the correspondence directed to me at my Beatles website, www.Sgt.peppers.co.uk, is from teenagers needing help with Beatles projects they have been set at school. What I suspect they are often learning about is more a fairy story than the truth.

Useful, objective explanations of the Beatles are treated with wariness. Each new and challenging Beatles book – particularly Ian MacDonald's *Revolution in the Head* and even the Beatles' very own *Anthology* book – is treated in the media with the same desperate assertion: 'We thought that nothing new could be said about the Beatles, but you can go out and buy this book safe in the knowledge that this is the very last Beatles book you ever need to buy.' One assumes that people generally like the myth of the Beatles and do not want a rational explanation.

Our views on the Beatles must evolve. Just as every generation produces a new analysis and opinion of figures like Mozart or

Shakespeare, so our attitude to the Beatles will change. Crucially, new evidence is still emerging on the Beatles. Already Philip Norman's thrilling biography of the group, *Shout!* from 1981, looks to have gaping holes in it. Since its publication many figures from the Beatles' past have emerged to tell their own stories as the Beatles nostalgia industry has provided public speaking opportunities. At the 2001 Beatles convention in Liverpool it was interesting to hear Cavern DJ Bob Wooler denounce as myth the idea stated in many Beatles books that it was 'Cunard Yanks' working on ocean liners that docked in Liverpool who introduced rare rock 'n' roll and R&B records to Liverpool. And who should know better than Liverpool's foremost early 1960s DJ that such records were easily available on order in Liverpool record shops? During my own research, I came across numerous interviews not drawn upon by other books – part of it on the relatively new medium of the Internet. John Lennon and Paul McCartney have been prolific givers of interviews, yet even widely available interviews such as John's interviews for *Rolling Stone* in 1970 and *Playboy* in 1980 are fruitful after repeated reading.

We resist too much deep thought on the Beatles as their songs are often simple and light. At the same time by contrast we often find their success so incomprehensible that for many of us it is easiest to portray them as gods. Understanding the Beatles' methods is something that can improve our appreciation of their music and is of use for anyone making music or contemplating a pop career. To be able to see them as human beings and not deities should, too, make them more appealing to a younger generation irritated with their parents' gloating memories of having been closer in spirit and time to the Beatles.

What pass for explanations of the Beatles' music today are shaggy dog stories. We are kept amused with tit-bits of trivia about the making of their music. There is the endless and disappointing retelling of the creation of 'Yesterday'; of how with no lyrics Paul used the words 'scrambled eggs' to scan out the melody and of how 'Hey Jude' was originally 'Hey Jules' in honour of Julian Lennon. These tales are dead-ends and do not illuminate us on the Beatles' artistry; if anything, they diminish the songs in question. By contrast, we have little such trivia on the making of Shakespeare's plays. Instead we are left with his works, which we must grasp and analyse.

Analyses, of course, have been made of the Beatles music, two of the best being Ian MacDonald's *Revolution In The Head: the Beatles' Records and the '60s* and Steve Turner's *A Hard Day's Write*. MacDonald's book is largely an analysis of the intuitive and conscious musical workings of the

Beatles, while Turner's is a result of his extensive research of the anecdotes and events surrounding each song. In parts our research has overlapped, but neither of these books seems motivated strongly to demystify the way we see the Beatles.

One of the key myths I have set out to disprove is that the Beatles' music was so artistically strong it could not fail to get to number one. This belief fails to take into account their huge ambition for fame and its rewards. In today's usual reckoning of the Beatles as pop 'artists', we tend not to examine any of their baser motives, preferring to see them as purely motivated by a love of music and a need to communicate with the world. The Beatles themselves, it should be noted, have attempted to point out that actually they were not all that holy and not all their motives were pure. John in particular wielded the biggest attack against the Beatles myth – as he himself referred to it – in his 1970 *Rolling Stone* interview. To make it to the top he said you had to be a 'bastard' and the Beatles were in such a context the 'biggest bastards on earth'. Albert Goldman's *The Lives Of John Lennon* seems to have taken this remark to heart and pursued it relentlessly, missing the point of what John was trying to achieve with this comment. By making such knowingly sensational remarks, he sought to counter what he saw as widely held misconceptions of the Beatles. His remarks also served to emphasise that the Beatles were not gods, but ordinary human beings. It is from the last perspective that I have written this book – the Beatles not as four gods, but as four highly motivated, but otherwise normal, Liverpool lads.

While the Beatles did more than any other pop group to make the term 'pop artist' a valid one, to see their first five albums, for example, in purely artistic terms is to misunderstand them completely. If anything, the Beatles' early career involved the suppression of their artistic urges for monetary gain and a high media profile. (The importance the Beatles gave to getting rich is revealed unashamedly in many interviews they made between 1963 and 1965, especially in those set question-and-answer-style profiles in pop magazines, where often their answer to the 'Ambitions' section is simply 'to be rich'.)

To reach the top, the Beatles faced more commercial than artistic battles. Their early five-year struggle (1957–62) left its mark on them, unlike, for example, the Rolling Stones, who achieved national fame a mere two years after their formation. By contrast the Beatles needed to present themselves smartly to gain the few early gigs they could muster in Liverpool, they needed dramatic stage showmanship and a broad repertoire of songs to win over a disinterested German public on their first visit to Hamburg, and they needed to wear suits to secure lucrative bookings in large theatres and make an impression on London record companies.

These compromises shaped the Beatles' outlook but encouraged them to put one over on the staid, out-of-touch UK music industry and re-write the rules. Unlike Mick Jagger, who had an open invitation to return to the London School of Economics any time his pop career fell through, the Beatles had staked everything on making it in the music business and their first concern was to gain enough commercial success to secure their livelihood. Probably the only time the Beatles truly relaxed enough to produce material that appealed to their artistic sensibilities alone was on *The White Album* in 1968.

The Beatles' key commercial strategy in their first few years of recording was to write lyrics emphasising their eligibility as young handsome men to impressionable girl teens – one of the most loyal markets of record buyers. John's marriage and child (which admittedly he never publicly sought to deny) were kept secret for as long as possible, as were Paul, George and Ringo's girlfriends. As cynically as any boy band of recent years, the Beatles lyrics portrayed the group as a fantasy of true, devotional love and unthreatening masculinity. Intimacy went only as far as kissing, holding hands ('I Want To Hold Your Hand') and dancing ('I Saw Her Standing There' and 'I'm Happy Just To Dance With You'). The grand lie of this early Beatles era (and that for most successful boy bands today) was that between 1962 and 1965, John and Paul in particular were in fact so sexually active that the only true relationships they had time for were between themselves.

The irony was that the Beatles would probably have been far more comfortable with the raunchier style of the Rolling Stones at this time. What little mention of sex did creep into their music in this era was either coded or implied on album tracks and B-sides, such as 'Norwegian Wood', 'She's A Woman', 'Hold Me Tight' and 'Everybody's Trying To Be My Baby'. ('Please Please Me' arguably includes some of their more salacious lyrics, though this was written before Beatlemania and before the Beatles had entered the national consciousness.) It must have been a cause of enormous satisfaction and relief to the Beatles when they smuggled their first overt sexual reference onto an A-side with 'Day Tripper', where Paul smuggled in the words 'prick teaser'. Even here, though, the reference was largely included to impress their drinking buddies and contemporaries in the rock business.

By late 1965 the Beatles had all bought their big houses in exclusive neighbourhoods, had proved themselves 'as big as Elvis' and were free to explore other artistic ambitions. Meanwhile in Hollywood a younger, tamer version of the Beatles – the Monkees – was conveniently about to take over as the world's cuddly and puppet-like 'fab four'.

A further myth of the Beatles career occurs at this point. It has become standard to talk of the music they produced from *Rubber Soul* onwards as representing their 'mature' period. This period is seen as one in which the Beatles developed their emotional, spiritual and intellectual sides, but while they undoubtedly grew as individuals in this era, it is misleading to attempt to measure this development in their music and lyrics. By 1966, with little motivation to add to their fortune, John in particular lost the desire to create purely commercial songs. Yet if the terms of the Beatles' early contracts with EMI had been more lucrative, it is arguable that John could have attempted songs such as 'Tomorrow Never Knows' and 'Strawberry Fields Forever' as early as 1964–65. Such is the improved nature of contracts today that many 'artists', buoyed up by quick fortunes, attempt the artistic 'Strawberry Fields Forever' route on their second albums. In hindsight we have cause to be thankful for the small royalties accorded the Beatles in their early years which encouraged them to be so prolific.

The Beatles' early songs are in fact some of the most mature and clever they ever wrote. Songs like 'From Me To You' and 'I Want To Hold Your Hand' are deceptively simple, their lyrics written in a mock naive style aimed firmly at the hit parade. The wealth and power the Beatles gained from such records set them up for life. Once such riches had been gained, they had the luxury of relaxing, fooling around and experimenting to their hearts' content.

The Beatles' 'mature period' mirrors the development of pop culture in the 1960s. The commercial success of Bob Dylan in 1965 was a big incentive for them to drop their tin pan alley songwriting style. The new technological developments which became available at this time, such as compression (which allowed a louder guitar sound) and automatic double tracking, both of which were used on *Revolver*, and eight-track recording, which was used from 'Hey Jude' on, allowed increasingly complex arrangements.

This leads us to a third and important misunderstanding about the Beatles. The artistic freedom and control over their product that they enjoyed in their so-called 'mature' phase has become the holy grail for most serious rock bands of today. This artistic freedom, though, is largely a mirage for any band signed to a major label. The pursuit of an arrangement similar to the one enjoyed between the Beatles and their record company, EMI, in the late '60s is something that is bound to end in tears.

The artistic freedom enjoyed by the Beatles from late 1965 to 1969 came about largely through the sheer incomprehensibility with which EMI treated them. In an interview from 1988, Paul claimed bitterly that the profits graph from EMI's record label show a huge upward turn once the Beatles joined the label. The Beatles may not have seen their fair share of profits, but the scale of the money they were generating for EMI led the company to treat the Beatles like the goose that laid the golden egg. EMI did not understand where the Beatles were heading and indeed their establishment boss, Sir Joseph Lockwood, judging by the unsmiling photos of him standing stiffly with the Beatles awarding them gold discs, certainly did not appear to enjoy their product.

EMI's attitude to the Beatles seems to have been 'we may not like or understand what you are doing, but the profits generated are so huge we are going to let you carry on unhindered'. EMI knew something strange was going on with the *Sgt. Pepper's Lonely Hearts Club Band* [*Sgt. Pepper*] album, but such was their faith in their sales that they gave them free rein. Brian Epstein, the Beatles' manager, had the same attitude of incomprehension and, to his credit, faith in them.

The profits generated by rock 'n' roll in the late '60s allowed many purely experimental bands to enjoy similar artistic freedom. Record companies, knowing there were large profits to be made but unsure what the kids would be buying next, went out and signed up the highly experimental, but ultimately poor-selling Velvet Underground and Captain Beefheart in 1966.

For a while the Beatles and youth culture grew and changed at such a pace that the establishment was at a complete loss about how to deal with it. New musical forms such as punk in the '70s, rap in the '80s and electronic dance music in the '90s all enjoyed similar initial incomprehension from the establishment. The uniqueness of the Beatles' situation in pop is that record companies now well understand the developments they went through. The Brian Epsteins and Sir Joseph Lockwoods of today know how to package and market anything from revolution, protest, drugs imagery and sex to alienation, anger and anarchy, just as well as traditional gimmicks such as young, handsome and available 'boy' singers.

The beauty of the Beatles' late era, then, is that apart from their own desire to create commercial records, what they produced were pure artistic statements of a kind that only exist in today's pop in bands that work outside the main record companies and produce their records independently. Like the indie scene, of course, the Beatles' late period was not all a pretty sight – hence the ghastly misadventures of the *Magical Mystery Tour* cover and the 'Revolution No 9' track from *The White Album.*

The Beatles' progression from heavily commercial boy band to 'indie' music is unique in rock history and is much misunderstood by many of their admirers today. Radiohead and U2 may namecheck the Beatles as heroes, but they have followed very different paths. The Beatles' early career is echoed more by bands like N'Sync and Westlife than many would like to admit, while their later career is akin to that of today's obstreperous indie bands who refuse to follow the big labels' corporate line. When a Beatles' record made the charts in the late '60s, there was a genuine feel of an event about it. The same air of excitement is experienced today only when a left-field indie band gatecrashes the charts. This is something the big-league modern corporate rockers will never know.

An important part of understanding the Beatles' music and deconstructing the myths that surround it is accepting the influence of other artists on their work. Writing music from thin air can be a long and torturous process; it is often far easier to start from the basis of someone else's song and adapt part of it into something new. The Beatles often worked like this. How often is a matter of debate, though George Harrison once claimed that if you named him any Beatles song, he could tell you the record it was based upon. John, who stole records, a guitar, an amplifier and a harmonica during the Beatles' hungry days pre-fame, was hardly going to have sleepless nights about reworking someone else's tune. He once explained that he would often take another artist's song and change it to the point where he could not be sued.

This process of adaptation did not stop at other people's songs. John would often rework his own music, particularly 'It Won't Be Long' as 'Any Time At All' and 'All You Need Is Love' (itself adapted from 'Three Blind Mice') as 'Instant Karma', while 'Girl' is not a million miles away from Paul's 'Michelle'.

Working out the original songs that the Beatles based some of their music on is a fascinating but time-consuming process. Some suddenly leap out at you after years of listening to a song, e.g. 'Yer Blues' as 'Heartbreak Hotel'. Others are much less obvious; 'I Want You (She's So Heavy)' originates from the 1962 cocktail music classic 'Comin' Home Baby' and 'Please Please Me' owes inspiration to a Bing Crosby song.

It is not the case, though, that all the Beatles' tunes were the result of this process of reworking (George's rather exaggerated quote is, of course, something of a dig at John and Paul). Paul in particular claimed no knowledge of the origin of the tune for 'Yesterday' (though the amount of unconscious influence from other artists in Paul's work is remarkable) as did John for 'Across The Universe'.

There is a long and noble tradition of plagiarism in music, many classical composers including Mozart and Beethoven adapting popular folk songs into their symphonies. Ultimately there is something mean-spirited in analysing every song in a body of work that has brought so much joy to people in this way. Understanding this process of adaptation, though, is helpful in explaining the Beatles' success. The hundreds of songs they learnt to play whilst working arduous hours in Hamburg and at the Cavern between 1960 and 1962, and the thousands more they studied, provided a vast store of ideas, tricks and lessons from which to draw upon later in their career. Their musical knowledge was greater than we can easily comprehend today. While today's pop artists' knowledge of music is usually limited to the genre in which they work, the Beatles were familiar with songs going back to the turn of the century.

The rigours of the Cavern and Hamburg are one of the key factors in my final point about the Beatles. What was it, despite all their crude commercial strategies, that made them rightly become the most respected band of all time? The answer is a combination of natural talent, timing, location, luck and hard work. Firstly, while not a natural musician like Paul, John's great voice, quick wit and way with words were all-important to the Beatles' success. John's ability to connect with people through pop music is rivalled by few others – only Bob Marley and Bob Dylan come close. His perceptiveness, ironically, is perhaps due to his dyslexia; a recent report suggested that dyslexics often have a compensatory ability to be able to judge characters more deeply than other people. Secondly, the Beatles heard rock 'n' roll at its most influential point. The genre may have been purely American in origin, but it was mostly English performers who capitalised on it in the 1960s and '70s. While the impact of Elvis Presley's 'Heartbreak Hotel' was no doubt electric to those who heard it in the USA, to those who heard it in an equally free, but drab, grey and conservative Britain it was life-changing. Paul at 13 and John at 15 were at the prime age to be influenced by such music – music that was helpfully sung in English, too.

Why did such a phenomenon occur in Liverpool? Once England's second wealthiest city, the Liverpool of the late-'50s was much more prosperous than it is today and its population was higher. Away from the bright lights of London, the UK's entertainment capital, Liverpool was a much more open city for local talents to make a mark. Its large Irish population, too, carried with it traditions of live communal music, which flourished as a result.

What then of luck? Arguably the Beatles would never have had the impact they did were it not for the death of Buddy Holly, the brightest and most innovative of all '50s rock 'n' rollers. Holly was looking to extend the boundaries of rock 'n' roll, long before the Beatles. Holly shared the Beatles' fascination with what could be achieved in the studio. The off-room miking of the drums on 'Peggy Sue' predated the Beatles' own experiments with unusual mikings for drums on 'A Day In The Life' by ten years. Lyrically too the innovation of 'Peggy Sue Got Married', where Holly talks directly to his fans, and the ironic introspection of 'Well Alright', all predate the Beatles' similar strategies. If Holly had lived longer than the tragically young age of 22, he would have certainly progressed and matured in the same way the Beatles did. If he had lived, would the Beatles have been hailed for the artistic breakthroughs of *Rubber Soul* and *Revolver*, or would they have merely been following on his coat-tails? The Beatles, to their credit, recognised the importance of Holly to their own careers and also closely identified with him – like them, he was unique among early rock 'n' rollers in being suburban and well-educated.

Lastly, but most importantly, the Beatles worked hard to reach the top. Over the years between 1960–62 the Beatles were playing live almost nightly to audiences who often knew little of them and had to be won over. The musical grounding they gained, along with their knowledge of how to entertain people, was something no band has equalled to this day.

The availability of these gigs was fortunate for the Beatles. The early-'60s saw probably the greatest-ever opportunity for bands to play live. Since then a combination of strict music licences, coupled with the growth of discos and numerous forms of alternative entertainment, have taken their toll on live music.

The nature of rock bands has changed too. Bands now see themselves less as entertainers and more as artists whose work should be adored and not questioned. The idea of engaging audiences and winning them over is becoming a lost art. Bands would rather blast their audiences into submission with the power of their amplification. Unsurprisingly, many teenagers have turned their backs on live music and found more rewarding pursuits.

The Beatles' legend also rests on their amazing output. While today top bands might aspire to producing two or three 'classic' albums in the course of their careers, the Beatles produced at least ten. This was in part due to the onerous understanding they had with EMI that two albums should be produced every year. The Beatles became accustomed to working in this fashion and came to appreciate the benefits it brought. One of their greatest albums, *Rubber Soul,* was nearly entirely written and recorded in one two-month stretch. The Beatles recognised the powerful appeal of songs written under such pressure. John took the process to its ultimate extent with 'Instant Karma', a song written and recorded all in one day.

Despite the adoration of the Beatles today, the success of these methods is ignored. Three-year gaps between albums while writers stagnate are commonplace. The cult of the producer, the engineer, the 48-track studio and the overdub are the enemies of fresh-sounding music. The ability to perform in the studio takes second place to the process of tinkering with a song's sound. Like alchemy, this is so often a vain attempt to turn base metals into gold. The cult of the pop star as artist, too, intrudes on the process. Record companies accept extended deadlines for albums as commonplace. Any band with the ability of the Beatles today would make one acclaimed *Please Please Me*-style album and take the next three years off touring, taking drugs and going to parties. They would then attempt their equivalent of *Rubber Soul* without any of the same organic musical growth between albums.

Unless there is a change in work styles, pop will go the way of classical music and painting on canvas – an art form whose greatest artists are all long dead.

The point should be restated, though, that John Lennon and Paul McCartney, as much as they are mythologised, were two people who were fortunate enough to be in the right place in the right decade. Thousands of other people must be out there with the same ability that never got the same opportunity.

Lastly, I should explain my own processes in writing this book. While it was always my original intention to produce a credible analysis of the Beatles' music, it was if anything my intention to write a much more critical book. But my criticism has often been tempered with awe. One of the wonders of listening to the Beatles' music is the constant amazement it provokes at the quality and imagination of what they produced.

My opinions on particular songs and albums have evolved greatly over the 12 years it took to see this book published. An early draft of the book was being touted around publishers and agents in early 1994. *Revolution In The Head* and *A Hard Day's Write*, though, were both unexpectedly published that year in quick succession. This forced me into a three-year hiatus where I did very little new work on the book. The start of *the Beatles' Anthology* video/CD/book/interview blitz provided irresistible new material for research, as did the publication of Paul McCartney's official biography *Many Years From Now* in 1997. This prime source material, plus the gap in my work, has allowed me to approach the Beatles' music with a greater objectivity and wisdom than I did in my first and much weaker versions of the manuscript.

While, as mentioned before, I have culled much of my research from numerous interviews the Beatles gave, an equally important piece of that research has been tracking down the music the Beatles listened to themselves. One certain way of doing that has been to trace the originals of some 250 cover versions the Beatles are known to have performed live and on record, as listed in Mark Lewisohn's *The Complete Beatles Chronicle*.

1. Please Please Me

The Beatles were turned down by nearly every British record company between January and April 1962. When at last Parlophone, an offbeat subsidiary of EMI, showed interest they felt in little position to be choosy about the terms of the deal or their producer, George Martin. Furthermore, keeping Martin happy was a priority while their contract with EMI remained unsigned. In a telegram to the Beatles in Hamburg in May 1962, their manager Brian Epstein had misled them, saying: 'Congratulations boys, EMI request recording session. Please rehearse new material.' The 'recording session' was in reality merely a recording test to gauge their potential.

Showing the Beatles' timidity in the face of the big, important London-based record company, they brought to the recording test at Abbey Road studios on 6 June 1962 three of the politest songs they ever wrote, 'Love Me Do', 'Ask Me Why' and 'PS I Love You'. By all accounts, the nerve-racked renditions they gave of these songs did not do them justice. In spite of this Martin offered to sign the Beatles to record two singles. He has since claimed that this decision was based in part on the warmth and humour of their personalities, qualities he wisely predicted people would find hard to resist, and in part on an indefinable unique quality in their sound. What this account omits is that he could not have failed to notice the classic doe-eyed, pretty-boy looks of Paul McCartney and the cute matching mop-top fringes of John, Paul and George. All wore matching suits chosen by the meticulous and fashion-conscious Epstein. Such neat, attractive presentation, as Martin was surely aware, gave them strong commercial potential.

Unbeknown to the Beatles, Martin was desperately looking for an act to match the enormous UK chart success of Cliff Richard and The

Shadows, who tantalisingly recorded from the very same number two studio at Abbey Road that he worked from. Richard's boyish, unthreatening looks made him perfect for marketing watered-down rock 'n' roll to a wide audience. Martin (like the Beatles) had a low regard for him and believed that his commercial success could be copied.

Martin ruled out the Beatles' own compositions as too weak and asked them to return to Abbey Road to record a song written by a professional songwriter. Cliff Richard similarly had most of his big hits written for him by such tin pan alley writers. Likewise, Martin's offer came with the proviso to Epstein that a session drummer would be hired to play with the Beatles – Richard's debut single had also been recorded with the aid of session musicians who stood in for his regular bass and guitar players. It is generally accepted now that Pete Best, the Beatles' drummer of two years standing, was singled out because the performance of 'Love Me Do' from the June recording test reveals him playing an erratic beat. The Beatles, eager to keep Martin happy and already tempted by the prospect of working with the more highly regarded Ringo Starr, sacked Best in August.

Martin next touted around for songs for the Beatles to record. On discovering the catchy but lightweight 'How Do You Do It?' written by Mitch Murray, he fixed a recording date for 4 September.

Over the summer the Beatles worked out their own arrangement for 'How Do You Do It?' and even played it live, yet they were loathe to record it. Possibly it had received a negative reaction when played at the Cavern, but most likely John and Paul found it an affront to their five-year apprenticeship as songwriters. By contrast Brian Epstein, still nervous about losing the deal he had worked so hard to obtain, argued the Beatles down and ordered them to record the song.

When they returned to Abbey Road in September, the plan was to record 'How Do You Do It?' as the A-side of a single and 'Love Me Do' as the B-side. The Beatles, in an effort to sway favour for their song, produced half-hearted performances of 'How Do You Do It?' The out-take, released on the *Anthology* series, reveals John glibly and comically under-emphasising many of the lyrics. Martin protested in the face of the Beatles' stubbornness that 'How Do You Do It?' was a guaranteed number one single. The Beatles explained, as Paul remembered in 1997, that they would have loved a number one, but felt that a song like 'How Do You Do It?' not only compromised the more 'artistic' route they were taking, but would be laughed at by their fans in Liverpool.

Beatles
For Sale

'LOVE ME DO'
(McCartney/Lennon) Single released 5 October 1962

'Love Me Do' had been often played live by the Beatles and their faith in it was due to the positive response it received from audiences, something George Martin had not yet witnessed. Simple in melody and lyric, its strength was an expressive blues feel that had been lost at their nervy audition in June. John, later speaking in support of it, described it as 'funky', which suggests at least that the Beatles never did justice to it on record.

Numerous unsigned bands playing live in small UK clubs in the early 1960s were playing this same imitation of soul and R&B music, which valued a song's 'feel' more than its structure. The big, conservative London-based record labels were at first resistant to this trend, though as Parlophone showed it was only a matter of time before one of them proved its commercial potential. Tellingly, Keith Richards of the Rolling Stones said that on first hearing 'Love Me Do' he felt 'sick' that another band had made this breakthrough first. The Rolling Stones, then still unsigned, were causing a small sensation as a regular live act in and around London.

'Love Me Do' was written by Paul around 1958 with added help from John. Its form owed something to Elvis's 'Love Me Tender', which they had performed live. Further changes were made to its arrangement in Hamburg in May 1962, to prepare it for their visit to Abbey Road. It is likely that at this stage harmonica was added, as the rhythmic lilt of John's riff owes much to 1962 R&B hit 'Hey Baby' by Bruce Chanel, which the Beatles had also played live. The harmonica riff was decisive as it was the basis of George Martin's decision to record 'Love Me Do' in preference to the other songs he heard at the June recording test.

Its eventual recording was flawed by Martin's eagerness to mould the Beatles into the style of Cliff Richard. Looking to make one person the focal point of the group, he gave Paul the lead vocals, understandably picking him out as the best-looking Beatle. (A year earlier in a Hamburg recording studio German producer Bert Kaempfert had had the same idea.) Martin, still in a position of power, claimed that John could not play harmonica and sing lead. Yet why could the harmonica not be recorded separately, as it would be on 'Please Please Me'? Paul, looking back in 1988 said, 'I can still hear the shake in my voice when I listen to that record – I was terrified . . . John did sing it better than me, he had a lower voice and was much more bluesy at singing that line.'

George Martin was not finished with 'Love Me Do' and decided to re-record again on 11 September with session drummer Andy White in Ringo's place. Accounts of these early Abbey Road sessions are hazy and it can only be surmised that Martin had held back from using a session drummer for the 4 September recording, perhaps wishing to give Pete Best (Martin had not yet heard of his sacking) a second chance.

The most logical explanation of events would suggest that the decision to favour 'Love Me Do' over 'How Do You Do It?' was made at the 4 September session. This suggests that as a compromise for getting 'Love Me Do' made the A-side, the Beatles gave in to George Martin's wishes to use Andy White on its re-recording.

White, who played with dance orchestras, gave a rigid beat on this new recording, killing the blues feel of 'Love Me Do'. In its favour, though, this version features a much more confident vocal from Paul and was the one that Martin preferred. In some sort of mix-up, early pressings of the single 'Love Me Do' featured the version with Ringo on drums. Later pressings and the *Please Please Me* album used the Andy White version.

On release, 'Love Me Do' met a lukewarm reaction from the UK pop music press, who were subsequently surprised by its chart placing soon afterwards. A popular rumour spread that Brian Epstein had 'bought' it into the charts by fixing chart return slips at his record shop in Liverpool. As much as this rumour is appealing, it has been denied for so long and so adamantly by former assistants of Epstein, who now have nothing to lose from telling it, that it must be untrue. The rumour is perhaps more revealing of how out of touch the music press was with the huge popularity of the Beatles in the north-west of England. Before the Beatles even got their record contract they had a thriving fan club based in Liverpool. This local support helped 'Love Me Do' reach a chart peak of number 17 in December 1962. Crucially, the single gained the Beatles exposure on three separate local TV shows broadcast in the north-west of England, Wales and the London area.

'PS I LOVE YOU'
(McCartney) B-side to 'Love Me Do'

'PS I Love You' was written in answer to Brian Epstein's telegram to the Beatles in Hamburg requesting them to prepare new material for their recording test on 6 June. In many ways it is a superior track to 'Love Me Do'. Its polite, neat, Latin-flavoured melody seems tailored to mimic the chart hits of the day, suggesting it was written solely to impress George Martin. Indeed, its Latin flavour was not far from Elvis Presley's recent smash hit 'It's Now Or Never', a strong favourite of Paul's, which the Beatles performed in their live set.

Recorded at the second 'Love Me Do' session with Andy White on drums, White's clinical rimshot beat gives a professional touch that perfectly draws out the song's Latin rhythm. Unlike many of the raw recordings the Beatles became known for in 1963, 'PS I Love You' is also meticulous in arrangement, suggesting long rehearsals beforehand. So strong was its sound that there was some debate as to whether it should become the A-side. Ron Richards (George Martin's assistant producer), though, favoured the impact of 'Love Me Do', as he knew of another song named 'PS I Love You' (possibly The Hilltoppers' 1950s US hit).

The lyrics of 'PS I Love You' were long thought to have been inspired by Paul's letters to his girlfriend Dot Rhone who stayed in Liverpool while he was in Hamburg. In his 1997 biography, Paul rather ungenerously recalled them as being merely stylised and referring to no one in particular. This would back the explanation from John, who claimed that Paul took inspiration from the Shirelles 'Soldier Boy' which was a big US hit in May 1962. As such, 'PS I Love You' reads as a reply song to 'Soldier Boy', which was written in the style of a letter from a girl to her boyfriend who is far 'overseas'. This would fit in with tradition in the late '50s and early '60s of writing lyrics that 'replied' to other hits of the day. Such precocious use of this sophisticated songwriting device would have no doubt appealed greatly to Paul, then aged 19, who was looking to prove his name as a songwriter.

'PLEASE PLEASE ME'
(Lennon/McCartney) Single released 11 January 1963

Though lyrically simple, 'Please Please Me' is one of the Beatles' best-ever arrangements. In 1 minute 59 seconds they race through a song that crams in not one, but three separate riffs (harmonica, the chiming lead guitar and the accelerating rhythm guitar). The song finds time to stop for a drum fill and adds at the end, as if out of bravado, a coolly executed cadence, where John holds a single vocal note while the guitars descend in key and tempo to a final chord. Showing that the song's exuberance is for real, you can clearly hear John pause to catch his breath at 1.02.

The thrill of this performance transferred so well on to disc that the Beatles' new publisher Dick James secured them an immediate booking on UK national TV show *Thank Your Lucky Stars*, simply by playing it over the phone to the show's producer. This was the first of a long string of number one records for the Beatles and they would stick to its formula of short, fun and varied arrangements for nearly all their future singles. The formula owes something to George Martin, who had persuaded the Beatles to give the song a more uptempo arrangement (he also claimed credit for the song's closing cadence). When 'Please Please Me' was first played to him on 11 September 1962, it deliberately mimicked the slow pace of Roy Orbison's 'Only The Lonely'.

Martin's direction was significant, in that all the songs the Beatles had presented him with so far were slow-paced. It was almost as if they were frightened of revealing their true live power within the confines of a London recording studio. His direction encouraged them to show on record the guts their music had live in Liverpool and Hamburg. Credit should also be given to the sound Martin achieved. Often criticised for his lack of production ideas compared to producers such as Phil Spector, the clearness of tone here – especially on the lovely harmonica riff – captures the whole raw thrill of the Beatles' live performances. That Martin's production of 'Please Please Me' proved commercially astute too helped establish a relationship of trust between him and the Beatles.

The success of 'Please Please Me' was also a vindication of John's role as lead singer. On 'Love Me Do' Paul had studio nerves. The leap from singing live to singing to an engineer and producer behind glass in a control booth did not seem to inhibit John as much. Subsequently, John's vocals were favoured for all Beatles singles released in 1963, while noticeably Paul's vocals still sound inhibited on the vocal performances he contributed on disc from that year.

Lyrically 'Please Please Me' has been rumoured to refer to sex; Paul came close to admitting this in a 1967 interview for the *Observer* when he said the lyrics contained a double entendre. Shocking as this may sound for the early '60s, other hit records from this era also alluded to sex e.g. the Shirelles' 'Will You Still Love Me Tomorrow?' from 1960 and the UK number one hit 'Come Outside' by Mike Sarne from 1962.

'ASK ME WHY'
(Lennon/McCartney) B-side to 'Please Please Me'

John wrote 'Ask Me Why' in response to Brian Epstein's telegram to the Beatles in Hamburg, with Paul contributing to John's 'initial idea'. As it was written to impress George Martin, the intention was surely to write something good enough to be considered an A-side. Tellingly, its poised, finely crafted arrangement reveals that much time was devoted to it before recording. The next two Beatles B-sides, 'Thank You Girl' and 'I'll Get You', would feature nothing as fine as the vocal harmonies and the closing glissando on guitar featured here. The only rough edge is in the hoarseness of John's voice, which shows the effort of the searing vocals he had committed to 18 takes of 'Please Please Me' earlier in the day. These vocals are pushed way back in the mix, as if George Martin was embarrassed by them.

Like 'PS I Love You', which it was written alongside, the song's pretty and docile style is unrevealing of John's character, suggesting commercial considerations were foremost. The lyrics are especially untrue to him, if admittedly largely nonsensical in their mixed themes. It has been suggested that the line 'I can't conceive of any more misery', with its pause after the first three words, was put there to amuse live audiences in Liverpool. As this is the only Beatles' song that John was not asked about in his sprawling 1970 *Rolling Stone* interview, or his equally long *Playboy* interview from 1980, little more is known.

The contract the Beatles signed with EMI in July 1962 was for two singles only. A new lengthier contract was only signed after 'Please Please Me' began heading for the top of the charts in early February 1963. At this point EMI requested a quickly recorded album of the same name to cash in on its success.

PLEASE PLEASE ME
Album released 22 March 1963

Much legend has built up around the uniqueness of the Beatles' debut album, with its 'live' sound recorded in the studio, yet its formula was a straight copy. Cliff Richard and The Shadows also recorded their first album, *Cliff* (1959) live at the very same number two studio at Abbey Road, in front of a small audience of teenage fans. Staying in the British charts for over a year, it had successfully transferred on to disc the excitement of their live shows.

More used to recording comedy or novelty records, it seems natural that George Martin would look to use a tried and tested formula for the Beatles' album. In a revealing quote he gave to *Mersey Beat* at the 26 November recording session for 'Please Please Me', he talked of his plans to record the Beatles' debut album live. Knowing of the Beatles' popularity at the Cavern, he said he might record it there. Martin also told *Mersey Beat* that his alternative wish to recording at the Cavern was to have the album recorded in front of a small group of invited fans at Abbey Road. Martin opted for this choice after testing the reverberation at the Cavern and ruling that there was too much echo. The Beatles may have encouraged him along these lines. Their major complaint to him in late 1962 was that performing in the studio felt unnatural to them and they played better in front of a live audience.

The quick decision of EMI to authorise the recording of an album gave George Martin little time to organise a crowd to attend Abbey Road. In the middle of a national tour supporting Helen Shapiro, the Beatles returned to London on 11 February to record ten songs in a day. Ironically, *Cliff* had been recorded almost to the same day three years previously, on 10 February 1959. That no one ever openly admitted the link between the two albums is revealing of the antipathy felt by the Beatles for Cliff Richard, especially by John who was even quoted as saying he hated Richard's music.

Although not recorded in one continuous performance like the *Cliff* album, all recordings were essentially live group performances. To enhance this live sound, the amplifiers were faced to the studio walls to recreate the reverberation one would hear at the Cavern. This 'genuine' live sound was only broached for a vocal overdub on 'A Taste Of Honey' and the occasional overdub of piano or harmonica.

Recording stretched from ten in the morning till ten at night. Over the course of the day the music became tighter and the vocals stronger. This is evident in the following order of recording: 'There's A Place', 'I Saw Her Standing There', 'Hold Me Tight' (rejected and re-recorded for *With the Beatles*), 'A Taste Of Honey', 'Do You Want To Know A Secret?', 'Misery', 'Anna', 'Boys', 'Chains', 'Baby It's You' and 'Twist And Shout'. Arguably some of the songs would have benefited from more studio time, but the immediacy of the live performances on the last two songs especially would have been otherwise unattainable.

On record this raw sound was unlike anything else in the British charts in early 1963. While the Beatles may have emulated the harmonic twists of New York songwriters like Goffin/King and Phil Spector, they played in a simple three-guitar rock 'n' roll style that had fallen out of favour with record companies, if not fans. In stark contrast, in early 1963 ex-rock 'n' rollers Elvis and Cliff Richard were trading the number one spot with the tame pop of 'Return To Sender' and 'Bachelor Boy'.

Similarly the album cover was a world away from the glamorous airbrushed photos that most top pop stars had in the early 1960s. The Beatles, as Philip Norman, author of *Shout!* remarked, looked like they were hanging over a balcony on a council flat.

One illusion the album has since encouraged is that it is representative of the Beatles' live repertoire. A live set recorded six weeks previously in Hamburg, on 31 December 1962, features only one Lennon/McCartney number 'I Saw Her Standing There' among 30 covers. There is little evidence that the Lennon/McCartney songs 'There's A Place', 'Do You Want To Want To Know A Secret' and 'Misery' were ever regularly played in their live shows previously. Indeed the speed of the decision to record the album seems to have caught the Beatles on the hop, as the arrangements for 'Misery' and 'There's A Place' in particular sound barely thought out.

Other than the Beatles' original songs, it was George Martin who for the first and last time chose what cover versions they would play, after he had seen a Beatles set at the Cavern. A persistent rumour that a new addition to the Beatles' repertoire, 'Keep Your Hands Off My Baby', was recorded for the album, suggests it was heard and then rejected by Martin.

'I SAW HER STANDING THERE'
(McCartney/Lennon)

This was written in September 1962 as a pastiche of the Chuck Berry songs the Beatles were then playing live in Hamburg and Liverpool. The punchy bass line takes the main riff from 'Talkin' 'Bout You' and the lyrics borrow from 'Little Queenie', which was similarly a tale of sighting and falling for a girl aged 'seventeen' at a rock 'n' roll dance. This pastiche works surprisingly well, only Paul's accentuated plastic US accent giving the game away.

As he later recalled, Paul saw the song as marking a step up in quality for the Lennon/McCartney songwriting partnership. Written soon after they signed their recording contract with EMI, their songs were now being indelibly captured for repeated listens on disc and as such they were keen to iron out embarrassing lyrics. As Paul explained in 1988, 'I had the lyrics "Just seventeen, never been a beauty queen" which John – it was one of the first times he ever said "What? Must change that" and it became "You know what I mean".'

A popular live number for the Beatles, it seems possible that at some stage this may have been considered as a single.

'MISERY'
(Lennon/McCartney)

John and Paul wrote 'Misery' a week before starting a national tour supporting UK chart star Helen Shapiro in February 1963 with the aim of selling it to her management. Its simple but swooping melody is tailored for her big, expressive voice and its sorry put-upon lyrics match those of her first hits, 'Don't Treat Me Like A Child' and 'You Don't Know'.

Paul said later that he would have been happy for it to be just a B-side for Shapiro, who was then a household name in Britain. Shapiro's producer Norrie Paramour turned it down without informing her, who later said she would have been happy to have recorded it.

To be fair to Paramour, this was not one of Lennon/McCartney's strongest songs; the lyrics bear the sloppiness of being hastily written. On the album John and Paul sound embarrassed at singing the lyrics styled for Shapiro. John's vocals in their exuberance are particularly mocking of the song's theme and after a vocal gaffe from Paul at 1.22, he can be heard stifling a laugh. Such nonchalance extends to the guitar playing, where the opening chord is clearly out of tune.

Days after recording, George Martin felt the need to flesh out the arrangement and added some garish piano trills, while the Beatles were back on tour. Martin, who had played piano in his own band (which had a repertoire of pop, light classical and boogie-woogie) would go on to contribute occasional piano to nearly all the Beatles albums.

'ANNA (GO TO HIM)'
(Arthur Alexander)

Black singer Arthur Alexander was, in 1962, one of the hottest names on the R&B scene, his influential debut album being a source of many cover versions among British bands. 'Anna', 'A Shot Of Rhythm And Blues' and 'Soldier Of Love' were all played live by the Beatles, while the Rolling Stones recorded 'You Better Move On' and Gerry and The Pacemakers recorded 'Where Have You Been?' and 'A Shot Of Rhythm And Blues'.

Commercial success largely eluded Alexander, perhaps due to his somewhat nasal, overwrought vocal style. His 1962 version of 'Anna' too is melancholy with lush piano and strings, making the Beatles' arrangement seem scrawny in comparison. Yet the Beatles give it more power, especially in John's vocal, which brings alive the 'All of my life' bridge. While a strong performance, the melodramatic lyrics make this an ill-fitting song for John. Showing his unease, where Alexander tells the girl that once she gives back his ring that she will be free, referring to her as 'darling', John omits the word 'darling' and changes the tone by singing the more assertive 'and I will set you free'.

'CHAINS'
(Goffin/King)

The original version of 'Chains' by the Cookies, a three-girl vocal group who had graduated from being backing singers on such hits as Little Eva's 'Locomotion' and Mel Torme's 'Comin' Home Baby' to recording an album's worth of similarly inventive Goffin/King songs on their own, was the sort of innovative US single that belittled so much early '60s British pop. Written and produced by Goffin and King, it boasts neat vocal harmonies and an intricate score of saxaphone, guitar, drums and handclaps. The Beatles aspired to such standards, John admitting in 1970 that it was his and Paul's ambition at this time to become the English version of Goffin and King.

The Beatles' version of 'Chains' is a poor match, mainly due to George's offbeat vocal, but also maybe as it was new to their repertoire. The Cookies' version had been a small hit in the UK as recently as January 1963. Oddly John overdubbed an Arabic sounding harmonica intro which does not appear on the original. On the next album George's song 'Don't Bother Me' has an eastern-sounding intro too.

'BOYS'
(Dixon/Farrell)

In their early days in Hamburg and Liverpool the Beatles, while waiting to go on stage, to their horror often heard the band prior to them playing much of their repertoire. To overcome this they deliberately sought out covers of obscure or overlooked songs. 'Boys' was discovered as the slow and sultry B-side of the Shirelles 1960 hit 'Will You Still Love Me Tomorrow?', which the Beatles revved up into a wild rocker. In 1997 Paul remembered the lack of a gender change in the lyrics as being done for laughs. Whether Ringo, who inherited this song from Pete Best, found this funny too has not been recorded. Happier staying out of the limelight, Ringo often had to be persuaded to sing. For this reason, on the early albums great effort was spent in trying to record his songs in one take. Notably here John and Paul's screams goad Ringo into losing his self-consciousness. He duly gave surely his most exuberant ever vocal on a Beatles recording.

'BABY IT'S YOU'
(David/Williams/Bacharach)

One of the highlights of the *Please Please Me* album, 'Baby It's You' was recorded late in the day, with the Beatles in peak form. John especially gives an impassioned vocal, drawing out a drama in the lyrics not realised on the original by the Shirelles. The only blot on the track is what sounds like a metal xylophone backing up George's already ropey guitar solo. Such misplaced accompaniment would have surely been vetoed by the Beatles, yet they were back on tour when it was overdubbed at George Martin's direction.

'Baby It's You' was originally an unusual US top ten hit for the Shirelles in February 1962. The voice of the Shirelles' lead vocalist, Shirley Owens, was merely added to a demo version of the tune made by songwriter Burt Bacharach. The demo's low fidelity was hidden with a heavy echo applied to Owens' vocal. The Beatles got more mileage out of it, using only the barest guitar chords; their vocal harmonies carry the tune alone.

'DO YOU WANT TO KNOW A SECRET?'
(Lennon/McCartney)

One of John and Paul's early Goffin and King-style efforts. The slow, spoken intro mimics New York Brill Building songs such as 'Runaround Sue' and 'It Might As Well Rain Until September', all hits in 1962. Part of the lyrics too derive from 'Wishing Well', a song from the Walt Disney cartoon *Snow White and the Seven Dwarfs*, which John recalled his mother singing to him as a child.

John remembered writing it in the Liverpool flat he moved into after he got married, which would date it from August 1962 at the earliest. It seems hard now to believe that John's childlike lyrics here were crafted for himself. More likely it was part of the Lennon/McCartney game plan that they would initially become a songwriting team who wrote for other artists. George as the youngest Beatle was duly lumbered with promoting the song and on the recording John and Paul's backing vocals seem to mock George's embarrassment at the words; their inane (and heavily echoed) scat harmonies on the second verse provoke a barely concealed snigger from George (0.48). Billy J. Kramer's more straight-faced version went to number two in the UK charts and John later wrote him the similarly twee 'Bad To Me', a number one UK hit.

George Harrison pointed out in 1987 that the main downward chord progression here was copied from 'I Really Love You', a US hit in 1961 for the Stereos, a five-man black doo-wop group from Ohio, USA. This wonderfully inventive record has its descending bass line sung by the group's baritone singer and should have done better than its number 29 placing in the US charts. The Beatles came across the song when they provided backing at the Cavern for black Liverpool vocal group The Chants, who covered 'I Really Love You' live.

'A TASTE OF HONEY'
(Scott/Marlow)

During the five years the Beatles spent as a struggling live band, they learnt how to cater for many types of audience. The teenage girls who were the main audience at the Cavern in Liverpool in particular enjoyed ballads such as 'Over The Rainbow', 'It's Now Or Never', 'Wooden Heart' and 'A Taste of Honey', a cover of Lenny Welch's 1962 US hit. Mersey beat chronicler Spencer Leigh says that it was Pete MacClaine, a fellow Liverpool singer, who first performed 'A Taste Of Honey'. Possibly seeing how well it worked live, Paul decided to sing it too.

Lenny Welch had performed the song in a crooning Frank Sinatra style, which Paul copies, though any chance of matching the silky ambience of this original was scuppered by John's mocking, over-earnest backing vocal (especially 1.20). One of the two live recordings of 'A Taste Of Honey' in Hamburg, December 1962, shows him more openly distracting Paul, repeating the lyrics in a deadpan style seconds after Paul had sung them.

'THERE'S A PLACE'
(Lennon/McCartney)

An early attempt at the introspective lyrics John would become famous for. His theme about a place he could retreat to in his mind would be more fully developed on 'Strawberry Fields Forever'. The music, too, with its jolting stops and starts is unlike the simpler melodies on the rest of the album. The placing of this as the penultimate track on side two, traditionally a slot for an album's weakest track, shows George Martin's initial caution at taking an overtly artistic direction. On the early albums, Martin had total control over track listing and John's similarly introspective 'Not A Second Time' would get the same placing on the next album.

As the first recording for the album, the Beatles' playing had not yet fully warmed up. A drum roll comes in late at 0.53 and Paul's singing (an octave above John's) is often flat. In all this must be one of the worst renditions the Beatles gave of one of their songs – it deserved greater attention to detail.

Paul claimed that the inspiration for the title came from the song 'There's A Place For Us' in the musical *West Side Story*. Lyrically it is also similar in theme to the Drifter's 1962 hit 'Up On The Roof'. John said himself that it was an attempt to write in a 'black' style. While this is not obvious, the opening vocal gymnastics are similar to the intros on such records as the Isley Brothers 'Shout' and Dr Feelgood's 'Mr Moonlight'.

'TWIST AND SHOUT'
(Medley/Russell)

At the close of a full day's recording on 11 February the Beatles were playing instinctively, reproducing the sound they gained on the long nights playing in Hamburg. Aware that they would improve over the day, they held back 'Twist and Shout' till last as they considered it their strongest song. The contrast with 'There's A Place' recorded ten hours previously, could not be greater. The Beatles' sound is locked together tight, with each instrument struck with force and passion. Ringo's drumming particularly shows such driving force. The pleading intensity of John's vocal was in part due to a sore throat that left him battling against losing his voice. Providing a perfect foil for these last gasp vocals, Paul and George sing as if in a trance. One take captured this stunning performance and a second only got as far as the second verse, when John's voice finally gave in.

'Twist And Shout' was written in 1961 as a cash-in on the twist craze of that year, by top New York songwriter Bert Berns under the pseudonym of Medley/Russell. Its first recording by the Top Notes was so shambolic that Berns completely rearranged it with the Isley Brothers, who made it a number 17 US hit in July 1962. Their version has a Latin carnival sound, with brass playing the distinctive riff and the singing more restrained than the interpretation John Lennon would bring it. The proto heavy rock sound the Beatles brought to 'Twist and Shout' was a style they developed in Hamburg, where audiences demanded a heavier sound. Such a bold and energised approach was brought to nearly all their cover versions.

Gerry Marsden of Gerry and the Pacemakers said in his autobiography *I'll Never Walk Alone* that the Beatles 'nicked' 'Twist and Shout' from fellow Merseybeat group King Size Taylor and the Dominoes. This sounds plausible, as in a bid to keep one step ahead of other Liverpool beat groups, King Size Taylor had records especially sent over from the USA so that they could 'acquire' them for their live show before anyone else. The Beatles spent some time with the Dominoes at the Star Club in Hamburg and one innovation they may have copied from their version of 'Twist and Shout' was the ploy of repeating the rising crescendo of voices at the song's close. By contrast, the Isley Brothers' version fades out without any equivalent ending.

2. With the Beatles

'FROM ME TO YOU'
(Lennon/McCartney) Single released 11 April 1963

This was the Beatles' most commercially calculated single. Where only six months before they had rejected 'How Do You Do It' from fear of being seen by their fans in Liverpool as selling out, now the lure of chart success proved simply too overpowering.

On tour with 'Please Please Me' riding high in the charts, John and Paul set about writing both sides of a new single directly aimed at the teenage girl fans they had just gained nationwide. In 1988 Paul explained, 'We knew that if we wrote a song called "Thank You Girl" that a lot of the girls who wrote us fan letters would take it as a genuine thank you . . . "From Me To You" is another.'

A promise of fidelity to their new fans, the lyrics offer their fans a true heart, waiting arms to hold them and lips to kiss them. Such lyrics before and since have been a common ploy amongst songwriters marketing handsome 'boy' bands or singers to a young teen girl audience. Without the Beatles' looks it is difficult to imagine such a ploy working, and indeed for this reason bands like the Rolling Stones, The Who and the Animals did not or could not use it.

The Beatles' naked commercial ambition had been encouraged by the release of 'How Do You Do It?' by fellow Liverpudlians Gerry and the Pacemakers in late January. By late February, when 'From Me To You' was written, the Pacemakers were on the way to the UK number one spot with exactly the same song the Beatles had turned down. Although close friends with Gerry Marsden, the Beatles were jealous of their position as top Liverpool band and, according to Marsden, were peeved at the Pacemakers' success.

How much of the Beatles' commercial nous was their own is debatable. Brian Epstein had helped them take a step up in their career by making them smarten their appearances and even bow to acknowledge applause after every number on stage. George Martin too was encouraging them in a more commercial direction. Perhaps most significantly, in January 1963 the Beatles had signed an agreement to let Dick James act as their publisher. James, a shrewd music industry manipulator, had worked as both singer and songwriter and may well have advised them of the songwriting ploys mentioned above. The Beatles needed little encouragement; in February 1963 John told the *London Evening Standard* only half-jokingly, 'We all want to get rich so we can retire.'

Written at speed so as to follow up the impact of the single 'Please Please Me', 'From Me To You' was pieced together by John and Paul on a long coach journey from Shrewsbury to York on 28 February. While the lyrics are an exercise in simplicity, Paul rated the subtle chord change from the chorus to the middle eight as a sign of their growing sophistication. Recorded a mere five days later, the arrangement is sparse, with only the harmonica and John's strong vocal bringing the song alive.

Although a co-composition, Paul let John take lead vocals for the second Beatles single in a row, presumably as he did not wish to tamper with the successful formula established by 'Please Please Me'. The excitement of the Beatles' emerging fame is evident in their happy, buzzing performance. A strong impact on radio was ensured by George Martin's decision to place a chorus, which is faster than the opening verse, at the record's start to grab listeners' attention.

'From Me To You' spent an amazing seven weeks at number one in the UK charts and by the summer the growing signs of fan hysteria were evident wherever the Beatles appeared. Success came at a price. As the Beatles later admitted, they found their return visits to Liverpool an embarrassment. Although their performances were a blast of energy compared to the current pop scene that year, their fans and friends back home must have been well aware of how much the Beatles had toned down their attitude and appearance.

'THANK YOU GIRL'
(Lennon/McCartney) B-side to 'From Me To You'

Written alongside 'From Me To You', 'Thank You Girl"s promise of eternal love to their teenage girl fans is the same. 'Thank You Girl', which had been written first, reads as a dry run at the lyrics for 'From Me To You'.

Both songs were considered for the A-side, John and Paul first seeking the opinion of the other artists they were touring with in February 1963 as to which was best. Backing their own hunch, 'Thank You Girl' was less popular and so became the B-side. Recorded on the same day just after 'From Me To You', by the sound of it 'Thank You Girl' was given very little studio time. Thrilled at the knowledge they had just recorded their next hit single, John and Paul sound unable to concentrate on their vocals, giving them an insincere and slightly manic edge. A much better version of this song, recorded live, is on *Anthology 1*.

'SHE LOVES YOU'
(McCartney/Lennon) Single released 23 August 1963

A common record company policy in the 1960s was to prepare their top artist's new single for release as soon as the previous one started to fall out of the charts. Tellingly, 'She Loves You' was written the week after 'From Me To You' fell from the UK top 10 on 26 June 1963.

The Beatles, who toured the UK non-stop in 1963, had little time to spare and so John and Paul had to write the song in a Newcastle hotel room. As with 'From Me To You', they pooled resources to come up with one of their rare, start-to-finish 50/50 compositions.

Paul had the initial idea of having the words of the title answered 'yeah' by a chanted backing vocal, similar to the call and response vocals of early '60s US girl groups. Striving to make a lyrical step up from 'From Me To You', John said in 1980 that it was Paul's idea to write about a 'third party'. Paul had got the idea from Bobby Rydell's hit 'Forget Him', then in the British charts. Where in Rydell's song the third party is being lulled away from her lover, Paul here reverses the singer's role to one who is bringing two lovers together. That such mundane drama could be matched with such bold music is clearly daft and led one reviewer of the time to call it their worst single. Yet as John explained in 1980, for their early songs the lyrics did not count as much as the hook or sound of the record. The 'hook' that John spoke of rests largely on the infectious 'wooo' vocal sound which climaxes on the inane but irresistible vocal chant.

Overcoming its lyrical inadequacies, 'She Loves You' was a tour de force of sound. From Ringo's opening mock stumble on drums, through

John and Paul's chiming lead vocals, to the stark closing sixth chord, there is an ecstatic, infectious mood. Compared with other records in the British charts of 1963, 'She Loves You' stands out as a flash of raw brilliance among mostly grey limpid ballads and emasculated rock 'n' roll. The record's uniqueness endeared it to the British public so much that it sustained two separate stays at the number one spot and was for 14 years thereafter the highest-selling UK single of all time.

In comparison to the sometimes rushed performances of the first album, studio technique can now be heard coming to the Beatles' aid. At 1.23, a slightly off-beat edit reveals that 'She Loves You' is in fact two separate performances joined together.

'I'LL GET YOU'
(Lennon/McCartney) B-side to 'She Loves You'

Written alongside 'She Loves You', John and Paul seem to have decided here too that the 'hook' would be more important than the lyrics, the hook in question being the similar repeated backing vocal chant. On some of the dates of the Beatles' summer tour in 1963, audiences were asked to cheer for either 'She Loves You' or 'I'll Get You' to help choose the A-side of the next single. 'I'll Get You' lost and, like 'Thank You Girl' previously, it was given little studio time – notably, vocal gaffes between 1.14 and 1.17 went uncorrected. This, though, would be the Beatles last-ever throwaway B-side, increased competition between John and Paul over their songs and greater time in the studio both playing their part.

'I'll Get You' is notable for its opening line where John asks the girl he is addressing to imagine that he is in love with her. John would repeat this opening lyrical gambit on 'Lucy In The Sky With Diamonds', asking the reader to picture a fairytale land, and on 'Imagine', where he would ask the reader to imagine a utopian, peaceful world.

WITH THE BEATLES
Album released 22 November 1963

With the Beatles is *Please Please Me* volume two by public demand. Their debut album had spent most of 1963 at number one in the UK album charts and their second safely sticks to the same formula of uptempo stage favourites and new songs. The only change of direction is in the way the album is packaged. Enigmatically named, it bravely excludes their recent hit singles, which otherwise might have been used to attract wary record buyers. The cover, showing the Beatles in silhouette, was a hint of the more artistic approach they would soon take. It was also a sign of their increasing creative independence – not only did they direct the photo shoot, but they also fought both Brian Epstein and EMI to get the cover accepted.

While the songs were similar to the first album, they do show a great difference in mood. Each month in 1963 brought the Beatles a new and bigger success. The frenzy and lightheadedness of the times infects their new recordings with a relentless drive that makes even the songs about being sad sound happy. Such overnight fame might have overwhelmed lesser artists, but the Beatles took it in their stride, perhaps because they had waited so long for it. The darker, less welcome side to the mania that surrounded them was still to come.

Still working within the limitations of two-track recording, the album was made on six days between July and October 1963, allowing more attention to detail than the first album. The extra time was not always used wisely, as Paul admitted in 1997. 'It was such a thrill being let loose in the studio, that we almost OD'd on it.' This album particularly suffers from an overuse of double tracking. John in 1970 recalled such overuse with regret saying that he would love to remix it.

Double tracking, a process where a new vocal or guitar part is layered onto the tape of the original performance, when used judiciously can add a compelling force to a song. So enamoured were the Beatles with it that they often overruled George Martin's advice against overusing it – on two-track recording equipment it led to extra tape noise, blurring the sound quality. John's vocals consequently often lack the definition they had on their debut album, 'Please Mr Postman' and 'Money' suffering especially, while Ringo's poorly synchronised double-tracked vocals wobble all over 'I Wanna Be Your Man'. Double tracking was beneficial, though, in helping to overdub the difficult lead guitar parts to 'Roll Over Beethoven', 'All My Loving' and 'Devil In Her Heart'.

Despite such trickery the core performances here are still those of a 'live band' in the studio. Like the debut album, they vary in quality according to how well warmed-up the Beatles were. The 30 July session is typical. At 10 a.m. that day, 'Please Mr Postman' and 'It Won't Be Long' were recorded. The Beatles then left Abbey Road for a BBC radio recording session in central London. Returning at 5 p.m. they recorded, in order, 'Till There Was You', 'Roll Over Beethoven', 'It Won't Be Long (re-make)' and 'All My Loving'. The sharpness of the last track in particular shows the Beatles in peak form. In contrast the songs recorded on 11–12 September ('Hold Me Tight', 'Little Child', 'I Wanna Be Your Man', 'All I've Got To Do', 'Not A Second Time' and 'Don't Bother Me') are some of the weakest on the album, suggesting that on these dates the whirlwind schedule they went through in 1963 was taking its toll.

'IT WON'T BE LONG'
(Lennon/McCartney)

Starting off where their debut album had ended, 'It Won't Be Long' has the same raw impact as 'Twist and Shout'. Indeed it was inspired by another Isley Brothers song, 'Shout', a US hit in 1959, which the Beatles had performed live. The main 'Yeah! Yeah! Yeah!' chant here mimics the rising frenzy of the Isley Brothers' vocals on 'Shout'. That this works so well not only illustrates the growing advances in John and Paul's songwriting abilities, but also their abilities at incorporating other people's music within the bounds of acceptable (legally at least) plagiarism.

The energy of the music is let down by lyrics rooted in John's silly word game around 'be long' and 'belong'. Such tricks amused both John and Paul – a year or two later they would use similar double entendres to slip drug references into their lyrics. Although recorded after 'She Loves You', for a while this was considered as a single in its place, its demotion perhaps due to doubts over its lyrical impact.

'ALL I'VE GOT TO DO'
(Lennon)

Early '60s soul records by Smokey Robinson and Arthur Alexander appealed to John in the same way that Bob Dylan later would. Their vocals sounded as if they genuinely came from the heart, like Dylan's lyrics which seemed honest and truthful too – a stark contrast to most pop records from the early '60s.

'All I've Got To Do' is a rather plastic attempt to emulate such soul records. John's vocal (a rarity for the album, being unaccompanied and single tracked) winningly matches the passion of Smokey Robinson but again, as in 'It Won't Be Long', it does not seem worthwhile, as his lyrics are largely clichéd rhymes, lacking any of the directness he was already showing in interviews from this time. 'All My Loving', which follows, plainly shows that Paul is better at writing 'fictional' love songs. Such a contrast must have been apparent to John, who on later albums would only surpass Paul by drawing inspiration from his own life.

The stuttered tempo of the verses copies that of Robinson's 1962 US hit 'What's So Good About Goodbye' and Alexander's 'Soldier Of Love', though John only admitted to the Robinson influence. Musically this track is also notable for the high presence of Paul's bass, which on early Beatles records was barely discernable in the mix. Here it is turned up high to the point of distortion.

'ALL MY LOVING'
(McCartney)

As good as anything they recorded all year, 'All My Loving' was oddly never released as a single, although it would surely have made number one. The only recognition the Beatles gave of its worth was when it was used as the first song they played live on US television on the *Ed Sullivan Show* in February 1964.

Paul wrote it on a tour in May 1963, inspired by witnessing Roy Orbison compose 'Pretty Woman' when travelling on the same coach. Unlike most Lennon/McCartney compositions of this era, which were recorded within days or weeks of having been written, Paul had over two months until it was recorded to perfect its arrangement and words. The time spent is evident in the way the vocal melody is cleverly offset by the descending chord progression, a touch of class missing from most of their other 1963 output. The *coup de grâce*, though, was its magical studio performance. Like 'Twist And Shout' before it, 'All My Loving' was the last song recorded after a full day's playing, bringing out the absolute best in the band. Noteworthy are John's unusually fast, syncopated rhythm guitar and George's intricate Chet Atkins-style solo. Despite its breakneck speed, the performance ends as it starts with each instrument precisely in time.

'DON'T BOTHER ME'
(Harrison)

Uncontrived and with a driving rhythm, this track is better than several of the Lennon/McCartney compositions on *With the Beatles*. A quote recorded from an argumentative business meeting in 1969 suggests, though, that it may have been more of a Harrison/Lennon/McCartney collaboration than the sole credit suggests. John, answering George's complaint that his songs were often overlooked when recording Beatles albums, recalled that he and Paul had put much work into George's songs, naming 'Don't Bother Me' as a key example. It seems likely that John and Paul, with their experience at structuring and arranging songs, played an important part on this track. Yet for George to be seen to be writing his own songs was important for the marketing of the Beatles in this era. With many teen girl fans choosing a favourite Beatle, increasing George's profile was good for the group. Tellingly, the lyrics here sum him up as the group member who least liked the intrusion of fans and the media into his life.

George's account of the song was that he wrote it while lying sick in a hotel room in Bournemouth during a tour between 19 and 24 August 1963. Its recording several weeks later had an unusual mix of claves and loose-skinned bongos, which like 'Chains' before it appears to be an attempt to give George his own individual sound within the Beatles.

George's next composition did not arrive until 18 months later. George admitted to being overawed by the songs that John and Paul were producing, but he also suffered from being, unfairly as he saw it, locked out of their partnership. After all, pre-fame George had combined with Paul on 'In Spite Of All The Danger' in 1958 and with John on 'Cry For A Shadow' in 1961. Until his death George was the Beatle least enamoured with their legacy and much of his bitterness must have stemmed from what he saw as John and Paul's lack of team spirit. Memorably, in the *Anthology* video series he referred to them as 'egomaniacs'.

'LITTLE CHILD'
(Lennon/McCartney)

Paul excused 'Little Child' as a work song written at speed for Ringo to sing. But Ringo was particular about what he was given to sing and turned it down – he would later insist on a lyric change to 'With A Little Help From My Friends'. Paul later explained Ringo's decision by saying, 'If he couldn't mentally picture a song, you were in trouble.'

'Little Child' only works in that its 1-minute-45-second brevity means it is not long enough for its limited tune and purpose to be exposed. In its performance its strengths and weaknesses are both John's, who contributes a typically forceful lead vocal, undone by his artless and probably speedily overdubbed harmonica. Paul's confident contribution on piano, meanwhile, not only shows a willingness to widen the Beatles sound, but also harks back to their days in Hamburg when, owing to a lack of guitar strings, Paul would often have to play piano instead.

'TILL THERE WAS YOU'
(Wilson)

'Till There Was You' was written for the 1957 musical *The Music Man*, but the Beatles learnt their version from Peggy Lee who made it a small UK hit in 1961. Her arrangement innovatively changed the operatics of the original into a slow salsa – 'Broadway hits with an Afro-Cuban beat' was how the sleevenotes to her album *Latin A La Lee* described it. The arrangement of flute, guitar, piano and bongo, coupled with Lee's languorously sexy vocal, is so successful that it is easy to picture her singing the tune on a Caribbean beach.

The Beatles sped up Lee's version with John and George cleverly transposing the arrangement for acoustic guitar. This musical arrangement alone makes it preferable to the Lee version, yet Paul's vocal, though faithful, lacks the husky worldliness of Lee's, which suits the lyrics better. The point of covering 'Till There Was You' was that its unthreatening and old-fashioned style was useful when the Beatles played at the posher and more lucrative venues in and around Liverpool after Brian Epstein became their manager in 1961. It came in handy too when the Beatles performed four songs at the Royal Variety Show on 4 November 1963, in front of the Queen Mother and Princess Margaret. On record the song would have had the effect of convincing an older and less hip audience that the Beatles were acceptable and to be encouraged. Such acceptance inevitably led to the Beatles being awarded MBE medals by the Queen in 1965.

'PLEASE MR POSTMAN'
(Garrett/Bateman/Dobbins/Holland/Gorman)

One of the Beatles' best cover versions, this speeds up the tempo of the original by the Marvelettes, making for a rougher and more urgent rendition. John's vocal, if a touch melodramatic, realises far more of the lyric's potential. It should have been better, though. Where on the debut album John's single-tracked voice had proved a revelation on covers such as 'Baby It's You' and 'Twist And Shout', here his insistence that his vocal be double tracked means it loses a lot of its intimacy. George Martin, who recognised the power of his vocals, tried to persuade him otherwise, but John, who had become self-conscious about the sound of his voice on record, preferred the bigger, but blurred sound that double tracking gave.

'Please Mr Postman' was the Motown label's first US number one in

1961 and featured a pre-fame Marvin Gaye on drums. Its lyrics were written by Marvelettes singer Georgia Dobbins, who has since contested the way the song has been attributed to five writers. She claimed the only other credit should have been to William Garrett for coming up with the tune.

'ROLL OVER BEETHOVEN'
(Berry)

This innovative version of Chuck Berry's 1956 single captured the Beatles in peak form. Its exciting switch to a double-time tempo at 1.11 is not hinted at on the original. The added handclaps too make it a far livelier group performance than Berry's original – his backing band are distinctly muted. These changes were probably created playing live in Hamburg, where until 1961 it was sung by John.

The Beatles' version fails, however, in exposing George's limits as a lead guitarist. In order to match the wizardry of Berry's original, George had to record both the intro and ending separate to the band performance. Even then he sounds in difficulty and his embarrassment must have grown when the Rolling Stones' debut LP from May 1964 revealed Keith Richards to be far more adept at matching Berry's guitar work.

'HOLD ME TIGHT'
(McCartney/Lennon)

The arrangement for 'Hold Me Tight' caused the Beatles great difficulties. They had first attempted it on their debut album in February, but were dissatisfied and tried it again in September.

Out-takes from the recording session on 12 September 1963 that produced this finished version reveal Paul sounding tired and having difficulty with his vocal. Even on this 'best' take, Paul's vocal wavers in and out of tune, finally breaking completely at the song's end. Fatigue affects the rest of the production too; the tempo wavers and the guitars, which are double tracked, have a dull, clumsy sound. The overdubbed handclaps are a vain attempt to mask this lack of vitality.

The Beatles' heavy workload in 1963, when they crossed the country weekly in trains and coaches, seems to have caught up with them here. Or was it just too much celebrating the night before? The same week in September 'She Loves You' had become No 1 on all UK charts.

Written in 1961, 'Hold Me Tight' shows one of the earliest examples of the Beatles injecting some humorous smut into their lyrics. Although crafted as a simple love song, there is clearly nothing innocent in Paul's stated wish to make love all night long. On this line his vocal appears to be hiding an audible smirk. John said that 'Hold Me Tight' was mainly composed by Paul, who later credited it as an early attempt to write a song good enough to be a single.

'YOU REALLY GOT A HOLD ON ME'
(Robinson)

One of Smokey Robinson and The Miracles finest records, 'You Really Got A Hold On Me' had been a number eight hit in the USA in early 1963, but had failed to chart in the UK. Lack of promotion was largely to blame and consequently the Motown label would not gain its first chart hit until 1964. In the meantime, the Motown label developed a cult following in the UK and this would have been a deeply fashionable song to cover.

The Beatles and numerous other British beat groups saw the failure of such records as an opportunity to 'claim' them for themselves. Indeed much of the UK beat boom bands specialised in US hits that had not made the UK charts. Notably, the Rolling Stones also covered Marvin Gaye's excellent 1963 US hit 'Can I Get A Witness' for their debut album.

In the rush to stake their claim to 'You Really Got A Hold On Me', a version was broadcast on BBC radio on 24 May and it became the first song recorded for *With the Beatles*, on 18 July 1963. It was not an easy recording and several edits (the most obvious can be heard at 0.25) reveal that this is a mix of two takes. The Beatles' cover version, if a touch sloppy in performance, is a warmer, more impassioned rendition than the original. The slickness of the Miracles original by comparison owed much to the upwardly mobile aspirations of Motown label owner Berry Gordy. A notable difference between the two versions is in the ending; where the Miracles' version fades out, the Beatles improvised a closing drum roll and ninth chord.

'I WANNA BE YOUR MAN'
(McCartney/Lennon)

A chance meeting on a London street led to the donation of this song to the Rolling Stones. While window shopping for guitars in the Charing Cross Road, John and Paul were spotted by Mick Jagger and Keith

Richards from a taxi. They gave John and Paul a lift to their rehearsal studio a few streets away and boldly asked if they had any songs to spare. At the time Billy J. Kramer was at number one in the UK charts with 'Bad To Me', a song that the Beatles had 'given away'. To the amazement of Mick and Keith, who were still novices at songwriting, John and Paul turned a half an idea for a song (that Paul had for over a year), into a finished product within half an hour at the Stones' London studio. Unlike the twee song John had fashioned for the fresh-faced Billy J. Kramer, the Stones obviously needed something harder, explaining the absence of any distinctive minor chord-led middle eight from this straight-ahead rocker.

Improbable though this meeting may sound, it has been backed up by both Bill Wyman and Paul McCartney. Other versions of the story say that the Stones manager Andrew Loog Oldham, who had worked on the Beatles' early publicity, directly asked John and Paul to write a song for the Stones as a returned favour. Oldham himself says it was he who bumped into John and Paul in Charing Cross Road inviting them back to the Stones' rehearsal studio in a basement club, the Studio 51 at 10–11 Great Newport Street, next to Leicester Square tube station.

Two days after the above meeting the Beatles recorded their own arrangement but let the Rolling Stones release their version first in early November. The song's three-chord simplicity made it suitable for Ringo's vocal range and easy for him to sing and play drums. The Stones' version, which became their first top 20 hit, while messier musically is more suited to Mick Jagger's vocals, which draw out a bluesy sexuality from the lyrics. Ringo never really gets to grip with the song, which is only saved by enthusiastic backing vocals from John and Paul. Their added whoops and screams were, as on 'Boys', included to encourage a reluctant Ringo into singing.

'DEVIL IN HER HEART'
(Drapkin)

One of the most unusual Beatles cover versions, the original by US girl group the Donays was recorded as 'Devil In His Heart' in 1962 and featured a wildly out-of-tune lead vocal. Despite such failings, the Beatles recognised it as a good song and changed the lyrics gender for their version. It would have also appealed as a R&B number few other groups were likely to have heard. The Beatles had found a single copy of the record at Brian Epstein's record shop in Liverpool – Epstein at the time having a policy of ordering single copies of often quite obscure US records. It is difficult to believe that it was George who chose to sing this song, as his vocal struggles while John and Paul, on supporting vocals, appear to be having far more fun. Like most of the covers on *With the Beatles* this is a much faster rendition than the original.

'NOT A SECOND TIME'
(Lennon)

John admitted that this was a Smokey Robinson impression, making it his second tribute to the Motown singer on this album. The prominent syncopated piano chords bear close resemblance to 'Mickey's Monkey', a US hit for Robinson in September 1963. A blot on this pastiche, though, is George Martin's misplaced tea-dance-style piano solo – Martin presumably had not heard Robinson's record. Another more curious blip is found on the closing fade, where John's double-tracked vocals can be heard going wildly out of sync.

Hidden away at the end of the album, 'Not A Second Time' is often overlooked but represents John's most natural and convincing set of lyrics from this period. Indeed, a different approach appears to have been taken on recording too; the absence of backing vocals and the low presence of guitars has led to the suspicion that neither George nor Paul played.

'MONEY'
(Bradford/Gordy)

'Money', like 'Twist And Shout', was another crowd-pleasing end-of-album maelstrom, which by comparison falls slightly short. In a misguided attempt to top 'Twist And Shout', a wall of sound was added to its initial performance by double tracking not only John's lead vocals, but Paul and George's vocals too. This overloaded the two-track recording machines then in use at Abbey Road, distorting the sound and masking the energy of the basic performance, which only briefly shines through on the intro and the breaks between verse and chorus. When John commented in 1970 that he would like to remix the *With the Beatles* album (Is this technically possible? Are the extra vocals indelibly on tape?), he undoubtedly had this track foremost in his thoughts.

The original version of 'Money' was a small US hit for the 17-year-old Barrett Strong in 1959, although not credited to him, he claimed to have written the song's distinctive riff after trying to copy Ray Charles' riff from 'What I'd Say'. Released on the Anna label, a precursor of Motown, its lyrics were a dryly amusing account of the financial dire straits faced by Berry Gordy after setting up his new record company. The record now sounds remarkable for its tinny sound compared to the gloss of later Motown records.

The Beatles stuck to the arrangement of Barrett Strong's original, but like so many of his covers of early R&B and rock 'n' roll songs, John ups the emotional content at the expense of the song's humour. The way John interprets it, he appears to be asking not just for money but complete satiation, something that in the madness of Beatlemania it might have appeared he was being offered. His emphasis gives added weight to the closing lyric, 'I wanna be free', to which several Beatles books have since accorded great significance, even implying that John added this line to the lyrics. Though less prominent on the original, this line does appear on its fade out.

3. A Hard Day's Night

'I WANT TO HOLD YOUR HAND'
(Lennon/McCartney) Single released 29 November 1963

'I Want To Hold Your Hand' represents the high watermark of the Beatles' commercial ambitions. Its contrived 2-minute-45-second promise of unthreatening intimacy, makes it probably the ultimate boy band song. The lyrics are a wise reflection of their times; in the early 1960s million-selling girls' magazines *Judy* and *Bunty* gave no hint of sex in their content. It was also, just as importantly, the first Beatles' single aimed directly at the US market.

Always seeking new goals to motivate them, a US chart hit was the next big challenge. To date, in late 1963, the three number ones they'd had in the UK had done next to nothing in the USA. All lacked any significant promotion, having been passed on by Capitol (EMI's American subsidiary) and leased instead to small independent labels. In order to persuade them into releasing 'I Want To Hold Your Hand', Brian Epstein, carrying a copy of the Beatles' new recording, made a special trip to see the Capitol executives in New York in early November 1963. Apparently Epstein sold the record to Capitol as one specially designed for the US market. John and Paul never verified this story, though in its structure 'I Want To Hold Your Hand' matches recent US top ten hits 'You Really Got A Hold On Me' by Smokey Robinson and The Miracles and 'Please Mr Postman' by the Marvelettes. The lyrics echo the politeness of these songs and John and Paul's chiming lead vocals match their arrangements. It would be easy to imagine either group singing their own version of 'I Want To Hold Your Hand'.

Another factor in 'I Want To Hold Your Hand's' favour was that it brought a breakthrough in sound quality, being the first Beatles recording on four-track equipment. The new German recording machines introduced to EMI's Abbey Road studios in October 1963 gave greater clarity, particularly on vocals, which could now be recorded on separate tracks. So while John's lead vocals dominate, Paul's harmony vocals come through clearly for the first time.

While enormously successful – it was their biggest worldwide seller, along with 'Hey Jude' – the lyrics became quickly out of date in the rapidly evolving society of the 1960s. The Beatles would long be associated with its teen romance lyrics, inadvertently opening the door for bands like the Rolling Stones to take a calculatedly sexier and more rebellious approach. The lyrics were a cause of amusement for Bob Dylan. When he first met the Beatles in New York in July 1964 he offered them marijuana, for the first time as it turned out. Surprised at their inexperience, he asked snidely, 'Surely the lyrics to "I Want To Hold Your Hand" referred to the drug, with the line "I get high"'. 'No, those aren't the words,' John replied, explaining, as Dylan surely knew, that the Beatles were singing of a childish teen love they could not hide'. The most common accounts of this story see no intended sarcasm in Dylan's remarks, though years later John was to remark that he always felt paranoid and uncomfortable in his presence, never sure if he was mocking him or not.

Dylan's goading would seem to have had an immediate effect on their lyrics, which on their next album and single ('I Feel Fine'/'She's A Woman') contained both drug references and a much sourer take on the love song.

'THIS BOY'
(Lennon/McCartney) B-side to 'I Want To Hold Your Hand'

The D-Bm-G-A 'four-chord trick' used here was a staple of numerous '50s and early '60s vocal harmony records typified by 'Blue Moon' by the Marcels. On 'This Boy' John and Paul deliberately set out to write their own version of this style, with special reference to the vocal harmony classic 'To Know Him Is To Love Him' by the Teddy Bears, which the Beatles had sung live and which contains a similar soaring middle eight. John credited Smokey Robinson as an influence too, in which case he was probably referring to the singles 'Bad Girl' and '(You Can) Depend On Me' of 1959–60, both of which share the same pace as 'This Boy', and the same close harmonies and basic chord structure.

Great effort was needed to rehearse the vocal harmonies, somewhat to the loss of the Beatles' usual spontaneity. Their soulful sound, though, is let down by lyrics so bland they verge on meaningless, which makes the whole exercise seem a waste of energy.

'CAN'T BUY ME LOVE'
(McCartney/Lennon) Single first released in the USA 16 March 1964

Like their last three UK number one records, 'Can't Buy Me Love' was written to order as soon as the previous single vacated the number one spot, 'I Want To Hold Your Hand' being displaced on 18 January 1964. In the rush to prepare it for release, it was both written and recorded (at EMI's studios in Paris on 29 January) during the Beatles' three-week stay in France.

Paul's lyrics would appear to be a direct comment on the Beatles' first real taste of luxury. The Beatles, performing a series of shows in Paris, were staying in two adjoining suites at the five-star Georges Cinq hotel. Just off the Champs Élysées, the hotel is in one of Paris's most exclusive areas, dotted with upmarket clothes shops and jewellery stores. Such surroundings would explain the song's opening line, but it is hard not to believe that its carefree mood was not also influenced by the amazing news the Beatles received in Paris, that 'I Want To Hold Your Hand' had gone to number one in the USA. An alternative theory on the lyrics – sung with an unfortunate hammy US accent by Paul – is that they are a complete mirror image of those on the recently recorded 'Money'.

Musically 'Can't Buy Me Love' shows the honing of a song formula. As on 'She Loves You' the chorus is placed first, to start the song off to a fast pace, while the use of three major chords for the verse and two minor chords for the chorus was a formula used soon after on 'A Hard Day's Night', 'I Feel Fine' and 'I'm A Loser'.

A HARD DAY'S NIGHT
Album released 10 July 1964

One of the most relentlessly upbeat albums ever made, *A Hard Day's Night* caught the Beatles in an ecstatic mood following their unimaginable success in the USA. The welcome they were given on arrival in New York in February 1964 was their biggest career high. Explaining some of the mood of the album, the days devoted to songwriting in the US were spent in Miami, a place the relatively untravelled Beatles described as 'paradise'. For the chronically insecure John, such success and rewards gave a huge boost to his confidence. Casting aside his usual introspection, his songs for the album are among the happiest he ever wrote. Even his songs about heartbreak end up sounding euphoric. In a reversal of roles, Paul's songs are more contemplative and crafted. The gritty use of acoustic guitar and contemplative lyrics on 'Things We Said Today' suggest the influence of Bob Dylan, whose music the Beatles first heard in January 1964. At this stage the differences between John and Paul's characters were clearly emerging. On the cover photo John looks at the camera openly and head on, while Paul's gaze in contrast is evasive or guarded.

The songs were the first the Beatles had ever written on a commission basis. United Artists, the producers for the film that would become *A Hard Day's Night*, requested six new songs for the soundtrack. These were mostly recorded in the last week of February and appear on side A of the album. The song 'A Hard Day's Night' was recorded in April and added to the film at the last minute. The songwriting obligation to United Artists was something John and Paul found hard to fulfil, but once finalised it provided the temptation to complete an album full of their own compositions. John and Paul duly completed 'Any Time At All', 'I'll Be Back', 'I'll Cry Instead', 'When I Get Home' and 'Things We Said Today' once filming had been completed. All were recorded over the first three days in June.

Unlike most Beatles albums, *A Hard Day's Night* only contains 13 tracks. Another song was planned, but Ringo fell ill before the album's last recording session, on 3 June. The day after, the Beatles minus Ringo left on a world tour and the album had to be released with 13 tracks. Interestingly, in Ringo's absence the Beatles recorded demos of both 'You Know What To Do' and 'No Reply' – were either of these intended as the 14th track?

Filling an album with Lennon/McCartney tracks was also an act of bravado towards their rivals the Rolling Stones. The Beatles had held the number one spot for a whole year in the UK album charts before the Rolling Stones' first LP knocked them off in May 1964. The Stones' debut, like the first two Beatles albums, featured many cover versions. The Beatles, by demonstrating self-reliance in songwriting, were making a statement of their superiority.

Four-track recording equipment was used for the whole album and brought impressive results. Still recording from a group performance,

George Martin put drums, bass and rhythm guitar on track one, lead guitar on track two and lead vocals on track three. Tricky guitar parts and vocals were recorded separately and perfected at leisure on track four. This separation of sound gives more clarity to the vocals, one of the Beatles' greatest assets. It also gave clarity to the lead guitar, which paved the way for such riff-driven songs as 'I Feel Fine' and 'Day Tripper'. The more polished sound was offset by a loss in the live-feeling excitement captured on the first two albums, a sound the Beatles would eventually seek to return to on *The White Album* and *Let It Be*.

On the Beatles' trip to America in February 1964, George acquired a rare Rickenbacker 12-string guitar. Its distinctive wash of sound is heard on most of the album, though it was only occasionally used hereafter. Its use here inspired the Byrds' sound for hits like 'Mr Tambourine Man' and 'Turn, Turn, Turn'.

'A HARD DAY'S NIGHT'
(Lennon)

That Paul had completed 'Can't Buy Me Love' alone encouraged John's competitive nature to get the next A-side. Such was his keenness that on privately hearing that the new Beatles film was to be called *A Hard Day's Night*, he went home after filming and wrote the song that night, before Paul found out. The song was then presented to the other Beatles as a fait accompli the next morning.

John's coup over Paul was not complete. In writing the song so fast, he had not worked out its arrangement properly. To his embarrassment, when they came to record it John found he could not reach the high notes of the middle-eight/chorus refrain, which the higher-pitched Paul had to sing. Beyond the strong opening verse and middle eight John too had struggled to write much more on his own. In their partnership Paul traditionally helped out on the second and third verses of John's songs – here the second verse is notably weak and John, no doubt sensing he had got as far as he could, resorted to repeating the first verse three times. Completed at speed, the lyrics simply appear to describe John's return home after a day's filming. They are revealing as an honest account of the Beatles' tiredness – their schedule for filming was often from 8 a.m. until late. The music too borrows from the previous single 'Can't Buy Me Love', featuring a similar bluesy three-chord verse and a minor chord-heavy chorus/middle eight.

The film's opening sequence, for which this track was overlaid, dictated its arrangement. Under George Martin's direction the stark, suspended G chord from George's 12-string guitar announces the film's start, after the title credits. To fit with shots of running feet as the Beatles flee from chasing fans, a bongo plays double time, heightening the pace. Martin's other key input here was to create the unusual solo where George's 12-string guitar is matched note for note on the piano.

'I SHOULD HAVE KNOWN BETTER'
(Lennon)

John claimed the lyrics of this song meant nothing, implying that the 'love' he refers to here was fictional, yet the mood of the music and the lyrics is revealing. Recorded several days after the Beatles' first trip to the USA, the infectiously happy tone reveals his feelings over their new success. A rare example of John expressing unmitigated glee, this is arguably his happiest song in the whole Beatles catalogue.

This was also the Beatles best-ever arrangement for 12-string guitar – George's thick-as-treacle chords on his newly acquired 12-string Rickenbacker are layered one-a-bar over John's steadily strummed acoustic guitar. Despite this glorious effect, the Beatles were never ones for being stuck with a particular sound and did not use it again.

'IF I FELL'
(Lennon/McCartney)

'If I Fell' is often quoted as a rare example of John displaying his sensitive side through his songwriting, but his dry vocal betrays a lack of sincerity, or at least ill-ease, explained by the lyrics which are still rooted in sentimental clichés aimed at the Beatles teen girl fans.

The most successful part of the song is the pretty melody brought beautifully alive by the harmonies between John and Paul's vocals. Achieving this was obviously something that did not come easily, as even after 15 takes both John and Paul's vocals go out of tune in places. Within the Beatles' tight 1964 schedule they were typically recording three songs on each day spent in the studio, and so had little time to perfect each song.

'I'M HAPPY JUST TO DANCE WITH YOU'
(Lennon/McCartney)

Both John and Paul set out to write this for George. In his biography

Paul admitted the song was written to 'pander' to their fans. As most fans had their own favourite Beatle, 'I'm Happy Just To Dance With You' gave George's fans in particular another reason to buy the album and see the film. Unfortunately for George, neither John nor Paul gave away their best songs and this naff teenage dance hall tale typecasts George as the junior Beatle. This cavalier attitude to George extends to recording, where he struggles with the vocals, suggesting a rushed session.

John suggests himself as the main writer here, the jealous lyrics seeming truer of him than Paul. The syncopated rhythm guitar style copied from the Searchers' 'Sugar and Spice', a hit from 1963, was also a favourite of John's.

George's own songwriting, it would seem, was still suffering from a lack of support from John and Paul. A song he had begun for the album, 'You Know What To Do' (the demo of which now appears on the *Anthology 1* album) sounds promising but unfinished, something John or Paul could have easily helped with.

'AND I LOVE HER'
(McCartney/Lennon)

The time Paul spent mastering the Latin rhythms of 'Besame Mucho' and 'Till There Was You' were not wasted, as he showed here, writing his own Latin rhythm ballad. An exquisite arrangement, the subtle shift of key mid-song was a trick common among Brill Building writers such as Goffin and King, but way beyond the Beatles' immediate competitors and imitators. Such a trick was no doubt a self-conscious move by Paul, who was still looking to prove himself as a songwriter. Having the title of the song start in mid-sentence was a mannered ploy too, and Paul admitted he used it to sound 'clever'.

Despite such sophistication, the words convey little, other than in the reference to brightly shining stars, where the guitars evoke twinkling stars, film score-style.

John claimed a writing contribution on the middle eight here, but as Paul disputes this, it would suggest that John's contribution was small.

'TELL ME WHY'
(Lennon)

John said of 'Tell Me Why' in 1980 that United Artists 'needed another upbeat song and I just knocked it off'. Unusually, this quote suggests that the film producers United Artists to some extent dictated the style of songs commissioned for the film *A Hard Day's Night*. This, then, is a suitably amphetamine-fuelled jaunt whose mood mocks the heartache implied in the lyrics. Its recording is only notable for the use of multi-tracked vocals, which creates the probably intentional, comical choral effect in the verses.

Paul in his biography speculated that the lyrics spoke of John's marital difficulties with Cynthia.

'ANY TIME AT ALL'
(Lennon)

Looking back at the Beatles' discography in the '70s, John often expressed a desire to re-record all of it, such was his dissatisfaction with the arrangements and production. Arguably John began this task here by re-writing a song under a different name. 'Any Time At All' – one of *A Hard Day's Night's* most exciting performances – makes for a successful update of 'It Won't Be Long', John in 1980 admitting that the newer song contained 'the same chords with me shouting over the top'. Despite such amendments, the lyrics to 'Any Time At All' lack the emotional weight to match John's belting vocal performance, one of his best ever with the Beatles. 'Slow Down' and 'When I Get Home', which were recorded in the same early June recording sessions, similarly feature him in surely the best vocal form of his life.

'I'LL CRY INSTEAD'
(Lennon)

An early rebellion by John over the large number of Beatles songs that 'pandered' to their fans, this is a joke song styled as a corny country and western lament. The first verse, in which John declares himself 'mad' and then announces that he is going to have himself locked away, was a send-up of a similar line from Paul's 'A World Without Love', a song donated to Peter and Gordon who made it a UK number one in early 1964. John found Paul's unintentionally silly lyrics hilarious and could not resist repeating them here.

While typical of John's irreverent humour, such spoof love songs were not uncommon at this time. The Isley Brothers' 1964 single 'I'm Laughing To Keep From Crying' also mocked the Smokey Robinson and The Miracles' single 'I've Got To Dance To Keep From Crying'. The

Isleys' lyrics were a list of activities the singer has to do to keep from crying, culminating in the wonderfully daft staement that he will 'whistle' to stop himself from crying.

'THINGS WE SAID TODAY'
(McCartney)

Written below deck on a yacht while relaxing on holiday in the Bahamas with Jane Asher, Paul's ambitious song conjures up his thoughts on the future. The track succeeds as one of the few songs on the album that makes a strong connection between the words and the music. The verses with their minor chords are cautious, while the major chords of the chorus are more optimistic. Paul learnt this from one of his favourite songs, 'Besame Mucho', whose verses in G minor are cautious, breaking through to an optimistic G major for the more joyful chorus. If there is a fault with this otherwise perfect track it is that Paul's double-tracked vocals are somewhat out of sync.

'WHEN I GET HOME'
(Lennon)

It is easy to speculate that the lyrics for 'When I Get Home' originated as part of the original draft lyrics for 'A Hard Day's Night', for John once said that he did not like to waste lyrical ideas and its theme of returning home after work is identical. The cast-off nature of the lyrics is matched in the arrangement, which not even John's hollered lead vocals can save. John's boredom with the song is apparent when he inserts a colloquial line about the cows coming home on the middle eight which sabotages any of the song's sincerity. Clearly no longer seeing every song they wrote as a potential single, the Beatles were starting to master the skill of writing 'filler' songs as albums tracks.

'YOU CAN'T DO THAT'
(Lennon)

Here John reveals his 'Jealous Guy' persona, his scathing vocals and lyrics revealing his deep insecurity over girlfriends and wives. The words are matched by the menacing R&B thrust of the music, over which John lets rip with a rare guitar solo of inspired staccato thrash and stray notes. John rated himself as a better lead guitarist than Paul or George and his style here bears a resemblance to the rough three-string attack of Buddy Holly's solo on 'Peggy Sue'. He actually claimed the song was influenced by Wilson Pickett, but the stuttered tempo in fact reveals itself as a quite blatant copy of Marvin Gaye's 'Hitch Hike', a US hit from 1963.

Offered for the *Hard Day's Night* film, it was rejected by United Artists who no doubt found the lyrics and vocals out of sync with the cuddly image they were projecting of the Beatles.

'I'LL BE BACK'
(Lennon/McCartney)

Never released on single, this could potentially have been a big hit for the Beatles for its classic arrangement of vocal harmonies. Unlike the Beatles' best singles, though, the lyrics say little, having the appearance of a word game about hating to leave, coming back and then promising to go! Such illogical meanings suggest that this was a close John and Paul collaboration, with each adding consecutive but only tenuously linking lyrical ideas. Most thought was put into the music, particularly in the gorgeous verses, where descending guitar chords are answered by a vocal melody that falls too then rises. Curiously, the spindly guitar riff that starts the track is very close to that used on 'And I Love Her', which is itself close to that of the 'Harry Lime Theme' which the Beatles favoured as a warm-up tune.

LONG TALL SALLY EP

Enormous demand for Beatles' products in the USA led Capitol, the Beatles' record company in America, to request extra songs for release. In the USA the Beatles' albums contained only ten songs, so the songs that were spare could be used to make up new albums. The Beatles responded to the request from Capitol by knocking out cover versions that could be recorded in a couple of takes. In this way 'I Call Your Name' (a reject from the *A Hard Day's Night* film) and 'Long Tall Sally' were used to create what Capitol named The Beatles' Second Album. In the rush to meet demand, these songs with 'Can't Buy Me Love' came to be the first to be released in the USA – on 10 April 1964 – before their UK release date. Two further songs requested by Capitol, 'Slow Down' and 'Matchbox', were used to fill up another US-only LP entitled *Something New*. These songs received their first release date in the UK on 19 June 1964 as part of the *Long Tall Sally* EP which also included the latter two songs.

'LONG TALL SALLY'
(Penniman/Blackwell/Johnson)

At school Paul entertained his classmates by doing impersonations of Little Richard and went on to sing at least seven different Little Richard songs live with the Beatles. His rendition of 'Long Tall Sally' was one of the oldest, stretching back to his first performance with John's group the Quarrymen, when he was 15. Over the years his performance of the song improved to the point that 'Long Tall Sally' was often used to end live sets on a rousing note. The Beatles captured this atmosphere so well on this recording that some writers have claimed that it actually improves on the original. Yet unlike Beatles cover versions such as 'Twist And Shout' and 'Anna' which reinterpret the originals, this is still an impersonation. The Beatles' version might pack more physical power, but Paul's vocals miss out on the witty sexual insinuation in Little Richard's vocal that brings the words alive.

'I CALL YOUR NAME'
(Lennon/McCartney)

John claimed this as one of his earliest attempts at a song even before he had formed the Quarrymen. As such he remained fond of it in spite of its shortcomings, one of which was presumably an incomplete structure, to which Paul claimed to have helped on. In 1963 both returned to the song, writing extra lyrics and giving it a new arrangement. As such it was donated to Brian Epstein's pretty-boy protegée Billy J. Kramer, who recorded a pedestrian version as the B-side to 'Bad To Me'. The version the Beatles recorded in March 1964 is far better, benefitting from yet more improvements to the song, notably the bold switch to a ska tempo halfway through and the powerful use of 12-string guitar on the main riff.

'SLOW DOWN'
(Larry Williams)

Larry Williams was a black rock 'n' roll singer, whose close similarity in style to Little Richard meant that he was never accorded the status his talent deserved. John, though, championed him by singing six of his songs live and indeed the three songs that Lennon recorded with the Beatles provided Williams with a greater fortune than any of his own records.

'Slow Down' had been a minor hit for Williams in the UK in 1958 and featured a slick arrangement of tenor saxophones weaving their way round the main guitar riff. The Beatles give it a more obviously rock 'n' roll treatment, no doubt shaped by playing it endlessly live. Likewise where Williams sings it as a playful tale of a girlfriend's promiscuity, John gives it a dynamic life-or-death-style intensity that peaks on his enormous double-tracked scream before the guitar solo (at 1.40). In spite of, or perhaps because of this amazing performance and in the general rush to record it, two errors on the double tracking occured at 1.15 and 2.23 where John muddles up the lyrics.

'MATCHBOX'
(Carl Perkins)

Carl Perkins was on a rock 'n' roll revival tour of Britain in June 1964 when the Beatles invited him to Abbey Road and in honour of his presence recorded 'Matchbox'. Although sung by Ringo on this occasion, the song had been sung in turns by George, Pete Best and John since it entered the Beatles' live set in 1961.

'Matchbox's barely decipherable lyrics, derived from 'Matchbox Blues', a song by blues singer Blind Lemon Jefferson in 1927. From Jefferson it evolved into a country and western standard, with its verses being rewritten and improvised. Carl Perkins adaptation from 1957 injects a menace into the lyrics not hinted at by Ringo's happy singalong style, andlikewise Perkins' guitar solo is spidery, whereas George's solo is jolly. The solo recorded in his hero's presence is also one of George's most ham-fisted ever and George Martin judiciously buries it in the mix.

This was one of numerous covers the Beatles learnt from Carl Perkin's 1957 Dance Album. The Beatles, due to poor finances in their early days, were restricted in the number of records they owned and so exploited each to the limit. In all the Beatles either recorded or played live nine out of the twelve tracks from this album, including 'Blue Suede Shoes', 'Sure To Fall', 'Gone, Gone Gone', 'Honey Don't', 'Tennessee', 'Everybodys Trying To Be My Baby', 'Matchbox', 'Your True Love' and 'Boppin The Blues'.

4. Beatles for Sale

'I FEEL FINE'
(Lennon/McCartney) Single released 27 November 1964

In the 1960s boys often expressed a preference for the Rolling Stones over the Beatles, as while early Beatles records so obviously catered for teenage girls, the Rolling Stones did not seem to care who liked their music at all. 'I Feel Fine' goes some way to redressing this situation, with its wilfully macho burst of opening feedback and sharp metallic riff. On its release the Beatles were coy about their use of the feedback, claiming it was an accident, though Mark Lewisohn's study of the original tapes (*The Beatles Recording Sessions* of 1988), reveals it was actually rehearsed over all nine takes. The distinctive, chiming riff that follows was in places played together by George and John, giving the Beatles a harder edge than ever before on record. The device of starting the riff on one guitar (George) and then a couple of bars later having a second guitar (John) play it too for dramatic effect was a trick almost certainly learnt from the intro to Roy Orbison's 'Oh Pretty Woman', which was number one in the UK charts when 'I Feel Fine' was recorded on 16 October 1964. John, who created the now-legendary riff, said it was based on the simpler, but equally loud blues riff on Bobby Parker's cult 1961 R&B dance record 'Watch Your Step'.

John's lyrics follow the true love theme of the Beatles' 1963 singles and yet lack any of their conviction. Taking a lead from Paul's 'She's A Woman', completed the week before, John adopts the strategy of writing about a girl's emotions, but his words do not convince. The reference to a diamond ring so soon after its use in 'Can't Buy Me Love' (on the B-side, Paul's girl does not need any presents) sounds sarcastic. John's mocking tone throughout the verses makes you wonder if the chorus is really sincere. While the riff to 'I Feel Fine' must be one that most guitarists the world over at some time attempt, these unusual lyrics have made it one of the Beatles' singles least covered in its entirety.

'SHE'S A WOMAN'
(McCartney/Lennon) B-side to 'I Feel Fine'

It seems likely that this simplistic three-power-chord rocker was a pastiche on the Neanderthal rock of the Kinks' 'You Really Got Me', riding high in the UK charts when it was recorded. Other than the equally stylised 'I Saw Her Standing There', Paul had never written three-chord compositions previously. Its goofy, flippant lyrics, largely composed in the studio as the song was recorded, also seem to mock the simplistic vocals on 'You Really Got Me', telling an out-take of 'She's A Woman' reveals it breaking down into wildly exaggerated vocals and screaming.

BEATLES FOR SALE
Album released 4 December

The thousand-yard stares of the Beatles on the cover of this album reveal the fatigue of one feature film, one world tour, two US tours, one British tour, two albums, two singles and one EP, all squeezed out in one manic nine-month cash-in on Beatlemania. By several accounts the scenes backstage and in hotels post-concert on the Beatles' Australian and US tours of the summer of 1964 were the most debauched of their whole career.

In October 1964, when the Beatles should have been recuperating, they began touring Britain, fitting in recording on spare days. The seven days allocated to recording a new album were two less than for *A Hard Day's Night* and to catch up, songwriting often took place in the studio. The lack of new songs meant that cover versions which could be knocked out in one take were used to fill up the album quickly to meet their Christmas deadline. In one marathon session on Sunday 18 October, six songs were recorded.

The lack of time made for sparse arrangements; instead of the Beatles' characteristic vocal interplay, John and Paul often merely share lead vocals. Acoustic guitar too replaces the wall of electric guitar sound that dominates *A Hard Day's Night*. The Beatles were progressing, however.

Piano is used increasingly and Paul's songs 'Every Little Thing', 'What You're Doing' and 'Eight Days A Week' were their most adventurous productions yet.

The Beatles' weariness lent a jaded and often mocking tone to the new Lennon/McCartney lyrics. The hip influence of Bob Dylan, who they had met in New York in July, is at work too and John and Paul are clearly no longer pandering to their teen girl fans. 'I Feel Fine', 'She's A Woman' and 'I'm A Loser' openly subvert the simple true love themes of their earlier work, while other songs appear to comment on their heavy work load, e.g. 'Eight Days A Week' and 'What You're Doing'. Elsewhere a rebellious streak is emerging; after the feedback closes on 'I Feel Fine', someone can be heard muttering 'shit!' under his breath. The album's title, *Beatles For Sale*, is also a sour comment on their commercial exploitation.

As fast as the Beatles had changed the rules of pop music in 1963, they were changed again in 1964 as the Animals, the Kinks and the Rolling Stones brought a new macho edge to pop with their UK number one singles 'The House of the Rising Sun', 'You Really Got Me' and 'It's All Over Now'. While fans of this new sound, the Beatles largely steered clear of it for fear, it must be said, that they could not compete. The pyrotechnic guitar work of Keith Richards and Brian Jones on the Rolling Stones' debut album, released in May 1964, clearly outshone that of George and John, while the belligerent punk of the early Kinks hits was again not suited to the Beatles' strengths.

Temporarily the Beatles turned to country and western, which they had first heard in Liverpool prior to the advent of rock 'n' roll. The American radio stations they had listened to while on tour in the USA had reawakened their interest in this music and they reproduced its sound for five tracks on *Beatles For Sale*.

'NO REPLY'
(Lennon/McCartney)

One of the high points of *Beatles For Sale*, 'No Reply' was considered as a single and given more studio time than other tracks. Its arrangement benefited too from an early demo run-through during one of the *A Hard Day's Night* sessions in June. Notable embellishments were the calypso beat and the Latin touches of handclaps and a capo used on the guitar, which give a dramatic foil to John's tale of romantic intrigue. Underneath this arrangement George Martin's neat piano chords add a texture of sound missing from most of the album.

John's lyrics read like a picture story from a girl's comic, curiously a purpose for which several Beatles songs had already been adapted in 1964. Commenting on 'No Reply', John described the first verses as portraying an image he had of walking down a street and seeing a girl silhouetted in a window, not answering the telephone. The lyrics show John's first key use of alliteration in the first line of the second verse, with the emphasis on the sounds from the words tried, to, telephone, not and that. The sound of these words produces a percussive effect that adds a new texture to the rhythm track – in the context of the Latin sound, they are like castanets.

'I'M A LOSER'
(Lennon)

Although never folk fans, on hearing Bob Dylan the Beatles became instant fans of his powerful, direct style. Unlike the folk music they despised for its safe and twee style, Dylan's songs 'Blowin' In The Wind' and 'The Times They Are A-Changin'' were topical and held a powerful message. 'I'm A Loser' was their first and most obvious copy of Dylan, the corny way John addresses the listeners as a 'friend' is clearly traceable to 'Blowin' In The Wind'. Such a style sat uncomfortably with Dylan and even more so with John, whose judgement was clouded by infatuation. The chorus with its double tracking is more typical of the Beatles' style. Otherwise this is a strong group performance that reflects its initial consideration as a single.

The lyrics' origin lie in the Beatle's first full-length international tour in June 1964, which left John disillusioned with fame. The monotony of being cooped up in hotels and planes was often the reality of his existence rather than the non-stop party he may have expected. On stage, too, the Beatles might as well have been waxworks, as John later commented, since the screams of the audience prevented them from being heard. John also resented the Beatles' clean suit-and-tie image and the expectation for them to maintain a cheerful, endearing personality. Such an image was important for the Beatles' success, but was a strain for John.

Over the following years John would return to this theme many times, particularly with the more articulate 'Help!' in 1965. John summed up his condition succinctly in 1980: 'Part of me suspects I'm a loser and part of me suspects I'm God Almighty.'

'BABY'S IN BLACK'
(Lennon/McCartney)

A favourite track of the Beatles for its unusual (for them) 3/4 beat, 'Baby's In Black' veers between the banal and the sublime. Written in a hotel room while on tour, it is a product of a growing rebellion at the clean, safe image created by 'I Want To Hold Your Hand'. The lyrics are world-weary, sardonic and in places deliberately awful. The languorous pace and mood is symptomatic of their heavy workload in 1964.

John and Paul's equal writing input on this song is reflected in their dual lead vocals, sung on one microphone, a technique copied from the Everly Brothers.

'ROCK AND ROLL MUSIC'
(Chuck Berry)

Written in 1957 at the height of what the US media styled the 'rock 'n' roll craze', this is a wry, knowing look by Chuck Berry at a teenager's reasons for liking rock 'n' roll (Berry was then in his late 20s). By contrast, John interprets the song as if he were the teenager Berry wrote about, not only missing the point of the lyrics but also losing the song's intended humour. For John, simply recording a song entitled 'Rock And Roll Music' was an act of faith. The fervour in his double-tracked voice shows how passionate he was about singing it (it was recorded in one take to save time), so much so that he fluffs the lyrics, singing 'oughta got rock 'n' roll music' at 2.19.

'I'LL FOLLOW THE SUN'
(McCartney)

'I'll Follow The Sun' was written by Paul as a teenager, and a rare recording of a Beatles practice session from 1960 reveals the song at an earlier stage. Instead of the smooth arpeggio on the later version, there is a searing guitar line, similar to the intro on Buddy Holly's 'That'll Be The Day'. Vastly rearranged, the 1964 version is closer to Holly's 1957 track 'Everyday'. Similarly, Ringo copies Holly's drummer on 'Everyday', forgoing his kit to slap his knees as a percussion sound. The musical arrangement typical of him, and tellingly this track was recorded on the same day as the Beatles recorded Holly's song 'Words of Love' (see below). Clearly looking to try something different, the song also features an experimental vocal arrangement. Paul starts out singing alone, to be joined a few lines later by John, and for the chorus Paul's voice alone is double tracked. The song's lovely melody makes it a minor classic, yet for all its beauty this miniature (1 minute 44 seconds) song is so low key that it is easily overlooked.

'MR MOONLIGHT'
(Johnson)

In the early '60s in Liverpool and Hamburg live groups were largely judged on the originality of their repertoire. Rare songs were at a premium and as such 'Mr Moonlight' was found on the B-side of an obscure 1961 single by Dr Feelgood and the Interns.

This is one of the Beatles' most unusual tracks, Ringo plays bongos, Paul plays a very kitsch solo on hammond organ and, marking the distinctive silent breaks between verse and chorus, George hits an African drum! Neither organ nor African drums appear on the original by Dr Feelgood, although the Beatles do mimic its samba tempo. Like that of 'Devil In Her Heart' before it, the original version of 'Mr Moonlight' was hardly outstanding and the Beatles, largely by the virtue of John's bellowing vocal, surpass it.

This is an unpopular track among Beatles fans because of its corny lyrics and because of the belief that its inclusion on *Beatles For Sale* kept out the superior 'Leave My Kitten Alone', recorded on the same day. Now available on the anthology compilation, 'Kitten' features an outstanding vocal from John. Mysteriously it was consigned to the vaults, as reportedly John was unhappy with this vocal.

'KANSAS CITY/HEY, HEY, HEY, HEY'
(Leiber/Stoller/Penniman)

Little Richard recorded these songs separately, but played them as a medley in his stage act. Likewise the Beatles copied this routine after seeing Richard play in both Liverpool and Hamburg in 1962. Limited by time constraints, John egged Paul on to deliver a storming one-take performance, in doing so recreating the energy of the Beatles' live performances at their best. Yet Paul's efforts sound strained (especially compared to John's backing vocals) and this is his weakest Little Richard cover version. By comparison Little Richard's 'Kansas City' studio version has a swagger that brings out much more of the sexual insinuation of Leiber and Stoller's lyrics.

'EIGHT DAYS A WEEK'
(McCartney/Lennon)

In an effort to make this a single, a whole day was devoted to perfecting it – an unusually lengthy process for the Beatles in 1964. Harmony vocals and guitar intros were tried and tested over the day and further overdubs added days later. The finished song still lacks both conviction and the trademark upbeat mood of early Beatles singles – noticeably, John's vocal is tired. His exhaustion, combined with Paul's insistence on perfecting the track annoyed John, who still in 1980 tetchily recalled the struggle to record what he considered to be 'never a good song'. In the UK it was passed over as an A-side, unlike in the USA where more singles were released and it reached number one in the charts.

Lyrical inspiration came when Paul asked his chauffeur how work was going, to which he replied he had been working 'eight days a week'. The lyrics were completed with John's help.

'WORDS OF LOVE'
(Holly)

Buddy Holly was the most complex and ambitious of all the 1950s rock 'n' rollers. Typically, his 1957 recording of 'Words Of Love' was one of the first ever to use double-tracked vocals and guitar. To replicate this sound both John and Paul share lead vocals, while the lead guitar line is double tracked as per the original. This is a faithful and note-perfect cover, yet a touch too reverential and polite. On the original Holly imbues the lyrics at times with a romance and sensuality not hinted at here.

'HONEY DON'T'
(Carl Perkins)

The Beatles' taste for country and western made them a British beat group unique in their respect for Carl Perkins country-flavoured rock. The more fashion-conscious London bands would have viewed such music with disdain. Unfortunately, 'Honey Don't', as one of Perkins' simplest songs, is not a great advert for his music, its choice on this album being due to its simple structure which required little rehearsal and studio time. Usually sung by John, it was given to Ringo for his one song per album after he turned down the offer to sing 'I Don't Want To

Spoil The Party'. Ringo's vocals lose the raunch of the faster-paced Carl Perkins 1956 original, which was released as the B-side to 'Blue Suede Shoes'.

'EVERY LITTLE THING'
(McCartney/Lennon)

This was another attempt by Paul to write a single. Its arrangement of a neat 12-string guitar riff and booming tympani drums suggest ambitious plans, but they are let down by a tired performance. Instead of racing along like previous Beatles pop, it drags. Again John sounds out of breath. Unusually for a song that was largely written by Paul, it is John who sings lead (double-tracked) vocals.

'I DON'T WANT TO SPOIL THE PARTY'
(Lennon/McCartney)

John called this 'a very personal one of mine', which sets it apart from the tin pan alley fiction-style of 'No Reply' or 'Every Little Thing'. He never elaborated on the significance the lyrics had for him, but a tempting explanation comes from the Ronnettes' lead singer Ronnie Spector in her biography *Be My Baby*. She revealed that in February 1964, the Ronnettes were invited to a Beatles party at the Hotel Plaza, New York. Watching a private sex show put on for the Beatles' benefit in their suite of rooms, Ronnie at one point sat on John's lap for want of chairs before he lured her to another room. Here John made a pass at Ronnie, which she declined as she was going steady with Phil Spector. She made her excuses and left, at which point John slammed the door behind her, although he phoned to apologise the next day!

Whether this is the source of the inspiration for the lyrics or not, they make an embarrassing attempt at the openly autobiographical style that Dylan was pioneering at this time. Paul said in 1997 that the music was given a country and western style to encourage Ringo to sing it, though he apparently turned it down.

'WHAT YOU'RE DOING'
(McCartney/Lennon)

'What You're Doing' is one of the Beatles' most interesting early arrangements, yet both John and Paul were dismissive of it. The song is notable for the way the instruments and vocals echo each other. Ringo's bass drum on the intro is followed by tom-toms; when the bass plays a low note Paul sings a high note and vice versa. These contrasts of tone and octave were at the heart of the Beatles' music; as the main instruments on their best recordings, vocals rarely use the same octave.

Other fine musical touches are the 12-string guitar riff played by George, a forerunner of the riff on the Byrds' 'Mr Tambourine Man', as is the vocal arrangement where John sings the first word of each line that Paul sings. This trick was almost certainly learnt from Maurice Williams and The Zodiacs' single 'Stay', which the Beatles had covered live.

'EVERYBODY'S TRYING TO BE MY BABY'
(Carl Perkins)

Carl Perkins' influence on George's guitar playing was such that pre-fame George once used Carl Harrison as a stage name. Not surprisingly, this is a better Perkins cover than Ringo's 'Honey Don't'.

George, while staying true to Perkins' guitar style, took to some judicious cutting of his lyrics. Adapted from a country and western song dating back to 1936, the lyrics tell a tale of groupie sex, which Perkins presumably based on experience after his overnight fame with the hit 'Blue Suede Shoes' in 1956. While altering the 19 women knocking on Carl Perkins' door to a more Beatles-sized 50, George omitted the bawdier, more overtly sexual verses.

These lyrics may be true of the Australian and USA tours over the summer of 1964, which by many accounts were some of their most debauched, but revealing the Beatle's activities with groupies was in 1964 not in fitting with their clean media image.

5. Help!

'BAD BOY'
(Larry Williams) Single first released in the USA 14 June 1965

This was recorded to meet Capitol's request for an extra song to make up one of their repackaged albums – *Beatles VI*. Such contractual obligation perhaps explains one of the Beatles' least-inspired cover versions, which notably features several errors in John's double-tracked vocal.

Without hearing the original by Larry Williams from 1958 you might not realise that this was a comedy song, as the Beatles' version is so revved up that the lyrics are incomprehensible and their humour lost.

'YES IT IS'
(Lennon) B-side to 'Ticket to Ride', released 9 April 1965

Unusually for such an obscure Beatles song, this received much studio time to perfect its three-part vocal harmonies. These vocals, especially John's octave leap for the soaring double-tracked middle eight, are the strong point here, though they are wasted alongside George's inept use of a tone pedal effect on guitar. The oddness of the song was part of a growing trend by the Beatles to place their more unusual songs on the B-sides of their singles. The song is the third of John's to refer to a colour in its lyrics; in 'You Can't Do That' everybody was 'green', in 'Baby's In Black' he was feeling 'blue' and here the key colour is red. Such continuity is unlikely to have escaped John and was probably done for his own amusement.

'I'M DOWN'
(McCartney) B-side to 'Help!', first released in the USA 19 July 1965

A combined rewrite of Little Richard's 'Long Tall Sally' and 'Rip It Up', this was the highlight of the Beatles' famous Shea Stadium show in New York 1965, and ends up being more fun than either of the Little Richard songs they covered. The rough guitar sound and John's demented organ playing oddly became trademarks of the '60s US punk sound. That this was recorded minutes after 'Yesterday' in June 1965 shows Paul's willingness to make up for the Beatles' lapse from their rock sound.

Like 'I Feel Fine'/'She's a Woman', Paul's B-side parodies the A-side. 'Help!' (recorded two months previously) has John saying that he feels down; and here Paul goes one better, saying that he feels 'upside-down' which of course as the flip-side of the original vinyl single is exactly where he was in relation to John's 'Help!'.

HELP!
Album released 6 August 1965

Help! was the end of the line for the Beatles' output of upbeat love songs aimed at a loyal, teen girl audience. Such formulaic songs had lost their challenge and there is a clear feel on tracks such as 'Another Girl' and 'It's Only Love' that they were going through the motions. *Help!*, though, is no dead end, as both John and Paul introduced two bold songs that would signal a direction forward. The emotional depth and honesty of John's 'You've Got To Hide Your Love Away', recorded in February 1965, was matched a few months later on Paul's 'Yesterday', both heralding new and exciting standards of songwriting. The lyrics to the single were true to this new direction too, if its music was not.

The transition between the two styles might have been faster were it not for the Beatles' commitment to their second film. *Help!*, shot in spring 1965, required the Beatles to write six new songs for its producers, United Artists. Again, like *A Hard Day's Night*, the onus was on the Beatles to write something light and upbeat. Markedly, while the lyrics on songs they contributed to the film are often dark or sad, the music by contrast is light and happy.

The film, as it turned out, was one of the silliest commercial spin-offs from Beatlemania and the Beatles were bitterly embarrassed by it. Where a year before they had insisted on a good plot for their film of *A Hard*

Day's Night, they had let their guard down on *Help!*, John blaming their nonchalance on their new-found love of marijuana.

Help! is often overlooked as one of the Beatles' better albums, but it contains three of the most perfect pop moments of their career: 'Ticket To Ride', 'You've Got To Hide Your Love Away' and 'Yesterday'. It also marks a big improvement on *Beatles For Sale*, largely due to the lack of any hard live performance schedules between February and June 1965. Typically, the lyrics to 'Yesterday' were written while Paul was on holiday in Portugal. As John and Paul relied less on each other to meet deadlines, six of their songs were pure solo compositions. Working alone encouraged more introspective songs such as 'Yesterday' and 'You've Got To Hide Your Love Away', the latter's opening line ironically a wry comment by John on the difficulties of writing on his own.

Eight songs were recorded in February, from which United Artists chose their favourite six – songs two to seven on the album, with 'You Like Me Too Much' and 'Tell Me What You See' being rejected and thus appearing on the B-side. The single was recorded in April and added to the film, while a further five songs recorded from May to June appear on the B-side.

For the first time the Beatles were no longer recording proper group performances in the studio. Employing a new method of exploiting four-track recording, now only drums, bass and rhythm guitar would be recorded at the same time. Each of these instruments could now be given a single track, which could have its levels mixed before being 'bounced down' to one track. Lead guitar, vocals, piano and any extra instruments would then be added piece by piece. This process gave more polished performances for complex songs like 'Ticket To Ride', whereas on the simpler tracks, 'The Night Before' and 'You Like Me Too Much', it produced a lifeless feel.

The new recording process brought greater scrutiny to the playing of each instrument, particularly lead guitar. Norman Smith, the Beatles' recording engineer from 1963–65, recalled (in 1986) Paul being openly critical of George's playing and pulling rank on him to play lead on 'Another Girl' and 'Ticket To Ride'. While neither George nor Paul has openly commented on this, it was undoubtedly a source of great tension.

That Paul wanted a more prominent musical role is hardly surprising bearing in mind the low presence of his bass on Beatles records to this point. As the best musician in the group he was an equal guitarist to both George and John, a better pianist and a fair drummer too. Playing lead guitar to him was merely a way of reasserting the role of guitarist that he had held with the group from 1957–61.

The newest trick on *Help!* was the guitar volume pedal, a sensitive device used to emphasise certain notes or chords. George had difficulty coordinating it, so on some songs the effect would be reproduced instead by John kneeling down in front of George's guitar as he played and turning its volume control. The high-pitched whine on 'Yes It Is' suggests that here the volume pedal was used, whereas the clipped chords of 'I Need You' suggest that John was manipulating the volume controls on George's guitar as he played.

'HELP!'
(Lennon/McCartney)

This is Beatles formula pop at its best; a twisting chord pattern, a strong middle eight, perfect harmony vocals, a neat double-tracked guitar riff and a tight group performance. It was perfect for the jolly atmosphere of the film *Help!*, yet this was not how John intended it to be. In its original form it was styled as a slow lament and a genuine cry of unhappiness by John. Played at a faster pace he did not have time to sing all the words, and in places they came out garbled, their meaning was lost. John in later years named this as one of his favourite songs, but regretted the decision to speed it up, blaming this on commercial considerations. As with the next single, pressure would have come from both George Martin and the other Beatles to deliver something appropriate. As a promotional single for their new light-hearted film, a slow, self-loathing lament would have given the wrong commercial message.

Like 'A Hard Day's Night' before it, the song's title originated from Dick Lester, who midway through making the Beatles' second film gave it the name *Help!*. The lyrical possibilities of the title meant most to John, who responded quickly by writing the main lyrics and song structure, to which Paul notably added the brilliant counter-melody vocals. The title gave John a welcome excuse to side-step the usual Lennon/McCartney boy–girl romance lyrics and a chance to improve on the themes of the similarly confessional 'I'm A Loser'.

In early 1965, John was lost without the activity and purpose of touring. Like some dissolute lottery winner he gorged himself on food, drink and luxuries. Notably Bob Dylan, a visitor to the Lennon household around this time, came away critical of the way John had chosen to spend his money on useless luxuries. Growing fat and isolated in his mansion in suburbia, often idly watching TV, soon John also began to realise that this might not be what he wanted.

'Help!' proved a landmark song for John. Despite its production being untrue to his initial design, it showed that writing honestly about his personal experiences produced his strongest lyrics. From now on he would rarely write anything in the old commercial style of 'No Reply' or 'I Feel Fine'.

'THE NIGHT BEFORE'
(McCartney)

'The Night Before' makes a disappointing contrast to the emotional depth of the Lennon songs it is bracketed by on this album. Paul's tale of getting the chuck after a one-night stand is neither convincing (his lyrics to 'Another Girl' are much more believable) nor interesting. Also disappointing is the dumb mismatch of Paul's tale of woe with a piece of uplifting and harmonically warm classic Beatles pop. The song suffers from an uncharacteristically poor mix, with the vocals drowning out a murky backing. It seems likely that Paul's growing involvement in production may have overruled George Martin's better sense here.

'YOU'VE GOT TO HIDE YOUR LOVE AWAY'
(Lennon)

The lyrics to 'You've Got To Hide Your Love Away' have caused much speculation over the years, though John never elaborated further than to say that they were 'honest'. Notoriously, the lyrics, which hint at an extra-marital affair, have been seen as the admission of a homosexual affair. Pauline Sutcliffe in a biography on her brother Stuart – a member of the Beatles 1960–61 and a close friend of John – said she believed him to have had sex with John. A more believable interpretation is that John was writing – in the chorus at least – about Brian Epstein's homosexuality. In Britain at the time, homosexuality was a criminal offence.

John credited the lyrics as a stylised attempt to write like Bob Dylan in the way it drew upon his real emotions. He later referred to this era as his 'Dylan days', such was his infatuation for the American singer – at one stage he even wore a cap similar to the one Dylan sports on the cover of his 1963 album *The Times They Are A-Changin'*. The influence extended beyond the lyrics to copying Dylan's gruff vocal style and using a purely acoustic accompaniment. John also envisioned a Dylan-like harmonica solo, but, realising his homage had gone far enough, a flute solo was used instead.

'I NEED YOU'
(Harrison/Lennon)

In 1966 George described how he and John stayed up one night in early February 1965, putting the finishing touches to 'I Need You' and 'You Like Me Too Much'. These were the first decent compositions George had introduced for over a year and it is likely that he wrote the basis of each song, with John knocking off the rougher edges of both lyrics and chord structure. 'I Need You' in particular shows a key trademark of Lennon/McCartney formula pop – the use of dramatic emphasis within a song by the twin introduction of both backing vocals and minor chords, which suggests itself as John's contribution. The unusual rhythm guitar sound was another Harrison/Lennon piece of teamwork. While George played the chords, John knelt beside him swivelling the volume control on his guitar, producing the odd appearance and disappearances of sound.

The lyrics reveal George's affection for his girlfriend Patti Boyd, whom he was to wed in January 1966.

'ANOTHER GIRL'
(McCartney)

Paul wrote this in the sunken bath of a grand villa in Tunisia in February 1965, after finding the room's acoustics conducive to singing. The song was apparently recorded the next day when Paul returned to London. This rush perhaps explains why the carefree music was left so at odds with the caustic lyrics, which are revealing of Paul's spoilt pop-prince behaviour at this time.

Like 'The Night Before', this is one of the least successful productions on *Help!*, Paul's vocal and lead guitar drowning out all else. The only real edge given to the music is in Paul's closing wild, lopsided guitar solo.

'YOU'RE GOING TO LOSE THAT GIRL'
(Lennon/McCartney)

The inspiration for the lyrics of 'You're Going To Lose that Girl' would seem to lie with Betty Everett's 1963 single 'It's In His Kiss'. Similarly a tale of relationship advice given to a friend, where the call and response vocals with a wagging finger sing 'No' repeatedly, here Paul and George's vocals also emphasise John's words of warning.

Musically, 'You're Going To Lose That Girl' demonstrates well the frustration the Beatles felt at the low bass presence on their albums. At the time their record company, EMI, insisted that bass levels be kept low so as to prevent records from jumping. In the USA, where vinyl quality was more advanced, this problem had been overcome. Notably, from early 1965 the Byrds' 'Mr Tambourine Man' and the Temptations' 'Get Ready' both featured dominant bass. The Beatles, though, would have to wait until the recording of *Revolver* to pull off this kind of sound.

One musical innovation that does succeed here is the sharp attack of the opening drum roll, which was achieved by double tracking. The inspiration for this must surely have been the forceful percussion that opened so many Motown records from this time.

'TICKET TO RIDE'
(Lennon/McCartney)

A perfect piece of Beatles pop, full of fine touches, from the double-tracked drum rolls to the surprise coda. Throughout the song the unusual drum beat, thought up by Paul, neatly offsets John's delicate four-note riff. John's (double-tracked) singing in turn submits to this infectious rhythm, the words in the first line merging into each other for percussive effect. Cover versions often ignore this, giving emphasis to the words rather than the rhythm, but John's lack of emphasis suggests they held little meaning for him. Reinforcing this is the fact that a 'ticket to ride' was also a pun. Ryde was actually a town in the Isle of Wight, which John and Paul had visited in 1960.

Despite such pop perfection John claimed in 1970 that the sound he was really looking for was something heavier. Expressing a desire to go back and remix the track, in 1980 he somewhat grandly called it 'one of the earliest heavy metal records ever made'. John appears to be referring to his distorted rhythm guitar, which is pushed back in the mix.

'ACT NATURALLY'
(Morrison/Russell)

This cover of a 1963 Buck Owens country and western number one hit was chosen by Ringo when the weak and contrived 'If You've Got Trouble', written for him by Paul, was rejected. Out-takes of 'If You've Got Trouble' reveal that Ringo was clearly dissatisfied with his vocal; the three-chord simplicity of 'Act Naturally' would prove much easier to sing.

Buck Owens, like other beneficiaries of Beatles cover versions, gained a great deal of knock-on publicity. Clearly bemused by this, Owens returned the favour by playing 'Twist And Shout' in his live set, for which he and his band put on Beatles mop-top wigs. Such satire is also evident in his version of 'Act Naturally', in which he sings the self-pitying lyrics mockingly. Ringo, lacking such confidence, unfortunately sings it straight. Knowing of Ringo's unease, John captured it live in 1965 when he cruelly introduced 'Act Naturally' by saying 'Now here's Ringo all nervous and out of tune, to sing something for you.'

'IT'S ONLY LOVE'
(Lennon/McCartney)

The last song John specifically wrote for the teen-girl fan base of Beatlemania later caused him great embarrassment. In 1980 he said of it, 'I was so ashamed, I could hardly sing, that must be the worst thing I ever wrote.' His embarrassment is evident on the recording. At 1.06, he can be heard stifling a laugh. Interestingly, the last lines are double tracked and given an emotional emphasis missing on the rest of the song.

'YOU LIKE ME TOO MUCH'
(Harrison)

One of the weakest songs the Beatles ever recorded, its arrangement of electric and acoustic piano vainly tries to disguise its lightweight tune. George's feeble double-tracked vocals fail to add weight to his adolescent lyrics, which he later admitted were 'naive'.

'TELL ME WHAT YOU SEE'
(McCartney)

Like 'You Like Me Too Much', here an inventive arrangement tries to mask a bland song which even Paul later summed up as 'unmemorable'. As on several other songs on *Help!* the lyrics are revealing of the boredom and lack of inspiration both John and Paul now felt at writing fictional 'true love' songs to pander to their fans.

'I'VE JUST SEEN A FACE'
(McCartney)

'I've Just Seen A Face' is still a favourite of Paul's and he played it live until the 1990s. Paul's joy is evident on this recording, where at the end he breaks into scat singing. A showcase for Paul's virtuosity on guitar, it marked a break-up of the traditional musical responsibilities within the Beatles. From here on Paul would frequently take over John's role as the group's second guitarist.

'YESTERDAY'
(Lennon/McCartney)

Composing new tunes had became so important for Paul in the mid '60s that they not unnaturally started to occur in his dreams. In 1965 the melody for 'Yesterday' came to him in his sleep and on waking he leapt to a bedside piano to try it out. At first incredulous at its creation, he thought he must have simply recreated someone else's tune. Accordingly he played it to friends and associates to see if they recognised it. George Martin recalled hearing it in January 1964, during the Beatles' stay in Paris, while in 1965 John remembered hearing the tune 'months and months' before it was recorded. At this early stage Paul had no proper words and simply mouthed the nonsense verse as the first line. How long the tune existed before the final words were added is a matter of debate. Paul's own account of the song in 1984 was that the words came around two weeks after the tune.

The date the lyrics were written is much clearer; Paul recalled them coming to him during a long taxi ride from the airport in Lisbon to the resort of Albufeira, which sets it as 27 May 1965. Paul remembered Jane Asher sleeping at his side while he wrote the verses. In such company it seems unusual that he would write a song about being unhappy in love. Taken at face value the lyrics describe the end of a love affair and most cover versions have interpreted it as such. Yet from what is known of Paul's love life then, there had been little heartbreak. He had been going steady with Jane Asher for two years. An intriguing theory, first published in Chris Salewicz's biography *McCartney* (1988) suggests that Paul's regret over words he wished he had not spoken refers to his outburst on hearing of his mother's death – 'What are we going to do without her money?' Paul's mother had previously contributed towards the McCartney family income as a nurse. (Paul has a history of injudicious remarks. Notably, after John's death he was quoted as saying 'It's a drag.') The song's second line, where Paul emphasises the suddenness of his unhappiness, may refer to the surprise of his mother's death – cancer was only diagnosed two weeks beforehand. Tellingly, John encouraged Paul to record 'Yesterday' without the group. John's song to his mother, 'Julia', was also recorded solo. Paul rather frustratingly has only half-heartedly backed up this theory, by saying that he 'may' have been writing about his mother unconsciously.

Despite the song's obvious strength, Paul viewed it initially as inappropriate for the Beatles, fearing perhaps that it would be vetoed by the rest of the group. At least two artists, Chris Farlowe and Billy J. Kramer, have claimed since that they were offered the song by Paul. Both turned it down, seeing it as too soft for their image. Since Paul only finished the lyrics two weeks after his taxi ride in Portugal and recorded the song on 14 June, it seems more likely that he offered them the song after the Beatles recorded it, but before it was released on album in August.

Even when it was recorded for the Beatles, Paul's unease remained. He first rejected George Martin's offer of strings, only to be persuaded otherwise. George Martin arranged the string quartet, under Paul's direction that they should not use vibrato, to avoid sounding too sweet. Paul's voice is recorded plainly too, with double tracking on the chorus only. The strings and Paul's vocal give in turns a severity and a tenderness appropriate for the song's unacknowledged subject. Undoubtedly, while soppy as a love song, 'Yesterday' is very powerful as a song about death.

Paul's unease with the song continued; in the UK it was not put forward as a single, unlike the USA where it became a number one. Its placing on *Help!* is also a scandal, its closing notes blasted away by the artless racket of 'Dizzy Miss Lizzie' which follows.

'DIZZY MISS LIZZIE'
(Larry Williams)

This had been in the Beatles' live set since 1960, yet this shambolic run-through has none of the excitement it must have possessed a few years before. The Beatles' edge as a live band had been lost when they became famous. As John remembered in 1970, once they started headlining at big venues on package tours they reduced an hour's playing every night to twenty minutes. He concluded that the Beatles had then 'died' as live musicians.

As a testament to their decline this, the single truly live studio recording on *Help!*, sounds like death warmed up. George's piercing guitar is blameless, but John's vocal is absurdly over-echoed and the pace drags with Ringo's cymbals being artlessly plastered over every second of tape. The weakness of this performance makes a painful contrast with that of the taut, exciting rock of their competitors and friends the Rolling Stones' 'I Can't Get No Satisfaction' and the Animals' 'We've Got To Get Out Of This Place' from mid-1965. Tellingly, the Beatles made this their last-ever cover version committed to vinyl ('Bad Boy' was recorded at the same session).

Larry Williams' tight and inventive original (from 1958), which featured saxophones matching the guitar riff note for note, shows how good 'Dizzie Miss Lizzie' could have been. At 2 minutes 12 seconds, it is also 40 seconds shorter than the Beatles' bloated cover.

6. Rubber Soul

'DAY TRIPPER'
(Lennon/McCartney) Single released 3 December 1965

Released in August 1965, the sexy, cool, propulsive riff the Rolling Stones used on 'I Can't Get No Satisfaction' has been little bettered to this day. The Beatles, though, fuelled by an ambition to remain pop's premier band, used this as an emphatic reply. While avoiding the fuzz box style of 'Satisfaction', the riff here is double tracked on guitar and followed on bass for extra impact. John, as on 'I Feel Fine', created the riff by adding extra notes to a standard blues riff. The riff on Bo Diddley's 'RoadRunner' seems the likeliest source of inspiration, not least because the Beatles used to play it live in Hamburg and in Liverpool, but also because it is a put-down song aimed at a woman and uses travel as a euphemism.

The Beatles' lyrics, like Jagger/Richard's, are provocative and suggestive. 'Day Tripper', while a drugs reference, was also a term used by John to put down those he considered to be straight and who wanted to be hip only at weekends. Paul also sneaks in a dirty joke; after referring on the first verse to the girl as a tease, he almost imperceptibly repeats the phrase as 'prick teaser' on the second. The girl who plays at one-night stands too sounds like a piece of hip London rock fraternity speak. Paul explained in 1997: 'We were interested in winking to our friends and comrades in arms, putting in references that we knew our friends would get but that the Great British Public might not.'

The line 'she only played one-night stands' too sounds like a piece of hip London rock fraternity speak. Paul's vocals reveal that while John started this song, Paul made much of an input too.

Speedily mixed, at 1.50 and at 2.32 sound levels change alarmingly where overdubbed vocals were dropped in.

'WE CAN WORK IT OUT'
(McCartney/Lennon/Harrison) Double A-side of 'Day Tripper'

Recorded the day before 'Nowhere Man', Paul's song similarly draws on personal experience to offer some remarkably mature and optimistic advice. The closeness of the two songs suggests that even if John and Paul did not influence each other, they were at the time holding similar views or discussing related ideas.

A response to the row Paul was having with Jane Asher, the reasoning of his verses is given added urgency by John's cautionary middle eight, the exchange of views and voices creating the effect of a mini pop opera. John's message not to waste life as it is short would seem to have been inspired by John's 25th birthday only days before the song was recorded. Rock stars at this time did not sustain healthy careers into their late 20s and John greeted his birthdays with increasing anxiety – turning 26 the following year would inspire the similarly philosophical 'Strawberry Fields Forever'.

This is the Beatles' and probably pop's most compact A-side ever. In 2 minutes and 12 seconds there are four verses, four choruses, two middle eights, an intro and a coda. There is even a time signature change, George Harrison coming up with the idea of changing the tempo mid-song to waltz time. The added use of a harmonium played by John, an instrument alien to pop, is another act of amazing bravado. Its use came about as it happened to be sitting in the studio on the day the song was recorded.

Such strengths won support for 'We Can Work It Out' as the next single, but John understandably argued for the dynamic 'Day Tripper'. As a compromise both became the Beatles' first double A-side.

RUBBER SOUL
Album released 3 December 1965

The time spent making a new album and single between 12 October and 11 November 1965 was the most productive and disciplined of the Beatles whole career. Within these dates 'Norwegian Wood', 'Drive My Car', 'Nowhere Man', 'In My Life', 'Girl', 'Michelle', 'Day Tripper' and 'We Can Work It Out' were all written and recorded. While they would produce work of equal merit in the future, they would arguably never stretch themselves so much again. For John in particular this was the last Beatles album that he would truly labour over.

When the group convened at Abbey Road in mid-October few songs had been written and as with *Beatles For Sale* the previous year, there was a genuine panic that they would not complete an album in time for Christmas. That they did respond shows how accustomed they had become to the heavy work schedules of near non-stop touring and to writing songs at speed to meet the voracious demand for Beatles products.

Such working practices have now become alien in the pop industry, yet both John and Paul even in later years recognised the merit in them. The logic runs that pop songs are simple and direct in nature. If you have to labour over them then they cannot be any good, and there is often nothing so inspiring as a looming deadline. John notably applied this logic to its fullest on his solo single 'Instant Karma' which was written and recorded in one day in 1970. Paul too, less successfully, tried to rally a drug-addled and disunified Beatles to repeat the feat of *Rubber Soul* one more time before film cameras over the month of January 1969.

But the success of *Rubber Soul* cannot be explained only by discipline and hard work. The Beatles had successfully lobbied for less time touring in return for longer hours in the studio. The 1965 British tour was held off until *Rubber Soul* was completed and their 13 days spent in the studio (two extra for 'Daytripper'/'We Can Work It Out') was the most spent on an album so far. The extra time was used to explore the possibilities of arrangements and to do justice to each song.

The greater time they spent in the studio was necessitated by a flourishing music scene. Notably, in 1965 Motown started producing some of their finest records, and artists like Otis Redding, the Beach Boys, Bob Dylan and the Rolling Stones too were reaching their creative peaks. For the Beatles to remain at the top of the pack would require more recording time and better songs. In a foretaste of how the Beatles would evolve, Brian Wilson of the Beach Boys had in 1965 already given up on touring to stay in the studio, owing to the pressures he felt in keeping up with such a competitive music scene.

The album's greatest influence was that of Bob Dylan. In 1964 the Beatles had admired his wordy, peculiar songs from afar, but did little to alter the winning formula of their songs to match. Dylan's sudden commercial success in 1965 changed all that. His albums *The Freewheelin' Bob Dylan* and *Bringing It All Back Home* went to number one in the UK album charts, while four of his singles would reach the UK top ten during 1965. Numerous Dylan cover versions and imitators were also making the charts. The message was clear that pop was changing fast. In response Paul and especially John now dropped the tin pan alley vernacular of previous songs.

The change did not come easily. John, recalling the creation of 'Nowhere Man', said that he had spent the whole of the night trying to create a song that was 'meaningful and good'. Such creative anguish was certainly never something he experienced working within the boy–girl, love and romance themes of his previous songs.

The clearest Dylan influences were the singles 'Positively Fourth Street' and 'Like A Rolling Stone', two of the most vituperative singles ever released. John, Paul and George all jumped at the chance at writing their own put-down songs to match, writing in turns 'Nowhere Man', 'I'm Looking Through You' and 'Think For Yourself'. Taking Dylan's lead, the Beatles lyrics also take on more serious issues. For the first time there are clear references to death on 'In My Life', 'Girl' and 'Run For Your Life' and 'We Can Work It Out'.

For the change in their songwriting style to look credible, the Beatles needed to find a new image. The cover of their previous album, *Help!*, had portrayed them as pop puppets playing in the snow. For the cover of *Rubber Soul* they were portrayed as giants. At their suggestion too the photo was distorted in a way that suggests the altered reality of drugs. Significantly marijuana had become their drug of choice and was credited by Paul in particular as bringing a more surreal and abstract nature to their songs.

The term *Rubber Soul* was Paul's ironic comment on the album's other important influence, that of soul music. Paul had heard a black musician refer to the Rolling Stones' music as 'plastic soul' and self-deprecatingly used this term to refer to the Beatles' own mimicking of soul styles, while also punning on the meaning of a rubber sole for a shoe.

Recording was now on a one-song-per-day basis, with some sessions continuing past midnight. A typical day would be spent rehearsing a song and experimenting with new ideas for it, so that each now had its own idiosyncratic sound. Typical of the new experimentation and attention to detail is 'You Won't See Me' where the last 20 seconds feature a single constant droning note on organ. Paul recalled a growing culture clash with the engineers at Abbey Road studios in trying out these new ideas. In an interview from 1988 he clearly remembered having to demand an overload of treble for the guitars on 'Nowhere Man' and for John's voice on 'Girl', which was way beyond what the white-coated EMI-employed engineers had been trained to allow.

This emphasis on treble throughout the album favoured guitars and vocals, but detracted from other instruments. More than any other Beatles album, Ringo's drums are pushed way back in the mix, his bass drum being largely inaudible, Paul's bass too is barely heard.

The extra studio time available to the Beatles was also used to hone vocal arrangements, which are among their very best.

A capo, a device that wraps around a guitar's neck to raise its key and was much favoured by Bob Dylan, is used on 'Girl', 'Norwegian Wood' and 'If I Needed Someone'.

George used a tremolo arm, which wavers a guitar's sound level, on 'In My Life', 'Run for Your Life', 'Nowhere Man', 'Wait' and 'What Goes On'. The fuzz box, a recent invention allowing a controlled form of distortion, was popularised in 1965 by its use on the Rolling Stones 'I Can't Get No Satisfaction'. Paul used it on bass guitar for 'Think For Yourself'.

'DRIVE MY CAR'
(McCartney/Lennon)

One of the Beatles' cleverest recordings, 'Drive My Car' combines four musical styles while successfully establishing the double-entendre lyrics that would become their stock-in-trade for the rest of their career. The songwriting is a high watermark of teamwork. Paul's first lyrics were about a girl on the make in films, a 'bitch' in his description, who asks her boyfriend to buy her 'golden rings'. Knowing this was not good enough he sought help from John who at length came up with the more suggestive and promising idea that the girl should drive his car.

Matching the ambiguity of the lyrics, the arrangement starts from a copy of the strutting bass from Otis Redding's 'Respect' and layers other musical styles over it. As on 'Respect', George at his own suggestion laid down a guitar line that follows the bass line, though here the guitar is distorted adding a rock edge. For the chorus Paul gives the Stax strut a jazzy interpretation with five syncopated piano chords and following this he turns to blues, adding a slide guitar solo. Without losing track of their own special identity, over the top of this arrangement is a distinctive Beatles vocal arrangement. The origin of the 'beeping' car horn vocal riff owes something to Bo Diddley's 'Road Runner' which uses a similar device – a song the Beatles had previously played live.

John's contribution to the lyrics referred to his own predicament with cars. He had suffered a series of car smashes that had so knocked his confidence at driving that he now relied on a chauffeur (unlike the other Beatles).

'NORWEGIAN WOOD'
(Lennon/McCartney)

This tale of seduction is heavily coded. John recalled in 1970 that he wanted to write about an affair he'd had without making it obvious to his wife. The words were a combination of experiences and descriptions of girls' flats. The cute, but presumably untrue anecdote about the time he 'crawled off to sleep in the bath' avoids suggesting that sex took place. An early demo of the song, now on the *Anthology 2* CD, also reveals that John first clearly sang 'I once "had" a girl'. On the final version he appears to sing both 'met' and 'had', an effect achieved by singing a different word when he came to double track his vocal. Again this gives the song less of a sexual connotation.

A girl's identity is hinted at in the lyrics. Her flat is bohemian in description, with its rug and no chairs, where they drink wine and talk until the early hours ('Norwegian Wood' was the name of a range of wooden furniture, sold at the trend-setting Habitat shop). John hints that it is the girl who takes the lead in both meeting and seducing him. This fits the description of the independent career women that started to emerge in significant numbers in swinging '60s London. Around this time John is known to have pursued a journalist and an actress, both in their early 30s and both Oxbridge graduates. Such taste in women was borne out by his eventual marriage to the older, university-educated Yoko Ono.

Using Dylan's method of writing words first, John fitted a melody to his lyrics' metre. This inspired the jaunty, unorthodox melody, which was further emphasised by George's use of sitar. Paul helped John complete the song writing the middle eight melody and parts of the lyrics, notably the closing lines.

'YOU WON'T SEE ME'
(McCartney)

Motown's records provided a constant source of inspiration for the Beatles, but only rarely would they come so close to their sound as on this Four Tops pastiche. Double-tracked rhythm guitar and vocals all add to a wall of sound similar to that achieved on typical Motown records. Finished at speed on the last day of recording for *Rubber Soul*, the gruelling work on this through-the-night session is betrayed in John's hoarse backing vocal.

The upbeat tune, though, is largely at odds with Paul's mournful account of his temporary split with his girlfriend Jane Asher. She was acting in Bristol at the time and by the sounds of it was proving elusive. The lyrics are revealing of Paul's affection for Jane, a truer reflection of his feelings perhaps than the anger he expresses on 'I'm Looking Through You'.

'NOWHERE MAN'
(Lennon)

The strategy John took in writing 'Nowhere Man' sums up the mass appeal of his songs to this day. His inspiration was autobiographical, but the lyrics read as if they could be about anybody. The song expresses John's doubts over the direction of his career as a Beatle, after he had achieved all the fame and fortune he desired. 'Nowhere land' referred to the opulent suburban estate where he lived in a 20-roomed mansion, overlooking a golf course. Other than Ringo, who lived close by, John was alone there most of the day. Taken at face value many of the lyrics read like a conversation he was having with himself, an approach he would again follow for 'Strawberry Fields Forever' and 'Hold On' from his debut solo album.

While most writers would simply dwell on their own unhappiness, John manages to universalise his problems, letting the listener identify with the song too e.g. 'Isn't he a bit like you and me?' He also offers hope and persuasive solutions such as 'don't hurry, take your time . . .' Combined with an uplifting melody and John's bright and haunting vocal, these positive messages are the song's lasting impression.

John was undoubtedly influenced by Bob Dylan's 'Like A Rolling Stone', which was a hit single in the British charts from September–October 1965. The protagonist of Dylan's song is similarly directionless and unknown. The song contains the implication that Dylan was writing about his own experiences of turning up homeless and unknown in New York in 1960. Along the lines of 'Like A Rolling Stone', John may have originally been aiming at more complex lyrics. As he recounted the writing of 'Nowhere Man', he had spent a full five hours unsuccessfully trying to produce something 'meaningful and good'. Giving up he lay down defeated, at which point, to his relief and amazement, the lyrics and melody occurred to him on the spot.

'THINK FOR YOURSELF'
(Harrison)

While both John and Paul would copy Dylan but cover their traces, George's infatuation was obvious. The verses here adopt the same put-down tone of 'Like A Rolling Stone', while the chorus baldly sums up the message of 'It Ain't Me Babe' – that of not depending on a relationship or a lover for all your needs. George is never convincing though; his voice lacks the stylised drawl of Dylan and his words come across as cantankerous rather than worldly-wise.

Compounding such faults, Paul unforgivably employs probably the most misplaced piece of instrumentation on a Beatles record, that of 'fuzz box' on bass. Still a novice at songwriting, George would have allowed such experimentation, presumably in exchange for help on the song's arrangement, he would not have been aided much by George Martin either, who later admitted to giving little time to George's songs.

'THE WORD'
(Lennon/McCartney)

'The Word' can be seen as a prototype for the peace anthem style John would perfect with 'Give Peace A Chance' and 'Imagine'. Unlike these songs it fails by lacking persuasion; Paul said that he wrote it with John under the influence of marijuana, which might excuse its lightheaded feel. The arrangement, employing the happy discotheque bounce of Otis Redding's Stax records, does not help either. John would learn from these failings.

The irony of a previously violent and domineering man like himself suddenly preaching 'love' was not lost on him, but he later rationalised that it is those who have been violent that best understand the need for peace. Dylan paved the way for John to express himself in this way, with his early protest songs such as 'Blowin' in the Wind', 'Masters Of War' and 'Talking World War Three Blues'. Yet while Dylan's concerns were largely those of the threat of nuclear war between the USSR and the USA, John's focus was on the Vietnam war. As a voracious reader of newspapers John would have been aware of the escalation of this conflict in 1965. For the first and perhaps last time journalists were able to report back on the full horror of war, in doing so encouraging a strong movement against America's involvement in Vietnam.

'MICHELLE'
(Lennon/ McCartney)

Paul had the basic chord pattern for 'Michelle' several years before he turned it into a complete song, inspired by a Chet Atkins instrumental called 'Trambone'. He had styled it as a French ballad in imitation of a student who had performed such a song at a party in Liverpool, thrown by one of John Lennon's art school teachers. This would date the tune to between 1959–60. Lacking any real lyrics, at the time Paul merely mouthed nonsense verse that sounded French. The imitation must have been good, as John remembered it some five years later in the rush to find new ideas for *Rubber Soul* and suggested that Paul complete it.

Looking to add some genuine French words, Paul sought the help of the wife of Beatles' friend Ivan Vaughan, who taught French. He asked her to think of a French girl's name and two French words that would match. Paul's suggestion conjured up the second line, for which Jan Vaughan also provided a translation. She also provided diction lessons for Paul singing. Later, acknowledging her contribution, Paul sent her a 'royalty' cheque.

The same attention to detail was matched in the music. There is something of the high pitch of Edith Piaf in Paul's voice, while the guitar for the solo has had its tone switched so full on bass that it matches the broader tone of an accordion. The middle section with its repeated 'I love you' refrain was John's input. He had heard Nina Simone improvise the same line on her version of 'I Put A Spell On You'.

'WHAT GOES ON'
(Lennon/McCartney/Starkey)

The quality of most songs on *Rubber Soul* disguise the rush with which the album was made. Some desperate measures were taken to add new songs, explaining the inclusion of 'What Goes On' which had been rejected for recording by the Beatles as early as 1963. Written when John was a teenager, it shows none of the songwriting skills for which Lennon/McCartney became famous – John later excused its recording by saying he did not like to waste anything. The ploy in 1965 of adding extra lyrics by Ringo conveniently deflects full blame.

In the studio 'What Goes On' merited a single take, done in a competent country and western style, apart from John's punk-like rhythm guitar.

'GIRL'
(Lennon/McCartney)

While convincing and powerful, 'Girl' is made up of two opposing lyrical ideas welded together to give the impression of a complete song. The initial lyric came from John, who started the song in the first two verses as a description in his words of a 'dream girl'. At this point the song changes tack, giving a starkly negative portrayal of the girl. The third verse with its rhythmic alliteration is classic Lennon, but both John and Paul claimed credit for the fourth verse with its sombre attack on the supposed virtues of hard or 'back breaking' work. John said in 1980, 'I was in a way trying to say something or other about Christianity, which I was opposed to at the time', which would make sense as an attack on the protestant work ethic. If Paul actually wrote these lines, as he claimed, they would make sense in terms of his bust-up with Jane Asher. Pointedly their argument was based on Jane's insistence on pursuing a career that took her away from him, while he was 'breaking his back' completing *Rubber Soul* to deadline.

While on paper these verses do not sit logically, in performance they have an operatic tension in their clash of emotions. But the Beatles were never ones to take themselves too seriously and the background vocals mischievously sing 'tit-tit-tit-tit-tit', an idea they probably got from Betty Everett's 'It's In His Kiss' whose backing vocals sing 'bum-bum-bum-bum'. There is a salacious touch too with John's sharp, sensual intakes of breath, emphasised by placing maximum treble on his voice.

John credited the song as being his first composition to match its music to the mood of its lyrics, though the dramatic, spiky Greek-style Bosouki guitar part added to the last verse was Paul's idea. In the rush to complete songs for *Rubber Soul*, John openly admitted to stealing ideas for songs. Strangely, 'Girl' has a resemblance to 'Michelle', with a similar chord arrangement, and the same key and tempo.

'I'M LOOKING THROUGH YOU'
(McCartney)

Paul's temporary bust-up with his girlfriend Jane Asher inspired at least three separate songs. 'I'm Looking Through You' was the first, written straight after the split, at which point Paul was in a defiant mood, seeing their relationship as over. His anger, couched in an acoustic Dylan-style put-down song is unusually clumsy from Paul, who lets his emotions override his usual perfectionism. His final riposte that the girl in the song is 'nowhere' is not only lame, but derivative of 'Nowhere Man' which had been recorded only two days before.

Conflict between Paul and Jane arose as he had old-fashioned ideas about a woman's role that ran counter to her career ambitions. 'You Won't See Me' and 'We Can Work It Out', which also refer to the split, suggest the change of attitude that would lead to them getting back together.

'IN MY LIFE'
(Lennon/McCartney)

John's first drafts of 'In My Life' were much more complex than the finished song. Originally he produced a rambling description of the Liverpool landmarks he remembered from his youth and of how some were now knocked down and some still standing. Scrapping this as unworkable, his next draft for the song summed up these memories as 'places' he would always remember. That such apparent simplicity proved so powerful was a lesson John would learn for many of his later songs.

The lyrics also refer to his childhood friends, particularly Pete Shotton and the 'fifth Beatle' Stuart Sutcliffe, who died in 1962. Shotton, John's oldest friend, who was still close to him in 1965, felt that the song's resolution was false. At this stage the Beatles had never written songs that did not mention love and John, though tempted to stick to his original intentions, reverted to type by evolving the lyrics into a love song. He would rectify this the following year by writing 'Strawberry Fields Forever'.

John and Paul both disputed the composition of the tune. John only credited Paul with making a contribution to it, while Paul recalled writing the whole tune alone basing it on a Smokey Robinson song; the tempo and guitar intro of 'Tracks Of My Tears' suggests itself as a likely template.

Under such pressure to write more songs, John left George Martin to improvise the instrumental section while the Beatles were out of the studio. Martin experimented with a sound that would feature on many later recordings. He played a piano solo at half the tempo of the song. The recording was then speeded up to match the song and this changed the tonality of the piano so much that it sounded like a harpsichord. Such happy accidents of sound impressed the Beatles deeply and they would experiment greatly over the next two years to repeat such effects.

'WAIT'
(McCartney/Lennon)

Recorded on the last day of the *Help!* recording sessions in June 1965, 'Wait', like 'No Reply' a year before, seems to have been deliberately left over so as to gain a head start on the next album. A song of reassurance largely written by Paul (though mostly sung by John), the additional overdubs made in November seem to be an effort to subvert this theme. The additional maracas and tambourines fill out the sound but also create a feeling of edginess, particularly in the song's sinister closing tambourine shake, which sounds like the tail twitch of a rattlesnake.

'IF I NEEDED SOMEONE'
(Harrison)

George, as he admitted in the Beatles' *Anthology* book, was falling way behind the songwriting skills of John and Paul by the time of *Rubber Soul.* As such 'If I Needed Someone' in words and style already sounds like it belongs on *Help!* rather than *Rubber Soul.* Promisingly kicking off with a sparkling 12-string riff borrowed from the Byrds' 'The Bells Of Rhymney', his tune goes nowhere thereafter, led by a woeful monotone vocal. So weak is his vocal that George Martin often pushes John's backing vocals higher in the mix than George's.

'RUN FOR YOUR LIFE'
(Lennon)

An Elvis Presley pastiche, 'Run For Your Life' seems directly inspired by the Beatles' first and only meeting with their hero in August 1965 at the end of a US tour. John came to the eagerly awaited visit determined to quiz Elvis about why he no longer recorded in the style of his early rock 'n' roll records, which the Beatles loved. Elvis deflected John's question, citing commitments to films. 'Run For Your Life' was recorded little over a month after this meeting, taking its key opening line from 'Baby Let's Play House', one of Elvis's Sun records. Possibly John envisaged the song as one that Elvis might like to sing, or as his own attempt at reviving the 'Sun' sound with its distinctive acoustic rhythm and electric lead guitar mix. John's petulant, nasty lyrics might have worked better with Elvis's deep baritone vocal. Sung by John they end up, as he later admitted, sounding 'phoney'.

Paul made an interesting interpretation of the lyrics in his biography. He speculated that instead of being aimed at a 'girl' as the lyrics state, they were really about John and the pressures he was under keeping his affairs hidden from his wife.

7. Revolver

'PAPERBACK WRITER'
(McCartney/Lennon) Single first released in the USA 30 May 1966

While probably the most derivative single the Beatles ever made, 'Paperback Writer' still manages to sound original and new. The arrangement namechecks a whole host of raw and exciting records released in late 1965 and early '66, while seeking to go one better. The distorted guitars are tougher than those on the Spencer Davis Group's 'Keep On Running' or the Yardbirds' 'Shapes Of Things'. The main guitar riff borrows from The Who's 'Substitute', as does much of the verse structure. The drums fills too copy the pneumatic style of The Who's Keith Moon and the clashing rhythms on guitar match those on the Byrds' 'Eight Miles High'. Beyond this heavy rock style, the Beatles boldly added one of their most complex vocal arrangements, inspired by the Beach Boys. Notably, the backing vocals sing the French nursery rhyme 'Frère Jacques' behind the main vocal.

Many of the other songs on the album avoided the subject of love in their lyrics and this became the first Beatles single to do likewise. Styled as a letter from a writer to a publisher, the lyrics are in places clever but largely mundane (especially as they are fictional) compared to the dynamic heavy rock they are paired with. These somewhat cryptic lyrics and avant-garde sound led to a loss of favour with some, one journalist at the time calling the single 'pseudo intellectual rubbish'. This opinion was shared by some, as although a number one in the UK and USA, it was a low seller compared to previous Beatles singles.

Unusually for John and Paul's writing partnership, Paul said John's contribution on 'Paperback Writer' was to the music and not the words.

'RAIN'
(Lennon/McCartney) B-side to 'Paperback Writer'

Better than many of the songs John wrote for *Revolver*, 'Rain' has undeservedly suffered a lower profile as a B-side, even now consigned to the bitty *Past Masters Volume Two* compilation. A beautifully cosmic lyric inspired by the egoless state he entered into on LSD, seeing rain and bad weather as an outdated concept echoes the message of the hip, higher consciousness he was also communicating on 'Tomorrow Never Knows'. Like that song too, John aimed to create an entirely new recording process for 'Rain'. Noting how the textures of instrument are affected by altering the tape speed, the guitars and drums here were recorded at a fast pace, then slowed down on tape – the bass was overdubbed at normal speed. While undoubtedly interesting, the effect is somewhat leaden and loses the excitement of performance. A more successful experiment was the use of backward vocals on the fade, which provide a wonderfully bizarre coda.

REVOLVER
Album released 5 August 1966

By 1966 extreme wealth, success and long-term peer approval all encouraged the Beatles to use their own instincts as to what would make a good record. Tearing up the song formulas that had served them so well seemed to make commercial sense too in light of the chart success of *Rubber Soul*. Its lack of songs especially written for the 'meat market', as John put it, did not greatly affect sales. The public were apparently happy to accept a more progressive and experimental Beatles.

This was a win–win situation for the Beatles, who had become enraptured by the studio and the possibilities of creating new sounds and arrangements within it. Emboldened, they prioritised for even more recording time and the first six months of 1966 were kept free from touring to allow this.

Revolver consequently became the most experimental album the Beatles made. Unlike the simple, pleasing melodies of *Rubber Soul,* half of the songs on *Revolver* use musical discord. Where songs like 'Nowhere Man' and 'Drive My Car' had been unthreatening and warm, now the

Beatles
For Sale

Beatles were using unsettling, discordant lyrical images too. In stark contrast to *Rubber Soul*, where 13 of its 14 songs concerned the theme of love or relationships, there was only one real love song on *Revolver*, 'Here There and Everywhere'. Five songs on *Revolver*: 'Taxman', 'Eleanor Rigby', 'Love You To', 'She Said She Said' and 'Tomorrow Never Knows'; refer to death, while 'For No One' and 'Rain' both euphemistically refer to it. John and Paul were well placed to write about death. Both their mothers had died suddenly while they were teenagers and both had experienced the loss of fellow band member Stuart Sutcliffe three years before. No Beatles album hereafter would concentrate so much on this theme, suggesting that John and Paul had until 1966 kept this subject bottled up inside them, waiting for an opportunity to write about it.

The album broached other taboos. Four songs were defintely about drugs, 'She Said She Said', 'Dr Robert', 'Got To Get You Into My Life' and 'Tomorrow Never Knows' while 'Yellow Submarine' appeared to allude to drugs. John in early 1966 was living an LSD-induced lifestyle of tripping and then sleeping off the effects well into the next day. For the first three months of the year when the Beatles had no engagements – the longest time off in their whole career – and other than take drugs John did next to nothing. Maureen Cleave, a journalist with the *London Evening Standard*, interviewed him during these months and summed him up as the 'laziest person in Britain'.

John saw LSD as a way of inspiring him to write greater songs, yet the sharpness and purpose his songs and performances had on *Rubber Soul* were lost as a result of the sedentary lifestyle that came with it. The melodies on 'I'm Only Sleeping' and 'Dr Robert' are near non-existent and the lyrics for 'And Your Bird Can Sing' and 'She Said She Said' half-finished. John now rarely played rhythm guitar on songs he had not written.

Heavy LSD use also brought with it a loss of ego and John's competitiveness with Paul eased. He let Paul take both A-sides for the new singles from the *Revolver* sessions; where he had previously been inspired to better Paul's best songs, he now accepted being outshone. In words echoed in 'Tomorrow Never Knows', John said later that influenced by Timothy Lery's pamphlet *The Pschadelic Experience*, he had sought to destroy his ego with LSD – a process he bitterly regretted.

Paul resisted taking LSD for some time and rather than retreat to a suburban mansion like John, he used his free time to immerse himself in London's art world seeing plays, operas, bands and exhibitions. His frantic search for new stimuli (he was quoted in the *New Musical Express* in June 1966 as saying, 'I've stopped thinking anything is weird or different') inspired some of his best songs. Unlike John, Paul was if anything sharper and keener than he had been on *Rubber Soul.*

George got married during the early 1966 lay-off, went on honeymoon in Barbados and studied sitar. Three of the Beatles were now married, firmly breaking the illusion of their 'availability' and their link to their teeny-bopper past. George, of all the Beatles, seemed to relish this change the most and turned in three of the most unromantic, heavy and challenging songs on the album.

The two greatest influences on *Revolver* were the Byrds' single 'Eight Miles High' and the Beach Boys' *Pet Sounds* album. Both were released during the making of the album in the UK, but as both bands were using ex-Beatles publicist Derek Taylor, it is likely that the Beatles received them earlier than their UK release dates. Paul was the group's biggest fan of *Pet Sounds* and accordingly many of his songs now used a broader range of instruments and sought more imaginative vocal arrangements. John seemed to be most taken with the Byrds' 'Eight Miles High'. Often attributed as the first psychedelic record, its unusual mix of competing lead guitars was an attempt by the Byrds to mimic the sound of a sitar. Similar effects were used on 'She Said She Said', 'And Your Bird Can Sing', 'Rain' and 'Paperback Writer'.

Sitar music was itself another key influence. Its discordant sounds were copied on several songs, as were its use of single drone chords, which are heard on 'Tomorrow Never Knows' and 'Love You To'.

Revolver and *Sgt. Pepper* reflect the highpoint of the Beatles' love affair with the studio, before internal bickering broke the goodwill necessary for long periods spent in the studio together. Between April and June 1966, 30 days in all were spent recording the album and single, with sometimes two or three days spent on one track alone. This process gave nearly every track a unique sound, not just for the Beatles but for the pop world as a whole – on the album's release Paul boldly stated that 'They are sounds that nobody else has done yet – I mean nobody ever.'

The album also benefits from several new recording innovations. Artificial double tracking (ADT) meant that a vocal, once on tape, could be fed back onto the tape a second time, at a fraction of a second's difference. This gives a slicker sound than trying to synchronise a second vocal performance to the original recording. The Beatles' best examples of it are heard on 'Eleanor Rigby' and 'Love You To'.

The new improved use of compressors and limiters allowed higher sound levels to be recorded. Previously tape distortion had restricted this.

The new freedom this gave is best heard on the riff for 'Paperback Writer' and the guitar solo for 'Taxman'. Such innovations finally allowed the Beatles to get the bass sound they had long awaited.

Backward tapes are used on 'Rain', 'I'm Only Sleeping', 'Tomorrow Never Knows' and 'I Want To Tell You'. The guitar solo on 'I'm Only Sleeping' was achieved by playing to a reverse sequence of the song's chords and then turning the tape of the solo backwards.

'TAXMAN'
(Harrison/Lennon)

This was recorded 20 days after the British election of 31 March 1966, which saw the socialist Labour party re-elected. Under its leader Harold Wilson, Labour had introduced one of the highest income tax rates ever for top earners like the Beatles, who were at the time paying a 95 per cent rate. In the hiatus between January and March 1966 the Beatles had time to sit down and work out their money affairs, at which point George found to his horror, as the lyrics state, that he was paying 19 pounds in tax for every 20 he earned.

Not everyone sympathised with the Beatles' plight. The Kinks' 1966 summer number one 'Sunny Afternoon' was also inspired by Labour's taxes, but satirised the rich who suffered.

George, often critical of the way John and Paul would help with each other's songs but not with his, benefited from a strong group effort here. John helped with the lyrics, giving the line about declaring the pennies that traditionally were placed on the eyes of the dead to pay their way into heaven. Possibly he added more too, as in 1980 he bitterly contrasted the help he gave on this song with what he saw as the lack of recognition he got in George's autobiography *I Me Mine*, published the same year.

Paul's contribution was to the arrangement. Underneath George's fake 1, 2, 3, 4 count-in, you can hear Paul's actual count-in. For the first time his bass is the dominant instrument on a Beatles song – he also contributed the punk-like guitar solo which, though unremarkable today, was in 1966 new and astonishing.

'ELEANOR RIGBY'
(McCartney/Lennon)

When John and Paul stopped writing fictional love songs that catered for their fans, they took very different lyrical paths. While John started writing about his own life, Paul evolved the fictional style to write about subjects other than love. As such he took inspiration for 'Eleanor Rigby' from a newspaper story about a 'lonely person'. From this idea he developed the first lines of the song about a woman – a dreamer – who picks up rice scattered after a church wedding. Paul lacked a name though, and recalled choosing the names Eleanor and Rigby separately, the latter from a shop name in Bristol. Curiously, in the 1980s it was pointed out that there is a grave with this name in St Peter's Church, Woolton, Liverpool – the same place John and Paul met in 1957. In an added twist, in the same graveyard there is a family plot containing that of a Mr McKenzie, his wife and daughter – a reference to the Father McKenzie in the lyrics? In the *Anthology* book Paul said he thought it likely that these names lodged in his subconscious. Indeed, the fact such key songs of his as 'Yesterday' and 'Let It Be' also emerged during his dreams makes this more believable.

As one of the Beatles' most acclaimed songs, the origin of the lyrics to 'Eleanor Rigby' was the cause of major disagreement between John and Paul. Most sources point towards Paul as writing the majority of them and yet John in one interview claimed that 'the first verse was by Paul and the rest by me'. Did John make this false claim to get back at Paul? In his long interview for *Playboy* magazine in 1980, John discussed his anger towards Paul and was duly asked to give examples of the times Paul had hurt him most. John immediately cited the writing of 'Eleanor Rigby', saying that Paul had started the lyrics then approached not only John but also the Beatles' assistants Mal Evans and Neil Aspinall to help him finish the lyrics, the inference presumably being that Paul at this time saw John as on the same level as the assistants. John said in 1980 that he had been 'insulted and hurt' by Paul's behaviour.

John's actual involvement can only be guessed at, though the line about the vicar writing a sermon that nobody will come to church to hear is classic Lennon imagery. The song's more sentimental key images, particularly the chorus, all back up Paul's assertion that he wrote most of the lyrics.

There is in fact a stronger argument for attributing a writing credit to George Martin for his score of Paul's piano arrangement. One of the best uses of strings on a Beatles record, rather than sweeten the tune, as on 'Yesterday', they have a severity that powerfully brings the lyrical images alive, an effect helped by keeping the microphones as close as possible to the violins. Martin copied the taut, slashing style from Bernard Herrman's film score for the 1960 film *Psycho*. Such was the success of this partnership between George Martin and Paul that they combined to write the music for the British film *Family Way* in late 1966. Here Paul would similarly write first on piano with George orchestrating.

'I'M ONLY SLEEPING'
(Lennon/McCartney)

Maureen Cleave's interview with John at his home in Weybridge in March 1966 for the *London Evening Standard* reveals an air of festering boredom in the Lennon household. Surrounded by unused luxuries, broken toys and a TV permanently on, he admitted to Cleave that he could sleep almost indefinitely. The need for sleep was a by-product of his steady LSD use; tellingly, in 'Tomorrow Never Knows', where John sang of drifting 'downstream' here he sings of floating 'upstream'.

While, to his credit, John manages to make the mundanity of his life interesting and amusing here, compared to the profound nature of songs like 'Nowhere Man' and 'In My Life' the lyrics are well below par. They were not particularly original either, both lyrics and music here owing much to 'Daydream' by the Lovin' Spoonful, a chart hit in early 1966. Musically too the only real merit in 'I'm Only Sleeping' is in George's suitably yawning backwards guitar solo. Oddly the song's only *real* yawn was delivered by Paul; just before it at 1.57, you can faintly hear John instruct 'Yawn Paul.'

'LOVE YOU TO'
(Harrison)

In this song George echoes the quasi-religious tone of 'Tomorrow Never Knows', which was recorded five days previously in April 1966. Reflecting his interest in Indian religion and culture the lyrics style him as a love-guru instructing his followers to spend their days making love and singing. One of the most fortunate uses of the new automatic double tracking open to the Beatles, the delay it allows on George's voice matches both the chanting of monks and the resonance of a sitar.

George, although fast learning sitar, may not actually have played on this track at all due to his inexperience. Beatles researcher Mark Lewisohn found studio documents that suggest Ayana Deva Angadi actually played sitar. The record sleeve at the time only credited Anil Bhagwat as playing tabla (drums).

'HERE THERE AND EVERYWHERE'
(McCartney/Lennon)

Like 'Yesterday,' Paul had the tune of this song long before he added the lyrics. In the *Anthology* book Paul recalled playing the tune on tape to John when they stayed in Austria in March 1965, suggesting that like 'Yesterday' Paul was only willing to use it once he found lyrics good enough to match.

Lyrical inspiration finally came on hearing the Beach Boys' single 'God Only Knows', a record Paul described at the time as the 'best ever made'. Seeking to match the same sentiments Paul wrote lyrics inspired by his then girlfriend Jane Asher. The Beach Boys' influence is apparent in the way the words 'Here There And Everywhere' echo the themes of infinite love in 'God Only Knows'. Mostly written by Paul, John's contribution was only likely to have been of help in smoothing out weaknesses in the full draft of the lyrics.

In the studio most time was spent on the vocals. Striving for a delicate touch on the lead vocals, Paul said he tried to imitate the tone of Marianne Faithful's voice, explaining his falsetto pitch, though actually he sounds (logically) more like Carl Wilson on 'God Only Knows'. To emphasise this sound, guitar, bass and drums were pushed back in the mix allowing Paul and the harmony vocals to glide over the top.

Paul has commented since that this was the only song he wrote that he could remember John openly praising him on at the time of its writing. After the Beatles' split, John would consistently praise the song in interviews too.

'*YELLOW SUBMARINE*'
(McCartney/Lennon/Donovan Leitch)

This has become famous as a kids' party song, though a whole welter of evidence suggests that it is crammed full of drugs references. Tellingly, only two weeks before John had disguised his own drug song, 'Dr Robert', with childlike lyrics.

The most commonly stated clue is that a yellow capsule-shaped amphetamine was nicknamed a 'Yellow Submarine' in the 1960s. This reference links to John's description of his first LSD trip in 1965, when he described ending the evening at George's Surrey bungalow, hallucinating that he was actually in a submarine in which his wife, George and Patti Boyd were the occupants and he was the captain. This link becomes compelling when you consider that it is John imitating a captain who makes the 'full speed ahead' interjection mid-song.

The arrangement of the song is a clue as well; its brass band, big bass drum sound is similar to that of Bob Dylan's ode to drugs, 'Rainy Day Woman No 12 and 35', with its singalong chorus of inviting us all to join him in getting 'stoned'.

Paul, who has always claimed to have genuinely intended it as a children's song, nevertheless had to start defending it almost immediately after its release. The only part of the song that is clearly free from drug references, however, was the phrase that Paul's friend and folk singer Donovan added about the sky and the sea.

Written for Ringo, its simple melody and phrasing fitted his limited range, while the natural weariness in his voice too fits the old sea-dog character the lyrics suggest. As often happened with Ringo, some encouragement was needed to get him in the mood and so a crowd of the Beatles' friends and associates came to the studio to create a party atmosphere and join in on backing vocals.

'SHE SAID SHE SAID'
(Lennon/Harrison)

This was inspired by an incident that took place in August 1965, when John, George, Ringo, the Byrds and actor Peter Fonda all took LSD together at a house in Los Angeles. John began writing the lyrics soon after, during the *Rubber Soul* sessions, when they were entitled 'He Said He Said', referring to a remark Peter Fonda made in John's company while the effects of LSD were starting to take hold. Fonda recounted how he was once technically dead on an operating table. This alarmed John who was worried the story would encourage a 'bad trip', like his first frightening experience of LSD in February 1965.

That it took John until June 1966 to complete the lyrics suggests that they caused him problems. Indeed, the ambitious opening lyrical gambit, is not logically resolved, John eventually settling on the familiar theme of a longing for his childhood which he had already used on 'Help!' and would use again on 'Strawberry Fields Forever'. Such were John's difficulties with the lyrics that he even turned to George for help, and he provided the lyrical link between the two halves.

Acknowledging the Byrds, who were with John during the episode that provided the song's initial lyrical inspiration, the music uses jarring, discordant guitars similar to those used on 'Eight Miles High'. Similarly here, John and George's guitars play the main lead riff in unison while occasionally using different notes.

As Paul recalled in his biography, he had an argument with the other Beatles during the recording of 'She Said She Said' and stormed out of the studio, leaving George to play bass. Significantly, Paul's voice is absent from the backing vocals. As the last song recorded for *Revolver*, it is possible that after all of the musical developments on the album, Paul wanted to try out a new idea for this track which was vetoed by the others.

'GOOD DAY SUNSHINE'
(McCartney/Lennon)

The Lovin' Spoonful's 'Daydream' was one of John and Paul's favourite records of the spring of 1966 and while John picked up on its references to sleep, Paul picked up on its celebration of fine weather for 'Good Day Sunshine'. Almost entirely based on the lyrics to 'Daydream', in this song Paul too writes of a sunny day spent with a girlfriend, walking and lying down outside. Yet where the lyrics of 'Daydream' are infectious and convincing, the stiff formality of the delivery on 'Good Day Sunshine' never captures the free and easy mood its lyrics are trying to convey. Using an old-time music hall style, there is something stiff about Paul's vocals and only at the song's end, where his vocals are doubled up and overlap, does it convey a convincingly dreamy, happy mood.

The authentic honky-tonk piano played here by George Martin impressed Paul enough for him to replicate it for both 'Lovely Rita' and 'Rocky Racoon'.

'AND YOUR BIRD CAN SING'
(Lennon/McCartney)

Never one to neglect a successful songwriting formula, this reads like another attempt by John at the pop philosophy of 'Nowhere Man'. There is a hint that the lyrics, as well as being directed at an acquaintance of John's, could also be about himself. The 'possessions' he speaks of sound remarkably like the luxuries he surrounded himself with at his own home. Unlike 'Nowhere Man', though, the message here is never clear. John admitted as much years later when he referred to this track as a 'horror'.

The failure of the lyrics is disappointing as this is a great group performance. The dynamic dual lead guitar sound was achieved by John and George (some sources state Paul and George) playing slightly varying and hence discordant notes simultaneously. Pioneered by the Byrds, this is possibly alluded to in the song's title, in the same way that the Beatles' instrumental 'Cry For A Shadow' from 1961 referred to the Shadows.

'FOR NO ONE'
(McCartney)

The success of the classical-style arrangement of 'Eleanor Rigby' early on in the recording of *Revolver* encouraged Paul to look at arranging more of his songs in such a manner. This was not always necessary or appropriate. While 'Eleanor Rigby' loses much of its power whenever it is given a live performance without its distinctive string arrangement, countless Beatles tribute bands around the world have shown that 'For No One' works well, if not better, with a conventional guitar, bass, piano, drums line-up. One motivation Paul may have had in giving 'For No One' its unusual arrangement was to disguise its main chord sequence, which bears a close resemblance to the Moody Blues' 'Go Now', a UK number one hit in 1965.

Starkly unromantic in tone, Paul's sour lyrics were inspired after yet another row with Jane Asher while on holiday in Switzerland. The clipped use of harpsichord and French horn match this tone, but Paul's oddly passionless vocal never brings either the lyrics or melody alive. Paul notably gave the song a very different arrangement when he re-recorded it for 'Give My Regards To Broad Street' in 1984.

'DOCTOR ROBERT'
(Lennon/McCartney)

A mischievous swipe at the Beatles' blindly adoring fans and their straightlaced record company EMI, this supposedly innocent song is an in-joke intended for the Beatles and their friends. Styled as a gormless tale of a 'national health' service doctor, the song was in fact based on a notorious Doctor Robert Freymann, who freely prescribed illicit drugs (mainly amphetamine) to the New York art world in the 1960s. John, according to his close friend Pete Shotton, took great delight in the thought that Beatle fans would sing along unaware of the lyrics' connotations. Indeed, John's glee at the song made these some of his best lyrics on the album, though musically the song lacks any similar invention.

'I WANT TO TELL YOU'
(Harrison)

George's attempts at matching the songs of John and Paul must have been all the more painful for his natural reticence and reputation as the 'quiet Beatle'. As such the lyrics to 'I Want To Tell You' grapple with his feelings of inarticulacy, a subject that he would return to much more successfully on 'Something'. *Revolver's* spirit of experimentation tramples all over George's sensitive lyrics – where he seeks reassurance, Paul's discordant piano and bass on the verses create an unsettling feel.

'GOT TO GET YOU INTO MY LIFE'
(McCartney)

Paul's mastery of new musical styles on *Revolver* marked him out for the first time as the Beatles' prime mover. More musically literate than John, Paul had quickly become as much at ease arranging his songs for brass or strings as he was for guitar. Paul brought 'Got To Get You Into My Life' to the studio and experimented with several arrangements before hitting on the idea of styling it with a Motown sound. Little different to the instrumentation used on contemporary Motown hits such as 'Uptight' by Stevie Wonder and 'Love Is Like An Itching In My Heart' by the Supremes, the bass and brass are used as the dominant instruments. Paul also copies the distinctive Motown beat of a snare drum synchronised with the beat of a tambourine. This is no straight imitation though, for while on Motown the saxophones would normally dominate, here trumpets played by London's top jazz musicians are the lead instruments, providing a more distinctly jazzy sound.

Paul spent a total of six days' studio time trying to perfect the sound on this (a good first version minus brass is on the *Anthology 2* album) and it is probable that he intended it as a single, before 'Eleanor Rigby'/'Yellow Submarine' got the vote. That he thought it would have been a good single is backed up by the fact that he produced a version for his old Liverpool chums Cliff Bennett and the Rebel Rousers which became a UK hit in 1966.

This is one of the many disguised drug songs on *Revolver*; Paul in his biography said the lyrics were an 'ode to pot'.

'TOMORROW NEVER KNOWS'
(Lennon/McCartney)

Having reached a peak in his songwriting career on *Rubber Soul* John, with his naturally radical impulses, needed something new to satisfy his ambition. 'Tomorrow Never Knows' is his attempt to redefine what a pop song could be. Motivated in part by what he often found to be the tiresome, difficult process of songwriting, he resolved to write a song on one chord alone. This was an idea the Beatles had flirted with before on songs like 'The Word', but the encouragement he needed came from the Indian music he was now listening to, which largely modulated around a single chord.

Being written around one chord (C major) alone, 'Tomorrow Never Knows' demanded a new lyrical style too. Taking the mystical sound of Indian music as a key, John looked to turn the experience of taking LSD into a quasi-religious hymn. John's key influence for this was the book written by renegade US psychologist Timothy Leary, called *The Psychedelic Experience*. This book itself was inspired by the ancient religious text *The Tibetan Book of the Dead*, a guide for monks in helping those on the verge of death into a peaceful afterlife. Leary wrote of the process of taking LSD as one of similarly taking your soul into a better existence while you were alive.

John's lyrics are in places directly lifted from Leary's book, describing the process of destroying your old ego with LSD, to create a new and more aware ego. Elsewhere the lyrics refer to textbook LSD hallucinations, where the user becomes so sensitive to colours that they appear to speak.

The music attempts to capture the altered reality of an LSD trip. On top of a hypnotic bass and drum riff, both John and Paul create a collage of backwards tapes and electronic noise. John's voice too was much distorted and echoed to meet his request to sound like the 'Dalai Lama on the top of a mountain'. While apparently excited at these new sounds on recording, John later expressed dissatisfaction with them. His original request had been to have thousands of chanting monks, but the instinctively conservative George Martin discouraged him, fearing not only the cost but the logistics. The electronic sounds used on 'Tomorrow Never Knows', while meeting John's original intention to redefine pop music, end up defeating the lyrics. Rather than being a hypnotic song aimed at promoting the enlightenment John felt he was gaining from LSD, it sounds more like a nightmarish warning against the drug.

(Subconsciously perhaps this was John's intention, as nearly all his LSD-influenced songs are sad in tone). The slowed-down backwards guitar that creates the whining noise on the track in particular sounds like the shrieking of a monstrous seagull. John's reticence is evident in the title. Originally entitled 'The Void', he changed it to the more lighthearted 'Tomorrow Never Knows' after one of Ringo's malapropisms.

8. Sgt. Pepper's Lonely Hearts Club Band

'STRAWBERRY FIELDS FOREVER'
(Lennon) Single first released in the USA 13 February 1967

What is arguably John's greatest song was written on a long, curative break between 19 September and 7 November 1966. In Spain to act in the rather lame anti-war film *How I Won The War*, John's supporting role, to his disappointment, meant more hanging around than work. Staying at a house not far from the beach in Almeria, southern Spain, largely apart from his friends and family, he found the time and space to reflect on his life. So deep in thought was he that his chauffeur recalled John barely uttering a word to him in Spain. In an admission John made public only months before his death, foremost in his mind was his turmoil over whether to leave the Beatles or not.

John's disaffection stemmed from the events of the Beatles' world tour in the summer of 1966. An ordeal from start to finish, it was dogged by death threats in Japan, a terrifying scramble out of the Phillipines after being chased and beaten by a government mob and yet more death threats in the USA. This last crisis, to John's horror, was caused by a careless but innocent remark that the Beatles were more popular than Jesus. In the deep American south, where the Beatles were due to play, John's words led to mass bonfires of Beatles records. Forced to make a public apology to save the tour, John's usually tough exterior was cracked by what he saw as the very real possibility that he or the other Beatles would be assassinated. He reportedly cried after a press conference in Chicago on 12 August, where the American press repeatedly asked him to recant his words. Film footage of the conference tellingly shows him looking haggard. While publicly the Beatles showed a united front over the remarks John made, in private they let John know their resentment at the danger he had put them in.

John now began to question his career as a Beatle and for a while considered acting instead. Only his experience of endlessly hanging around during the making of *How I Won The War* deterred him. What saved the Beatles from splitting at this point was their decision to give up touring. In effect a semi-retirement, it meant that they would never contractually be obliged to perform in public again. Meanwhile John, still shaken by the events of the tour and not yet foreseeing the artistic growth of *Sgt. Pepper*, slumped into depression and self-doubt on the set of *How I Won The War*.

Normally a speedy writer, it took John the full six weeks he spent in Spain to complete 'Strawberry Fields Forever'. He seems to have gone to great lengths over the words for a song he had attempted in many guises before. 'There's A Place', 'I'm A Loser', 'Help!', and 'Nowhere Man' had all explored similar themes of self-doubt, though the starting point for 'Strawberry Fields Forever' is more obvious on the recent *Revolver* album. The line which is left unresolved on 'She Said She Said' is fully explored here.

As a contrast to his worries, John idealised his memories of Strawberry Field (John added the 's' to make it scan), a large imposing garden and house converted for Salvation Army orphans close to his home in Liverpool where he played as a child. Now knocked down the large gothic style house (of which many similar houses still stand in its street) must have looked to John like the setting for one of the Lewis Carroll 'Alice' stories he loved so much. A place were nothing literally appeared to be real. John saw Strawberry Field as a symbol of freedom and happiness, a place where nothing bad happened to him. (Were these childhood memories stirred by John's first short-back-and-sides haircut since he had been a schoolboy, necessitated by his film role as a soldier? Looking in the mirror, John must have had an eerie flashback to his youth.)

An instinctive optimist, John used these happy memories of his childhood in the chorus as an uplifting contrast to the self-doubt of the verses, which show a clear end to the commercial compromises he had employed in his earlier work. Rarely addressing the listener, they read like a conversation with himself concerning his career crisis. The lyrics conjure up his feelings of isolation and unhappiness and by way of contrast hark back fondly to the blissful ignorance and innocence of his youth. John in 1970 summed up the lyrics as psychoanalysis put to music.

The changes John was making in his lyrics were matched in his appearance. Symbolically, he gave up his mop-top hairstyle and on his return to London grew a moustache. No more would he wear contact lenses to maintain his pop star image; instead he continued wearing the spectacles he had used to stylise his film role as a doomed soldier in *How I Won The War*. John was basically looking to be truer to himself. Pointedly, the song title 'Strawberry Fields Forever' offers a different world view to the banners fans held up at Beatles concerts, which proclaimed 'the Beatles Forever'.

Back in Abbey Road studios in November 1966, John spent a month searching for a sound to match his lyrics. Ironically George Martin (the Beatles' producer) rated the best version as the one John first played to him on acoustic guitar – a version that was sadly not recorded.

John tried out two very different recordings. The first was built up on 24, 28 and 29 November, and 8 and 9 December 1966. Tapes now released on the *Anthology 2* CD show its evolution from a slowly strummed lament into a light psychedelic mood piece featuring Paul on the newly invented Mellotron, a proto-synthesiser that you could only use in short 11-second bursts, hence its brevity here.

Back amongst the camaraderie of the Beatles, John's crisis must have eased as he now sought a more uplifting mood. A new version, scored with cellos and trumpets by George Martin, was recorded on 15 December.

Without the time constraints of touring, John contemplated the two recordings at leisure. Deciding he liked the first half of the group version and the second half of the other, he boldly asked George Martin to join them together. They were a note apart but Martin, by speeding up the first half and slowing down the second, made their keys meet around B flat on 22 December. The cut takes place exactly one minute into the song. The change of tape speed helped the two halves mix in an unexpected way. The slowed-down string and brass gained a ghostly sound that fits the otherworldly sound of the mellotron. The speeded-up drums in the first half too slipped easily into the more frantic second half.

An extra addition to the mix was the closing fade-out and fade-back, which is almost certainly a direct copy from the fade-out to the Beach Boys' 'Caroline No'. The ringing bell on the latter track is identical in tone and repetition to the guitar note that Paul plays, while Ringo's drums imitate the sound of a train passing over the tracks, a sound also used at the end of 'Caroline No'. The Beatles often put references in their records that they knew only their friends or associates in the pop business would understand. It is probable that this coda is a nod to the Beach Boys, whose *Pet Sounds* album they so admired.

The lyrical depth and musical wizardry of 'Strawberry Fields Forever' have made it a favourite with music journalists, who often quote it as the greatest single of all time. It made a big impact on the Beatles too. The six days spent recording it was more than any other song they had worked on. That the results were so successful encouraged them to continue working in such a fashion for the album that would become *Sgt. Pepper*.

'PENNY LANE'
(McCartney/Lennon) Double A-side with 'Strawberry Fields Forever'

The nine studio days spent recording this, the most spent on any Beatles song, shows the ambition Paul felt in trying to match the sonic triumph of 'Strawberry Fields Forever', which had been completed a week before recording began on 'Penny Lane'.

A breakthrough in sound quality, 'Penny Lane' combined more instruments on the limited four-track recording machines employed at Abbey Road than ever before. Aiming for a huge piano sound, three piano tracks and a harmonium track were recorded and mixed separately, then 'bounced down' to a single track. This cleared three tracks for the recording of brass, drums, bass, vocals and flutes. Only with the great experience of George Martin – operating under Paul's instructions of getting a very clean sound – was this mix possible without loss of sound quality. To this day the depth of tone on 'Penny Lane' is astonishing. Emphasising the peak of this sound is the piccolo trumpet played by London Symphony Orchestra musician David Mason, whose notes reach as high as the blue skies of summer the lyrics suggest. Mason was hired after Paul heard him playing on a performance of Bach's Brandenburg Concerto, where his trumpet plays the main melody, unlike the merely decorative role it performs here.

The roots of the creation of 'Penny Lane' go back to November 1965 when Paul was quoted as saying he wished to write a song of the same name. It seems probable that John and Paul discussed this together as 'In My Life', which was written by John at the same time, also referred to Penny Lane in its first draft. Impetus too may have come from the

Beatles' lightweight Liverpudlian rivals Gerry and the Pacemakers, who surpassed themselves with their haunting paean to Liverpool, 'Ferry 'Cross The Mersey' in early 1965.

John's 'Strawberry Fields Forever' reawakened Paul's plan of writing a song about Penny Lane in early December 1966 (John contributed lyrics to the third verse). Both songs are tinged with an air of sadness; the Beatles' enormous success meant they were unlikely to go back to living their old lives in Liverpool.

In contrast to John's isolation, Paul's lyrics are a celebration of street community. Strawberry Field was a place John could be at one with himself, yet Penny Lane – an area near a large crossroads close to a street with many shops – was where Paul could be like everybody else. The two places are actually only a stone's throw away from each other in Woolton, Liverpool.

That Paul and John wrote two of their best songs in recognition of the city that raised them and shaped their characters is commendable. Yet to this day there are many in Liverpool who feel bitter at the lack of recognition the Beatles gave to their hometown. The success of the Beatles' career paralleled a long-term decline in the prosperity of the city.

SGT. PEPPER'S LONELY HEARTS CLUB BAND
Album released 1 June 1967

Sgt. Pepper is the extent of the Beatles' ambition within the studio. Released from the schedules of touring deadlines, interviews and TV appearances, the unlimited time they had for recording must have seemed like one long summer holiday. Allowed to unleash their musical imagination to the full, the resulting album suitably stunned the public on release. For many this is the Beatles finest hour, yet *Sgt. Pepper* is in truth largely the work and design of Paul alone. John contributed two of its best songs but these, like most of *Sgt. Pepper*, were chiefly arranged under Paul's direction. Such was Paul's enthusiasm and energy for the project that in the face of a lacklustre input by John and George, he had become the album's musical director and was able to cover up for his bandmates.

Much of Paul's drive came after he heard the Beach Boys' 1966 album *Pet Sounds*. Amazed at its level of invention and breadth of sound, he thought it the best album ever made. He also realised that the Beatles would need to raise their standards if they were to compete. His imagination fired to go one better than the Beach Boys, Paul came up with the exciting and amusing idea of recording a Beatles album under a pseudonym while travelling on a flight back from safari in Africa in

November 1966. For this 'band' he wrote the album's opening song and wanted each Beatle to assume an alter ego for each song, e.g. Ringo as Billy Shears. The idea was that under a pseudonym, the Beatles would feel less inhibited about creating new sounds and songs. Yet despite Paul's domination the Beatles were still a democracy and neither John nor George responded with anything that could fit into Paul's concept, which only survived on the cover photo.

Some of Paul's ideas, though, were irresistible. Through reading imported copies of US underground newspapers the *Oracle* and the *Berkeley Barb*, he learnt early on of the new San Franciscan counter-culture that would soon sweep the world in the summer of 1967. Many songs on *Sgt. Pepper* contain the Utopian ideals of this new San Franciscan scene, which owed much to the city's position as a centre for anti-Vietnam war activists and also its abundant supply of LSD. At the forefront of this scene were San Franciscan 'hippy' rock bands such as the Grateful Dead, Jefferson Airplane, Quicksilver Messenger Service and Country Joe and the Fish. The outlandish names of these bands, that often lived in communal houses and played free concerts in the city, were Paul's inspiration in the album's long title name.

Despite these links to the emerging counter-culture, many of the drugs and political references people read into the album are simply not there. For instance, the offer to take some tea with me on 'Lovely Rita' is not a reference to marijuana and 'When I'm 64' is not a criticism of capitalism!

Paul ironically blamed the lack of input from John and George on LSD. In 1988 he said that he resisted LSD as he saw it 'making them sit around very dopey and making them hear noises I couldn't hear.' The use of different drugs by the Beatles would mark the beginning of their split; noticeably here it made John and George more introspective. John in particular was at the height of his LSD use, which made him placid enough to accept Paul's takeover as prime mover within the Beatles. John had already, wittingly or not, made his mark on the album with the enormous achievement of 'Strawberry Fields Forever'. As the first song recorded for the project, the fantastical nature of its lyrics and vocals and its innovative production techniques had a big influence on the rest of the album.

George's input was less obvious. Paul, who ended up playing the lead guitar on both 'Being For The Benefit Of Mr Kite!' and 'Good Morning, Good Morning', in 1986 criticised George for hardly being present during recording. George, whose interest in Indian music and religion was taking precedence, admitted later he had 'lost interest' in being a Beatle at this time.

There were other reasons for George's absence. Both George and Ringo became bored during recording. The large attention John and Paul gave to perfecting arrangements often gave them little to do. Over the 14 days of recording from the beginning of December 1966 to the end of January 1967 all George was required to do was to make 'aaaah' noises on 'When I'm 64', ring a fire bell and beat a conga drum on 'Penny Lane' (his lead guitar contribution for this was cut), and shake maracas on 'A Day In The Life'. Typically, later on George's role on 'Being For The Benefit Of Mr Kite!' was limited to harmonica, while on 'She's Leaving Home' he did not appear at all.

Paul brought to the album a wide variety of musical styles. Looking to develop the Beatles beyond straight pop, he was listening to classical composers such as Stockhausen, Bach and Benjamin Britten. Motown was still a big influence, though not as big as the Beach Boys' album *Pet Sounds*, whose variety of instruments and multi-layered sound are copied here. The wilful strangeness of Frank Zappa and The Mothers Of Invention's 1966 double album *Freak Out* encouraged the Beatles' bolder experiments on *Sgt. Pepper*, which at one stage was also planned as a double album.

It is difficult to imagine now, but prior to *Sgt. Pepper* many were writing the Beatles off. The failure of some US concerts to sell out in 1966 and the relatively low sales for *Revolver* caused some journalists to claim the Beatles had run out of steam. The Beatles were, of course, far from finished and Paul in particular actually worked harder to prove these critics wrong, relishing how silly they would look on the album's release, although as John later admitted in 1970 none of the Beatles were completely sure of how the album would be received.

As a result of working so hard on *Sgt. Pepper*, though, the Beatles' public profile was lower than at any time since the start of their fame. This fuelled further rumours of a split, yet this absence from public view was useful as it allowed them to put distance between their old mop-top image and their new ambitious music. Their record company and manager Brian Epstein, though, were panicked by their low commercial profile and requested the release of a single for February 1967. Duly 'Strawberry Fields' and 'Penny Lane' were released and subsequently left off *Sgt. Pepper*.

Many regret these song's omission and there has been much debate over which tracks could have been dropped to make way. George Martin went as far as to name 'Lovely Rita' and 'When I'm 64' for the chop. Arguably 'Being For the Benefit Of Mr Kite!', one of the most mannered *Sgt. Pepper* tracks, would make a better omission, along with the misplaced 'When I'm 64'.

Each song on *Sgt. Pepper* is given the perfect sound balance, with great clarity of tone for all instruments and vocals. Unlike previous albums, there was unlimited time for perfecting instrumental and vocal performances. Often songs were returned to again and again to repeat individual parts. For example, the brilliant drum track on 'A Day In The Life' was perfected on a separate overdub after the main track had been made. Notably, the vocals are some of the most perfect the Beatles ever recorded.

The basic recording process for most tracks was to find unique sounds for the drums, bass and guitar before recording them together as the backing track. The numerous overdubs beyond this often necessitated that several instruments share the same track. In such cases, for clarity of sound the instruments would often queue up to appear, e.g. a piano on the first verse, a tambourine for the chorus and a sitar for the second verse.

Many of the album's sounds relied on on-the-spot studio innovation from George Martin and engineer Geoff Emerick. Amplifiers were tampered with and set at unusual angles or distances and instruments were enhanced with extra-close miking, particularly the drums. Vocal speeds were raised for 'Lucy In The Sky With Diamonds', 'When I'm 64' and 'Lovely Rita'; on 'A Day In The Life' two four-track recording machines were used then mixed onto one tape, to give a greater range of sound. This search for perfection dragged out recording from December 1966 to April 1967, at that time an incredible length to spend in the studio.

'SGT. PEPPER'S LONELY HEARTS CLUB BAND' (McCartney)

Paul's introduction to the album as an old-fashioned master of ceremonies shows him at his most corny. What saves him is the song's musical dramatisation, as if played by the Jimi Hendrix Experience. In early 1967 Jimi Hendrix was causing a sensation in London's small rock clubs. Stories spread of his amazing prowess on guitar, of how he would play guitar with his teeth, behind his back and on one occasion with his feet! What most impressed London's rock fraternity, though, was his ability to appear to be playing rhythm and lead guitar at the same time, a trick best heard on 'Foxy Lady'.

Paul's proximity to central London meant that he could easily catch Hendrix live. Prior to and during the making of *Sgt. Pepper* he saw him at the Scotch of St James club on 25 October 1966, with John at the Bag of Nails in Soho on 25 November and by himself at the same club on 11 January 1967. Several unnamed Beatles again saw Hendrix play at the Marquee on 24 January, while Paul and John went to see him supporting The Who at the Saville Theatre on 29 January, where they saw the show from a private box and later invited Hendrix to a private party. The *Sgt. Pepper* title track recorded on 1 February, not surprisingly, is strongly influenced by Hendrix, particularly 'Foxy Lady'. (Jack Bruce, who was at the same gig, went home and wrote 'Sunshine of Your Love' inspired by Hendrix.) Thundering heavyweight chords are followed by lead fills at every chord change, both using the distorted sound Hendrix favoured. Paul mimics Hendrix's throaty vocals and his lyrics too are probably inspired by the dry wit with which Hendrix often spoke to his audiences. Presumably flattered at the tribute, Hendrix returned the compliment by covering this title track at a gig in London in Paul's presence, days after the release of the *Sgt. Pepper* album.

In the same way that 'Strawberry Fields Forever' mixed separate brass and rock segments, here an arrangement of French horns was added to the Hendrix rock workout. French horns are traditionally used in classical music to announce either a beginning, or the entrance of a hero or a god. Their triumphal fanfare here typifies the ambition Paul felt during early 1967.

There has been some speculation as to the identity of Billy Shears, who is announced at the end of the song. It is likely that the name lodged in Paul's memory and subconsciously re-emerged later on. This may have been the case with 'Eleanor Rigby' and also for 'Sgt. Pepper'; while the Beatles toured Canada in 1965, they met a policeman who was looking after them with the name of Sergeant Pepper. Notably, on the front cover of *Sgt. Pepper* Paul wears a badge given to him by the Ontario Police Precinct. Paul's explanation is that he was playing around with the words 'salt and pepper', and decided that Sgt. Pepper was a more amusing variation.

'WITH A LITTLE HELP FROM MY FRIENDS'
(McCartney/Lennon)

Many accounts of the making of *Sgt. Pepper* tell of the good atmosphere that existed among the Beatles. Their relief at having given up touring was the main cause. These happy vibes seem to have encouraged them to set aside normal rivalries, to the extent that John and Paul combined to write one of the album's best songs (and many people's favourite) for Ringo. The lyrics acknowledge the group's currently healthy partnership.

For once, too, time was given to record Ringo's vocals, which so often before had only been given one take. In particular, the last line of the song was recorded separately, to help Ringo reach surely his highest note ever.

Hunter Davies' book *the Beatles* gives a first-hand account of John and Paul finishing the last verses to this song at Paul's house before entering the studio to record it the same day. The tune and first verse were by Paul and the latter verses were co-written with John, who added the typically jarring, sexual innuendo on the third verse. The music uses a distinctive Motown sound in the way the rhythm guitar accents each beat, rather than playing across it. The call and response vocals here are almost certainly inspired by contemporary black US vocal acts.

The song caused some controversy when it was released, for its clear and intentional reference to marijuana. This overshadowed the song's main message about friendship so much that John was forced to emphasise in 1970, that the lyrics were sincere.

'LUCY IN THE SKY WITH DIAMONDS'
(Lennon/McCartney)

Shortly before John died in 1980, he said that it was an aim later in life to write a story in the same vein as Lewis Carroll's *Alice In Wonderland*. This ambition is evident in the fantastical imagery of 'Lucy In The Sky With Diamonds', whose opening verse John admitted to being based on images from *Alice In Wonderland*. Carroll had been a favourite of John's since childhood and his poem 'The Walrus and the Carpenter' would inspire 'I Am The Walrus'.

Another input into the song came from John's son Julian, who was then three years old. John recalled, 'My son came in one day with a picture he painted about a school friend of his named Lucy. He had sketched in some stars in the sky and called it "Lucy in the sky with diamonds".' John was to retell this story many times to refute what many saw as the song's hidden promotion of LSD, in the initials of its title. Yet while the title has a genuinely coincidental link to LSD, many of the lyrical images do not. The 'marmalade skies', 'flowers of yellow and green' and 'kaleidoscope eyes' relate to the increased sensitivity to colour caused by LSD. The line 'grow so incredibly high' too is quite clearly the type of knowing wink to the effects of drugs the Beatles had been putting in their songs since 1964. Interestingly, only several months prior to the recording in March 1967 of 'Lucy In The Sky With Diamonds', Jefferson Airplane released their drug song 'White Rabbit', which made direct and unashamed links between the fantastical imagery of Lewis Carroll and the effects of LSD. Elsewhere in the song, it was Paul who added the chorus melody and who contributed the lines 'cellophane flowers' and 'newspaper taxis' to the lyrics. Intriguingly, John's opening words to the song are a lyrical gambit he would repeat on 'Imagine'.

Some of *Sgt. Pepper*'s most innovative sounds feature on this track. John's voice has been speeded up, phased and echoed as if to make it sound like a voice from a dream. The organ played by Paul, using a Celeste key, has its sound enhanced so acutely that it is always a surprise to hear. (To overcome the limitations of four-track recording, the organ and lead guitar share the same track. The organ plays on the first half of each verse and the guitar takes over for the second half.) Adding another layer of mystery to the track, Paul's sleepwalking bass line on the verses plays a counter-melody, styled like that for incidental music in Hollywood thrillers. John's vocal too adds a layer of percussive texture to the music, in the same style as Gene Vincent's on 'Be-Bop A Lula'. A similar effect is used on 'A Day In The Life'.

Despite this track's popularity, John felt it was never recorded properly, referring to it as 'abysmal'. His unhappiness was almost certainly due to the way each chorus clumsily breaks up the dreamlike verses, the second chorus also noticeably entering faster than the first.

'GETTING BETTER'
(McCartney/Lennon)

No one track better illustrates the pay-off for the long hours spent working on *Sgt. Pepper*. Over three separate eight- and nine-hour-long recording sessions, within what is mostly a simple F, C, G chord pattern the Beatles built an exciting mix of sound textures from a variety of instruments, whose sound has all been acutely enhanced. The arrangement allows in turn the rhythm guitar, lead guitar, drums, vocals and tambora (a stringed Indian instrument played by George) a separate chance to shine. The vocals too add to the multi-rhythmic layers with their emphasis on the prevalent 't' sounds in the lyrics. Paul almost certainly got the idea for the arrangement from watching the way a classical orchestra works.

The optimism of the lyrics were inspired on a walk Paul took on Primrose Hill in London on the first sunny day of spring. Taking the words 'getting better' as the basis of a song, he sought help on more lyrics from John. Paul turned his comical put-down that they lyrics would not get much worse to his advantage by incorporating it as a harmony vocal line. John's other lyrical contribution, the similarly dark admittance of a past misogynistic treatment of women, is a jarring and powerful contrast to Paul's verses, its emotional impact similar to the lyrics he added to other songs by Paul, especially 'We Can Work It Out' and 'She's Leaving Home'.

Some of the longest hours on *Sgt. Pepper* were spent perfecting this track, but the other Beatles became impatient with Paul's attention to detail and such meticulous recording was rarely attempted by them again.

'FIXING A HOLE'
(McCartney)

The teasing lyrical double entendres in this song show the influence of John's songwriting on Paul. In the same way that the drugs prescribed by 'Dr Robert' on *Revolver* could be illicit or purely medicinal, here 'Fixing A Hole' could either be an innocent, mundane description of DIY or a description of the effects of drugs. Where on 'Tomorrow Never Knows' John instructs us to free our minds to the effects of LSD and to let it move upwards, here Paul similarly talks of setting his mind free to let it explore. Tellingly, John praised the lyrics as late as 1980 and also referred to them in his lyrics to 'Glass Onion'.

For those hip enough in 1967 to tune into the song's drug references, Paul's giveaway clue are his strung out, heavily echoed vocals. The backing too, with its disorientating mix of jazz, rock and classical music, hints at altered states. Paul's reticence in explaining the true meaning of the song at the time of its release has led to it becoming the most misinterpreted of all the Beatles' songs. On first explaining the lyrics in 1967 Paul had played down their drug connotations. By 1997, when his drug use had become public and police knowledge for some time, Paul stated that the DIY theme in the lyrics was largely an analogy for the effects of marijuana, though as he has had to point out over the years, it was never about 'fixing up', i.e. heroin.

This is one of several of Paul's songs that sum up the initial optimism of the new counter-culture in early 1967 (John would follow later with 'All You Need Is Love'). His opinion that what is seen as 'wrong' is 'right' connects to the counter-culture's challenge to straight society's values.

'SHE'S LEAVING HOME'
(McCartney/Lennon)

The hippies of San Francisco, with their values of spirituality over materialism, were in early 1967 causing ripples worldwide. On both 'Getting Better' and 'Fixing A Hole' Paul had injected first-person references to these new values. Yet where John was at his most compelling when writing about himself, Paul was for the time being at his best when writing in the third person. On 'She's Leaving Home' he summed up the mood of change of 1967 perfectly, with his adaptation of a story he had read in the *Daily Mirror* published on 27 February 1967. Telling of how 17-year-old Melanie Coe had run away from home, the story quoted the girl's father saying: 'I cannot imagine why she should run away. She has everything here. She is very keen on clothes, but she left them all, even her fur coat.' Paul dryly narrates most of this tale in the lyrics, but in a great example of how their songwriting partnership worked, John added a cutting emotional edge by voicing the parent's reaction. His lines about parental sacrifice and money were words he recalled his Aunt Mimi saying to him.

In the early 1990s Steve Turner, author of *A Hard Day's Write*, traced Melanie Coe in England and asked her about the song. Amazingly she credited Paul's lyrics as accurately interpreting her reasons for leaving home, even though for obvious reasons she was not quoted in the original article. Paul's only mistaken embellishment to the newspaper story was that she ran off with a second hand car salesman – he envisaged her going off with a 'sleazy guy with a flash car'. Melanie Coe actually left home to live with a croupier from a gambling club.

All instruments are played by session musicians conducted by George Martin, which encouraged some observers at the time to suggest that the music school-trained Martin was the talent behind the Beatles. Such opinions led to friction between the Beatles (especially John) and Martin, to the extent that his role as a producer was diminished on the *Magical Mystery Tour*, *The White Album* and *Let It Be*. The sound here is actually directly attributable to Paul's growing interest in classical music in late 1966, which led him to take up formal piano lessons. The music, with its evocation of daybreak to match the opening lyrical images, is reminiscent of Dvorak's 'New World Symphony' and Greig's 'Peer Gynt'.

'BEING FOR THE BENEFIT OF MR KITE!'
(Lennon/McCartney)

This is John's weakest contribution to *Sgt. Pepper*, its steam organ solo, made from randomly spliced tapes, in particular shows the contrived quaintness encouraged by the album's concept. John came to be embarrassed by the song and in 1970 blamed its weakness on having to write quickly to match Paul's prodigious output of songs. John claimed that if he had not written quickly he would have had barely any songs on the album. This was something of an exaggeration, as when 'Being For The Benefit Mr Kite!' was recorded on 1 March 1967, John had also recorded 'A Day In the Life' and 'Good Morning, Good Morning'. The final tally of songs for *Sgt. Pepper* shows Paul as the main songwriter for eight songs, with John the main songwriter for four.

On release many assumed the lyrics were a product of John's imagination. Some saw the dancing horse as a drug reference, as horse is also slang for heroin. Yet in 1968 John revealed that the lyrics were largely lifted from an original 1843 poster advertising a fair, which he bought in an antique shop (Paul claimed to have helped John compile these lyrical images). He even went to the length of being photographed standing next to the poster to make his point. The reading of hidden messages into the song infuriated him. In 1968 he complained to the Beatles biographer Hunter Davies, 'People want to know what the inner meaning of "Mr Kite" was. There wasn't any. I shoved a lot of words together and then shoved some noise on. I didn't dig that song when I wrote it. I didn't believe in it when we were recording it. But nobody will believe it. They don't want to. They want it to be important.'

Such was John's irritation that he was inspired to write 'Glass Onion' as a spoof song, to bamboozle all those who read too much into his lyrics.

'WITHIN YOU WITHOUT YOU'
(Harrison)

George's input into *Sgt. Pepper* was the lowest by any Beatle on any of their albums. Disillusioned with his image as a Beatle, his first (rejected) contribution to the album 'It's Only A Northern Song' seems to mock the new experimental sounds of *Sgt. Pepper* with its sardonic lyrics. Effectively a solo track, 'Within You Without You' by contrast contained his most powerful lyrics so far. Their spirituality and rejection of materialism appear a riposte to the fantastical artifice of Paul's vision for the album. For this reason, on its release in 1967 this was many people's favourite *Sgt. Pepper* track. Its message that the love generated by the new enlightened youth of the 1960s was capable of saving the world summed up the new San Franciscan scene more succinctly than any other song from 1967. Today such connections are lost and now George's optimism merely sounds deadened by his mournful vocal and an arrangement that does not shift key for a full five minutes. His case is also not effectively made by George's typically vague song title.

This track's weaknesses could have been helped by harmony vocals from John and Paul, yet although they were present in the studio for the song's recording, respecting George's greater knowledge of Indian music, they let him work solo. George Martin took a firmer role. Unimpressed with the track, which he later called 'dreary', he added an arrangement of classical strings for extra harmonic interest.

To get a glimpse of George's state of mind in 1967, the following is a quote from a long rambling interview he gave to the English hippie newspaper *International Times* in May 1967. 'The buzz of all buzzes which is the thing that is God, you've got to be straight to get it . . . be healthy, don't eat meat, keep away from those nightclubs and meditate.'

'WHEN I'M 64'
(McCartney)

Paul wrote most of 'When I'm 64' when he was 16, envisaging it as a song for a musical. At the time he was not certain of success with the Beatles and he was quite wisely keeping all career routes open. The tune only came to be played by the Beatles whenever the amplifiers failed at the Cavern, a common occurence owing to the humidity 'shorting' the electricity. At this stage John recalled it was only half completed and when Paul resurrected it for *Sgt. Pepper* he added new lyrics.

Recorded largely solo with help on the arrangement from George Martin, Paul strove for an authentic 1930s sound, perhaps explaining why his vocal was speeded up on tape as if to mimic the often whiny pitch of records made in this period.

The lightweight, easy-listening style of 'When I'm 64' caused friction with John and George. John said dismissively of the song, 'I would never even dream of writing a tune like that.' Despite this band unity was still good during the making of *Sgt. Pepper* and both John and George added fine backing vocals here. A further interesting point on John's dislike of 'When I'm 64' is that it was completed partly in honour of Paul's dad, who turned 64 in 1966. Paul's father always saw John as a bad influence, an impression vindicated when John hospitalised disc jockey Bob Wooler at Paul's 21st birthday party at his family's house in Liverpool. John in turn saw Paul's father as curbing Paul's wilder rock 'n' roll instincts and generally treating him like a child. John's thoughts on Paul writing a song honouring his father are thus easy to imagine.

'LOVELY RITA'
(McCartney)

A slight song yet a great performance, the humble Rita is treated to a 'Lucy In The Sky' style arrangement, her praises being sung from heavenly-sounding backing vocals. What gives these vocals emphasis is that they are recorded at normal speed, while Paul's main vocals are speeded up, giving both quite different sound textures.

The effort Paul put into dramatising this fictional song about a traffic warden left John exasperated. Now clearly diverging as songwriters, John was saving his greatest efforts for writing about the extraordinary or capturing true emotions, and was beginning to see songs such as 'Lovely Rita' as an embarrassment. The inspiration for Paul's lyrics, though, based around the phrase 'meter maid' which was US slang for a traffic warden, are not as innocent as they seem. As he later admitted, they were his rather sordid revenge fantasy for receiving a parking ticket, that of seducing the 'meter maid' in question. English traffic warden Meta Davies, who gave Paul a ticket outside Abbey Road studios, claimed it was she who gave Paul further inspiration after he saw her name (which rhymes with both Rita and meter) on a parking ticket. Playing on the song's key words, Paul uses a device typical of John, that of cramming the lyrics full of words with hard 'ter' and 'ker' sounds to emphasise the song's beat.

'GOOD MORNING GOOD MORNING'
(Lennon)

A tale of the mundanity of the everyday home life that John was settling into, the opening line with its admission that he did not feel like going to work either sums up his diminished output in 1967. His lifestyle then consisted of sleeping in, rarely venturing out of his house and watching daytime TV, such as the lightweight comedy sitcom mentioned in the lyrics, *Meet The Wife*.

The song's description of everyday life could easily have earned it the title 'A Day In The Life', which had been recorded two weeks earlier in January 1967. John was perhaps trying to repeat the powerful images of that song, and that he later dismissed 'Good Morning Good Morning' as 'garbage' suggests that he saw it as a failure to capture the mood of 'A Day In The Life'.

The title was taken from a Kellogg's cornflake advert, which had a jingle that started 'Good morning, good morning'. This Kellogg's reference also appears at the song's start with the tape of a cockerel, the company's emblem. Some writers have stressed that John got this inspiration for the song accidentally while watching television, but it seems probable that he was already looking for an image of daily mundanity, like those found in a newspaper for 'A Day In The Life'.

On a musical level the track works brilliantly; it is a rare example for this era of adrenalin fuelled rock 'n' roll by the Beatles. Ringo's energetic drumming unusually drives the band along, compared to his normal behind-the-beat style. This accentuates John's rhythmic lyrics and their unusual shifting time signature. Paul's waspish guitar solo is another stand out, which again like the album's theme song was recorded shortly after John and Paul's inspirational visit to see Jimi Hendrix on 29 January 1967.

The gimmicky ending of animal noises seems to be another reference to the Beach Boys' *Pet Sounds*. To George Martin's astonishment the sound of a chicken clucking at the end of these noises fitted neatly into the pitch of the guitar that starts the next song, getting, as he remembered, an edit luckier than he could ever have hoped for.

'SGT. PEPPER'S LONELY HEART'S CLUB BAND'
(Reprise) (McCartney)

In April 1967, with *Sgt. Pepper* near completion, the Beatles' assistant Neil Aspinall came up with the smart idea of a reprise of the album's opening track, recorded as if it were the farewell to a live performance. It was traditionally Paul's role with the Beatles to announce their departure before the last song of the night, and thus it fell to him to write this corny showbiz farewell to match the album's introduction. This track then gives the album a rather thin concept of a Beatles' live show, acknowledging their fans who would no longer be able to see them tour.

Completed at speed with the minimum of overdubs, perhaps to give it a live feel, its only innovation was that the bass was plugged straight into the mixing board to give it a higher presence. The Hendrix imitation of the title track is transformed here to more straightforward heavy rock, played faster and at a higher key. The last bar moves up several notes to end on G, neatly introducing 'A Day In The Life' which starts in the same key.

'A DAY IN THE LIFE'
(Lennon/McCartney)

This collage of mundane and tragic media images is revealing of the drug-induced haze in which John spent much of 1967. His near-emotionless vocal emphasises detachment to the world around him, particularly to the stories of ordinary people in the newspaper. It makes a stark contrast with Paul's songs 'Lovely Rita' and 'She's Leaving Home' with their empathy for ordinary people. Such was John's surrender to LSD that the double-entendre in the song's key offer to 'turn us on' was put there more for its drug connotations than its sexual overtones. John's mood at the time of writing was also one of resignation and depression over the course of his career and his life.

John wrote the first verses with a newspaper propped up in front of him on the piano. They start satirically; inspired by a newspaper story that had a photo of a rich man sitting in an expensive car. Although refers to a different story, about the death of the Beatles' friend Tara Browne in a car crash on 18 December 1966. The double meaning in this line coldly links a joke about the effects of mind-blowing rugs to the head injuries that killed Browne. Browne's father was a titled aristocrat and, as the lyrics imply, neither John nor Paul were sure if he was eligible to be a member of the House of Lords in London. Coldly, his death is trivialised by the inclusion in the lyrics of a 'News in brief' item about 4,000 holes in the roads of Blackburn, Lancashire. John also cynically manages a plug to his soon-to-be released anti-war film *How I Won The War* which John had acted for in late 1966, with his sarcastic line about the English army winning the war.

John sings the verses in a mournful, bored voice, as if the weight of this 'news' was consuming him. This mood was enhanced by feeding the echo of his voice into his headphones, causing his haunting, disembodied phrasing and unusual timing. John's vocal, which shifts from the right speaker to the middle and then to the left speaker, highlights this echo. Accentuating the vocal is Ringo's closely miked, booming bass drum. This appears unusually high in the mix, the result of his drums being given a separate overdub, which allowed greater freedom in mixing sound levels. The free yet supporting role of the drums here has since been much praised as a landmark in the development of rock drumming.

The orchestral crescendo was a noise that John requested to sound like the world ending. This is revealing as, like 'Tomorrow Never Knows', it shows that subconsciously, the LSD experience for John was one of nightmare rather than optimism. To match John's vision, Paul created the idea of a rising orchestral crescendo, based on music he had heard by classical composer Stockhausen. To emphasise the power of this crescendo a whole orchestra was used.

Paul's middle verse was added after John asked him to help finish the song at Paul's house. As John remembered, Paul was initially shy (and probably awed too) at adding to what he clearly recognised as a great song. Paul's verse enters like a twist in an illogical dream, yet identically to John's opening verses its resolution of going upstairs on a bus to smoke alone (the intimation is that it is marijuana) again presents the cold detached world of drugs. Paul recently said that he had this section written before hearing 'A Day In The Life', as its reference of catching a bus to school links it to his local bus terminal at Penny Lane. Possibly this may have been part of an initial verse for the song 'Penny Lane'.

The thundering massed piano makes for a brilliant ending, the grandness of which may have made the Beatles self-conscious, as the gibberish backwards chant (they are shouting 'It really couldn't be any other') seems to mock it and lessen its impact.

9. Magical Mystery Tour

'ALL YOU NEED IS LOVE'
(Lennon) Single released 7 July 1967

'All You Need Is Love' is a rarity as a good song the Beatles recorded badly. Commissioned by the BBC to write a song for the very first worldwide television link-up, the Beatles, still enthralled to the medium of the studio, decided to let the world witness them in the act of recording at Abbey Road. The resulting single would thus have the exciting bonus of being one that millions would have seen at its creation. While an effective gimmick in its month of release, for posterity 'All You Need Is Love' suffers from the low sound quality of live recording and not least from the nerves of the band, playing before a worldwide audience.

While some instruments such as the harpsichord had been recorded on to a guide track prior to transmission and the opening drum roll and John's vocal re-recorded later, the sound is still very poor compared to the recent high definition of *Sgt. Pepper*. A more sympathetic production (the swaggering brass misses the point) too would have given higher prominence to John's vocals, in doing so highlighting what are some of his best lyrics. Much mocked for its naivety, John's message is misunderstood, largely as the verses to 'All You Need Is Love' sound unclear due to its muddy production. Normally it is the chorus alone that people hear. The verses, though, with their message that anything can be achieved if you only try, make it plain that rather than being a statement, the chorus is in fact a suggestion. A couple of years later John went some way to rectifying this misunderstanding on the much more persuasive 'Give Peace A Chance'. As he explained, he was not saying you must give peace a chance, just give it a try for a change.

There is another explanation for the simplicity, or naivety, of the chorus. The BBC had asked the Beatles to write a song that could be understood by those with little English. Accordingly John used five simple words for the chorus and repeated them over and over. How much of the song was written to meet this commission is open to question. Paul in his biography recalled that the song was already nearly complete when the BBC approached them.

'BABY YOU'RE A RICH MAN'
(Lennon/McCartney) B-side to 'All You Need Is Love'

This was originally recorded for the *Yellow Submarine* soundtrack, but a week later when it became known that a single would be needed for the Our World telethon it ended up as the B-side to 'All You Need Is Love'. While not without merit, the Beatles approached the recording of 'Baby You're A Rich Man' with some ill-will. Contractually obliged to provide new songs for the *Yellow Submarine* cartoon, a project over which they had little creative control, they decided not to labour too hard over each contribution. Eddie Kramer, a studio engineer who worked on this song, expressed amazement at the speed and sloppiness with which it was recorded.

While this slack attitude is evident in the cavalier use of the Clavioline (a plastic toy keyboard) and in Paul's off-key bass, its strength lies in John's beautifully sung verses. A combination of two separate ideas, the verses were written by John and the chorus by Paul. Both are topical, relating to the new 1967 'love generation', the verses lampooning several press stories the Beatles had read about the new hippies, whom some journalists were already calling 'the beautiful people'. (Beautiful, it should be noted, in this context referred to personality as well as appearance.) The chorus echoes the sentiments of the hippies, mocking those who only live for financial gain.

MAGICAL MYSTERY TOUR
Album released 27 November 1967

Without Paul's enthusiasm for the *Magical Mystery Tour* it is probable that the other Beatles would have taken an extended holiday instead. Both bemused at Paul's oddball project and resentful of his leadership, John and George approached the prospect of both a new film and an album in a begrudging mood.

John's drug use – photos of John taken during filming show him as pale and drawn – meant that he was by his own admission too weak to assert himself at this time. If he had been stronger he would almost certainly have vetoed or modified Paul's plans. Tragically too, the Beatles lost the cautionary managerial guidance of Brian Epstein who died in August 1967. Deciding against a new manager, Paul took on many of his responsibilities. Towards the end of the year Paul, who underestimated how long it would take to make the film, also found himself bogged down with its editing and the music for the first time took second priority. Indeed, many of the recordings were made more as film music than as songs in their own right. Typical of the lack of attention to detail is the cheap and garish packaging for the eventual EP, easily the Beatles' worst-ever cover.

Paul's idea for the project was, like *Sgt. Pepper*, another half-baked concept album. Beyond the theme song, again none of the other songs follow the concept. Lyrically they say more about the influence of the San Franciscan alternative counter-culture which valued spirituality over materialism and inward beauty over outward appearance. This is evident in the sarcastic mention of policemen in 'I Am The Walrus', the anti-materialism of 'Baby You're A Rich Man', the utopian vision of the title song, the questioning of popular opinion on 'The Fool On The Hill' and the anti-war 'All You Need Is Love'.

Psychedelia reached its heights in the summer and autumn of 1967 and temporarily groups were competing to produce increasingly 'far-out' sounds that often led to wasteful hours spent experimenting in the studio, as opposed to writing tunes or lyrics. While the Beatles' first recordings for the *Magical Mystery Tour* in April 1967 maintained the standards of *Sgt. Pepper*, over the summer of '67 their sense of purpose was lost and sessions descended into anarchic jams and experimentation, from which little could be salvaged. The breakthrough in sound the Beatles were probably looking for at this point would have been much better served on eight-track equipment, which would not be available to them for another year. Most of the productive work on what would become the *Magical Mystery Tour* EP took place between September and November 1967.

The Beatles relied increasingly less on George Martin for guidance, and he was likewise disaffected by their new attitude to recording. Martin later described a 'schism' taking place between himself and the Beatles in this period. Indeed, from the *Magical Mystery Tour* until *Let It Be*, the Beatles would on many occasions produce recordings in Martin's absence. Bad feeling also arose after the release of *Sgt. Pepper*, from which opinion grew - as one commentator put it – that George Martin was the 'brains' behind the Beatles' music.

Despite the experimentation that went into recording the *Magical Mystery Tour*, it relied most on tested gimmicks like backwards tapes, varied tape speeds, sound effects and the phasing of vocals through the process of automatic double tracking.

'HELLO GOODBYE'
(McCartney) Single released 24 November 1967

'Hello Goodbye' is unusual as a Beatles single in that it makes no kind of artistic progression; rather, its purpose seems to have been solely an exercise in making a slice of perfect pop guaranteed to hit the number one spot. While John was angry that his bold and sublime 'I Am The Walrus' had the indignity of becoming its B-side, Paul's piece of uplifting pop was exactly what the *Magical Mystery Tour* project needed.

Paul put into the song almost every trick he had learnt with the Beatles. The simple, happy, sing-along lyrics hark back to their early singles. Musically the tune offers an upbeat roller-coaster melody, featuring several stops and starts as well as a surprise ending to catch the attention of a radio audience. Unusually for a Beatles record too, the percussion is pushed way up in the mix to capitalise on its infectious, bouncy melody. In hindsight the only drawback is its muddy production, which shows none of the care lavished on 'Penny Lane' earlier in the year.

John's dislike of 'Hello Goodbye' may have come from paranoia that the lyrics were an attack on him. The words, which contrast Paul's positivity with another's negative outlook, were clearly aimed at somebody. Possibly they compare Paul's feelings for the Beatles with the sapped enthusiasm of John and George.

'I AM THE WALRUS'
(Lennon)

John's masterpiece of lyrical surrealism carries three strands of inspiration. Where before he had sewed separate lyrical ideas together to create the impression of a unified work, here he took delight in doing the opposite. The first lines, with its statement that 'I', 'you' and 'we' are all the same, tell of the ego death brought on by LSD and read like the start of one of his more conventional lyrics. A year earlier John might have pursued these to a more logical and commercially acceptable conclusion.

Writing now purely for his own pleasure, he next took inspiration from a letter he had received from a pupil at his old school, telling how Lennon/McCartney songs were being used in English classes. Incredulous at such a twist of fortune, John saw a chance to renew the pranks that he had relished playing on his teachers, by writing a set of lyrics incapable of analysis. This inspired such notable creations as the 'boy' who has been 'a naughty girl' and the 'semolina pilchards climbing up the Eiffel tower'. In 1980 John also claimed that the song was a spoof on Dylan, saying 'I was writing obscurely á la Dylan, never saying what you mean, but giving the impression of something . . . I thought well I can write that crap too.'

The lyrics have a bitter, unhappy mood, enforced by the relentless falling chord sequence and the repeated words 'I'm crying'. John's vocals too tumble out in a torrent of pent-up anger and emotional pain. It is hard not to draw some connection with this mood and the death of the Beatles' manager only a week before recording; of all the Beatles, John was closest to him. While our knowledge of John's angry and aggressive side is well documented and understood, this is the first instance of him expressing truly convincing anger in song. If this was his reaction to the tragic death of yet another close friend, then it provides a marked contrast to the reported accounts of his reactions to Epstein's death, which range from nonchalance to shock.

The tune owes a debt to John's favourite record of the summer of 1967, Procul Harum's 'A Whiter Shade Of Pale', with its similarly somnambulant Hammond organ chord descent. Where on Procul Harum's record the tune is paramount though, here a swirl of discordant overdubs including George Martin's oriental-sounding string arrangement, random words and hiss from the radio and the shrieking inanities of a choir emphasise the confusion of the lyrical images. These overdubs, teeter over the song but never break its flow, creating a compelling tension throughout.

'MAGICAL MYSTERY TOUR'
(McCartney/Lennon) EP released 8 December 1967

This serves the same purpose as the *Sgt. Pepper* title song, to introduce the *Magical Mystery Tour* project in a hip, subversive spoof on the clichés used by masters of ceremonies. While one of the better songs from the eventual film and EP of the same name, this approach did not break any new ground for the Beatles, providing poor inspiration for what was to follow.

The fantastical concept of the *Magical Mystery Tour*, like that of *Sgt. Pepper* came to the creatively restless Paul on a long plane flight. Returning to London from a short stay in California, Paul was inspired by the legendary tales he had just heard of Ken Kesey's (author of *One Flew Over The Cuckoo's Nest*) travels in a bus around the West Coast of the USA, dispensing LSD to all who he met. Inspired to create his own bus tour as a film and music project, he gave his idea an English spin by combining Kesey's experiences with his own memories of surprise bus tours for Liverpool pensioners – 'mystery tours' as he remembered them – from his youth. While the lyrics suggest these surprise tours, the music, especially the dissonant jazzy ending, strongly hints at the druggy connotations of the 'mystery tour'; tellingly, it is referred to once in the lyrics as 'a trip'. Bringing only the germ of an idea to the studio, much of the lyrics were written on the spot with John's equal help.

Recorded four days after the final overdub for *Sgt. Pepper* had been completed in April 1967, this retains much of the high definition sound achieved on that album. In a trick first used on 'Lovely Rita', the massed backing vocals here, were recorded slowly, then speeded up for the mix, creating a disembodied sound that contrasts the entrance of Paul's clear lead vocal, recorded at normal speed.

'THE FOOL ON THE HILL'
(McCartney)

One of Paul's deepest songs, 'The Fool On The Hill' symbolised what he saw as society's attitudes to those with ideas that were either different or ahead of their time. This was a moot point in the fast-changing western world of the 1960s, when many people, the Beatles included, were suggesting new sets of values for society. Indeed it is clear that Paul identifies with the fool and probably took inspiration from his morning walks on Primrose Hill in North London, close to his St John's Wood residence. Primrose Hill offers a clear view of central London, which suggests one of the song's key lines about being able to see the world turn around. This line is also uncannily similar to the 'kaleidoscope eyes' mentioned in 'Lucy In The Sky With Diamonds' and also, of course, suggests the use of hallucinogenic drugs.

Paul's message does not sound a hopeful or persuasive one, sung against the sad and desolate arrangement of flutes and recorders – a pied piper reference? The original demo, now released on the *Anthology 2* compilation, offers a more upbeat and in many ways preferable version. Here Paul alone sings and plays piano.

Written in March 1967 'The Fool On The Hill', unlike most of the *Magical Mystery Tour*'s songs, was not written with the film in mind.

'FLYING'
(Lennon/McCartney/Harrison/Starkey)

Many experimental jams were recorded by the Beatles over the summer of 1967; this one from September was edited down from its original length of twenty minutes to the one-and-a-half minutes featured here. George plays the spaced-out blues progression, John is on mellotron while Paul plays the melody on a cheap-sounding organ. An extra 30 seconds of separately made backwards tapes were added to this jam.

'Flying' was intended as incidental music for a planned, but never filmed sequence to the *Magical Mystery Tour* film which was to portray the coach flying off into the clouds. Presumably not made for logistical reasons, the image was intended to emphasise the druggy connotations of the *Mystery Tour*.

'BLUE JAY WAY'
(Harrison)

An experimental mood piece which, like 'Flying', seems to have been created largely to emphasise the drug references in the *Magical Mystery Tour* film. Listened to without the images to support it, George's dirge, like most film music is repetitive and overlong.

To achieve its sound a plethora of studio tricks were used. Much of the percussion sounds are played backwards, the main organ sound and George's vocals are taped at different speeds to create new sound textures and heavy delay is used on automatic double tracking. The song was written by George while visiting Los Angeles and simply describes a wait for friends at a house in the Hollywood hills on a street named Blue Jay Way.

'YOUR MOTHER SHOULD KNOW'
(McCartney)

Where tracks such as 'Flying' and 'Blue Jay Way' emphasised the druggy side of the *Magical Mystery Tour* concept, this was written by Paul as a contrast and a chance, as he visualised it, to perform an old-fashioned 'production number' in the style of Hollywood musicals. Where 'When I'm 64' had been completed in honour of Paul's dad turning 64, 'Your Mother Should Know' was also in part influenced by the presence of his aunt and uncle, who were staying with Paul when he came up with the tune. Like the '30s style of 'When I'm 64', this undeniably fine tune suffers from a lack of orchestration and by comparison sounds like a raw demo version.

Paul tried to explain one of the Beatles' more baffling lyrics in his biography: 'I was basically trying to say your mother might know more than you think she does.'

10. Yellow Submarine

YELLOW SUBMARINE
Album first released USA 13 January 1969

In the spring of 1967, the Beatles were contracted to provide four songs for the *Yellow Submarine* cartoon, fulfilling their three-film obligation with United Artists. After the disappointment of *Help!*, the Beatles were wary about the cartoon and decided not to contribute any new songs of worth. George Martin remembered too that such songs also received scant attention to detail on their recording. The cartoon turned out better than they expected and they subsequently became proud of it, if not perhaps the songs they gave to it.

That the first three songs were completed by May 1967 suggests that 'Hey Bulldog', recorded in February 1968, was requested as an additional song, perhaps as a replacement for 'You Know My Name Look Up The Number', which had been offered. George Martin's orchestral score on the B-side of the album, which was also recorded in 1968, is of a high quality and often overlooked, but it is outside the scope of this book.

In 1999 *Yellow Submarine* became the first Beatles album to be remixed. The reason stated was that the re-released film needed an enhanced sound for cinema release. The remix notably puts vocals and guitars on many tracks higher in the mix; on some songs e.g. 'Eleanor Rigby' this is unwelcome, but on 'Hey Bulldog', 'With A Little Help From My Friends' and 'All You Need Is Love' the finished result is arguably better than the original mixes.

'IT'S ONLY A NORTHERN SONG'
(Harrison)

George has openly admitted this was written as a 'joke' and therefore must have been hardly surprised when it was rejected from *Sgt. Pepper*. Openly bored with the intricate and drawn-out process of making *Sgt. Pepper*, George started his lyrics while witnessing the cacophonous, discordant recording of the orchestra for 'A Day In The Life'.

'Only A Northern Song' is, in its defence, is not as awful as it was intended; the discordant trumpet – played by Paul – and glockenspiel (possibly by John) were only added in April 1967 after it had been rejected for *Sgt. Pepper* and consigned to *Yellow Submarine*. The original track, recorded in February 1967, has in its favour the distinctive *Sgt. Pepper* production sound of high-definition bass and enhanced vocals.

'ALL TOGETHER NOW'
(McCartney)

Written especially as a children's song, this was perfect for *Yellow Submarine*, if not for the Beatles 'official' albums. Recorded between *Sgt. Pepper* and the *Magical Mystery Tour*, it is remarkable for that period in having no extra orchestration or studio special effects, perhaps as George Martin was absent for its recording. Oddly, the absence of George's voice from the lead vocals, recorded in turn by Paul, John and Ringo, suggests that he may also have been absent.

'HEY BULLDOG'
(Lennon/McCartney)

One of the great rare and much under-appreciated Beatles songs, 'Hey Bulldog' is notable for its classic vocal from John, a great guitar solo from George and a driving performance from the whole band. Much stronger than the other contributions to *Yellow Submarine*, it seems likely that when it was recorded in February 1968 the Beatles had been impressed by early rushes of the cartoon *Yellow Submarine* and so decided to give something better than what they had contributed before.

Completed in the studio from a set of incomplete lyrics, John's offer to talk with a friend whenever they are 'lonely' is sung in a taunting fashion and reads like a nastier take of the themes on 'Nowhere Man'.

This refrain suggests itself as John's original idea, while the random images of the verses read as if they were created in the studio.

'IT'S ALL TOO MUCH'
(Harrison)

This sounds like a well-intentioned song from George that he lacked faith in. As on 'Only A Northern Song', cacophonous overdubs overwhelm his vocals. The lyrics were inspired by the 'liberating' effects of LSD said Goerge and yet, like every song the Beatles made on this subject, the lasting impression is one of sadness.

11. The White Album

'LADY MADONNA'
(McCartney) Single released 15 March 1968

'Lady Madonna' was not originally intended as an A-side – John's more ambitious and worthy 'Across The Universe' should have got that honour. While slickly performed Paul's ambiguous lyrical mix of strife and erotic images are not compelling, not least because there is a feeling that the Beatles were having a laugh with their boogie-woogie accompaniment. Record buyers felt likewise and in the USA the single could only manage a lowly number four in the charts. While in hindsight the single's poor showing could be blamed on John's failure to complete a satisfactory recording of 'Across The Universe', the Beatles were by this time often unmotivated by chart placing. They had also become weary of the constant pressure and expectation that their records would reach number one.

The simplistic production of 'Lady Madonna' must have left some fans, who had become used to the Beatles' more elaborate singles, feeling short-changed. Change was in the air again though, as psychedelia fell out of fashion in early 1968 and for a short while many classic 1950s rock 'n' roll records re-entered the UK charts.

Paul stylised his singing and sound from Fats Domino, a relatively easy feat for him, having sung at least four of his songs live with the Beatles between 1958–62, though the tune itself here is derived from a 1956 UK trad jazz hit by Humphrey Lyttleton, 'Bad Penny Blues'.

Paul called the lyrics a 'tribute to women', a part acknowledgement of guilt at the cavalier way he had both treated them and written about them. In their style the lyrics follow a tradition of 'social conscience' songs about women that he started with 'Eleanor Rigby' and 'She's Leaving Home' and would continue in his solo career with 'Another Day'. The origin of the lyrics would appear to come from Fats Domino's 'Blue Monday' which also traced the days of the week through a man's hard week at work. Unlike Domino, Paul, as he later admitted, forgot to put the day Saturday into the lyrics

'THE INNER LIGHT'
(Harrison)

The placing of this as a B-side must have produced mixed emotions from George. While happy at last to have his own song on a Beatles single, he must also have felt disheartened that the sitar was never going to gain him a starring role within the group. George too must have been frustrated that he still had to rely on outside musicians to record such Indian music. This was the last instance of sitar being used on a Beatles record.

Recorded in January 1968 when George visited Bombay to record music with local musicians for the soundtrack of the film *Wonderwall*, this track was set aside for the Beatles and the vocals, added back at Abbey Road. George, still struggling with his lyrics, adapted the words here from part of the *Tao Te Ching* by ancient Chinese Taoist philosopher Lao-tzu.

'HEY JUDE'
(McCartney) Single first released USA 26 August 1968

'Hey Jude' saw the Beatles excitement for the studio reawakened after a string of three relatively sonically lacklustre singles, 'All You Need Is Love', 'Hello Goodbye' and 'Lady Madonna'. After testing the limits of four-track recording for five years the Beatles had become bored with the extra effort it required whenever they wanted to expand their sound. In August 1968, though, the long-awaited advent of eight-track recording had finally become available to them at Trident studios in Soho, London and it was here that 'Hey Jude' became their first recording to explore its new range.

Recorded essentially from a single live performance, Paul's arrangement over the first four minutes teasingly introduces each of the eight tracks one by one. Throughout the song's length the listener is treated to a constant trickle of new activity that evolves tantalisingly from lament to fanfare. This evolution echoes the lyrics' emotions. The opening section is slow and sad, featuring Paul alone on voice and piano.

One by one other vocals and instruments enter and the mood and tempo lifts. The tension that builds up to the triumphant three-and-a-half minute coda makes for an entirely convincing expression of joy and release. It should be corny, but the subtle build-up of sound makes it seem totally natural. The origin of the lyrics would appear to come from Fats Domino's 'Blue Monday' which also traced the days of the week through a man's hard week at work. Unlike Domino, Paul as he later admitted forgot to put the day Saturday into the lyrics.

The impact of the coda is heightened by the long-drawn-out chord sequence of the verses. Beethoven's Ninth Symphony works in the same way, before its choral 'Ode to Joy' ending – Paul's explanation of the coda was that he enjoyed singing it so much that he extended much longer than originally planned. In its day the near seven-minute length of 'Hey Jude' made it the longest-ever song released on a single.

More than being a clever use of eight-track recording, Paul's hymn to 'keeping it together' also derives much of its warmth and power from being essentially a live performance captured within the studio. Legend has it that on the finished take, Ringo was on his way back from the toilet when Paul started singing and had to race back to his drums to join in on time. Recording live did not come without its glitches; the transfer of the song from vinyl to CD reveals at 2.55–2.59 someone (Paul, John or George) swearing after hitting a wrong chord.

Paul was initially inspired to write 'Hey Jude' as a song for Julian Lennon, who at the age of four had suffered the shock of seeing his father split from his mother and leave home. As such it was first called 'Hey Jules', yet Paul's oft-repeated tale does not fully explain the lyrics, which clearly refer to a woman and the start of a new relationship. John's account of first hearing the song is revealing in that he saw it as one of encouragement to him. Paul, though, reminded him that they were going through the same upheaval in relationships. John had moved in with Yoko Ono, while Paul had split with his long term girlfriend Jane Asher. Only nine days before the recording of 'Hey Jude', Jane had announced the end of her engagement to Paul in a TV interview. The suddeness of Jane's decision to split (sources say she discovered Paul in bed with another woman) apparently left Paul shattered. The lyrics, while ostensibly being about another person's loss and hope, thus clearly had a personal meaning for Paul too.

For B-side 'Revolution' see entry under album.

Beatles
For Sale

THE BEATLES ALBUM (AKA *THE WHITE ALBUM*)
Released 22 November 1968

Part triumph, part mess, while *The White Album* evolved a vibrant recording style it was flawed by band disunity. Disenchanted with the lengthy studio trickery they had relied on from 1966–67, all four Beatles happily returned to playing live as a band in the studio. In theory this should have been easy, in practice it relied heavily on teamwork and mutual respect, which was evaporating fast.

Significantly, the dynamics within the group had changed. Until 1967 both John and George had grudgingly respected Paul's musical skill and leadership. This respect, though, had been shaken by the wrong turn Paul had led them on with the *Magical Mystery Tour* project. No longer using the LSD that had sapped his ego, John now took an aggressive, confrontational approach to Paul's opinions. This ill-feeling limited the often crucial contributions John and Paul would make to each others' songs.

A back to basics approach was now used for everything from the music to the cover, whose simplicity was in itself a reaction to the awful job the Beatles had made of the cover for the *Magical Mystery Tour*. The style of recording John favoured now was to play live as a group. This often produced exciting results, but for complex songs it required endless takes to create a satisfactory performance. In some cases up to 100 takes of a single song were recorded and as a result tempers often became frayed.

Adding to the tension, Paul and George both resented and were unsettled by the constant, unsympathetic presence in the studio of Yoko Ono, who regularly sat on John's amplifier. Yoko was a source of strength and inspiration for John, but for Paul and George she proved the very opposite. Yoko, unlike almost everyone they came into contact with, not only seemed unaware of the extent of their fame but also appeared visibly unimpressed with their music.

Although it would take until September 1969 for John to formally announce his decision to leave the Beatles, the split was regularly rehearsed on *The White Album*. To avoid the risk of conflict the easiest solution became to record apart and at least half of the tracks on the album were recorded with only one, two or three Beatles present at any one time.

The bad feeling had started from day one. In May 1968, with rioting in Paris and similar unrest spreading worldwide, John started the recording of 'Revolution' as a topical message, intending it for release as a single. Paul and George, not considering it commercially viable, put a veto on it. A second, more commercial version of 'Revolution' was recorded and appeared on the B-side to 'Hey Jude' in July, but the heat of the moment had been lost. Bitter, John gained revenge by vetoing 'Ob-La-Di, Ob-La-Da' as a single.

Walkouts over the six months of recording were common. In July Geoff Emerick, the studio engineer who had worked with the Beatles since *Revolver*, walked out after facing the caustic remarks of John once too often, not to return until the *Abbey Road* album. In August, George took an unannounced holiday and several songs were recorded in his absence. Shortly after his return, Ringo quit the group in a rage at Paul's criticism and took two weeks out before being wooed back. George Martin, on the receiving end of the group's tension and annoyed at Yoko's unannounced visits to sit in the control room, took a month-long break from the album in September, during which eight songs were recorded. For a while Martin's new trainee producer Chris Thomas took over.

Where disagreements were put aside and the Beatles concentrated on the music alone, there were still moments of magic. The end product, though, was the roughest and rawest they had ever released.

Most of the songs on *The White Album* were composed during the Beatles' stay in India between February and April 1968. They wrote prodigiously – some reports say they composed 30 new songs during their stay, though only the following 18 songs released by the Beatles are known for sure to have been composed in India: 'The Continuing Story Of Bungalow Bill', 'I'm So Tired', 'Dear Prudence', 'Julia', 'Rocky Racoon', 'Mother Nature's Son', 'Back In The USSR', 'Ob-La-Di, Ob-La-Da', 'Junk', 'Yer Blues', 'Revolution', 'Sexy Sadie', 'Don't Pass Me By', 'Mean Mr Mustard', 'Polythene Pam', 'Teddy Boy', 'What's The New Mary Jane'.

Staying in a remote camp in the hills of northern India, the Beatles were away from distractions and spent their days either meditating or attending lessons on spirituality. Their new songs showed a new relaxed and playful attitude to songwriting attributable to their regime of meditation. The benefits of meditation include an unleashing of creativity, which would explain their high workrate. Meditation also encourages simplicity, calm, empathy for others, joy, spontaneity and clear thinking. The emotion of joy appears to be the biggest influence here as over half of the songs on *The White Album* ended up with either jokey or satirical lyrics. The album also contains the Beatles' largest number of musical send-ups e.g. 'Back In The USSR' (Beach Boys/Chuck Berry), 'Glass Onion' (*Sgt. Pepper*), 'Ob-La-Di, Ob-La-Da' (ska), 'Happiness Is A Warm Gun' (doo-wop), 'Rocky Racoon' (country and western), 'Yer Blues' (blues), 'Helter Skelter' (The Who), 'Revolution 1' (boogie-woogie) and 'Honey Pie' (1930s Hollywood musical).

The White Album was also influenced by the highly charged political atmosphere in 1968 which split pop music in two. Rock music evolved to cater for the tastes of those who were looking to challenge the establishment and was accordingly serious, favouring the format of albums to the cheap commerciality of singles. Lyrically it was adventurous and often steered clear of the subject of true love. Rock also favoured a heavy guitar sound, strident vocals and an emphasis on musicianship rather than tunes. Pop in contrast was commercial, apolitical and light. While John and George were happy to align themselves with the new rock identity, to their annoyance – and to the annoyance of many of the more radical hippies – Paul still kept a foot in both camps.

Where most Beatles recordings are marked by a great clarity of sound, many songs on *The White Album* suffer from poor, muddy productions. The first four songs on side one are especially weak in this respect. Lacking the group spirit of previous albums, the Beatles rarely united enough to allow songs to be perfected. George Martin too had a limited role on the album, where previously he would have been drawn into the creative process to help solve problems relating to sound and production. Now his only role was often to sit and judge when the Beatles had achieved a good take.

Several types of recording processes took place, as follows:

1. A live group performance of drums, bass, guitar and singing, onto which a minimum of overdubs would be added. Used for: 'Yer Blues', 'Everybody's Got Something To Hide Except For Me And My Monkey', 'Helter Skelter', 'Revolution', 'Bungalow Bill', 'Long, Long, Long', 'I'm So Tired', 'While My Guitar Gently Weeps', 'Sexy Sadie', 'Glass Onion' and 'Ob-La-di, Ob-La-da'.
2. Layer recording four-track. Used for: 'Cry Baby Cry', 'Piggies', 'Goodnight', 'Don't Pass Me By', 'Happiness Is A Warm Gun', 'Rocky Raccoon', 'Why Don't We Do It In The Road' and 'Back In The USSR'.
3. Layer recording eight-track (available from September 1968).

Used for: 'Dear Prudence', 'Martha My Dear', 'Honey Pie' and 'Savoy Truffle'.
4. Solo: 'I Will', 'Wild Honey Pie', 'Julia', 'Mother Nature's Son', 'Blackbird' and 'Revolution 9'.

The wah-wah pedal, a variation on the volume pedal, was popularised by Jimi Hendrix in 1967. Its swooping, distorted range of tone is heard sparingly on many tracks, particularly 'Birthday' and 'Happiness Is A Warm Gun'.

Pre-recorded sound effects are used on 'Back In The USSR', 'Blackbird', 'The Continuing Story of Bungalow Bill', 'Revolution 9', 'Glass Onion' (anthology version) and 'Piggies'.

There is disagreement over whether or not this should have been a single album. George Martin wanted a single album, however, with little common ground between John and Paul and feelings running high, it was easier to release everything recorded than choose tracks for elimination. A single album would not only have the benefit of the lack of weaker tracks but it should also flow better. One of the major weaknesses of *The White Album* is the way its weaker tracks are hidden among the good tracks, making continuous play unsatisfying.

A suggested track listing for a single album might be:

1. 'Back In The USSR'
2. 'Dear Prudence'
3. 'Glass Onion' (anthology version)
4. 'Happiness Is A Warm Gun'
5. 'Martha My Dear'
6. 'I'm So Tired'
7. 'Not Guilty' (from *Beatles Anthology*)
8. 'Why Don't We Do It In The Road?'
9. 'I Will'
10. 'Julia'
11. 'Sexy Sadie'
12. 'Helter Skelter'
13. 'Long, Long, Long'
14. 'Goodnight'

Beatles
For Sale

'BACK IN THE USSR'
(McCartney)

Spoof rock 'n' roll had been popularised by the Bonzo Dog Do Dah Band and the Mothers Of Invention in 1967. In the same spirit Paul wrote 'Back In The USSR' as a spoof on the asinine lyrics of Chuck Berry's 'Back In The USA' and the Beach Boys 'California Girls'. Paul is said to have got the initial idea from a government campaign in the UK in 1967 to get people to buy British products to try and reduce imports. Adverts on TV and posters came with the catchphrase 'I'm backing Britain'. Lampooning this, Paul's original title was 'I'm backing the USSR'.

One of the album's best group performances, the obvious joy with which it was recorded is ironic in that during rehearsals Ringo walked out of the group, upset at criticism of his playing by Paul. Undeterred, Paul instead played drums, John bass and George guitar. Numerous overdubs, the sound effects of plane engines and an uncharacteristically rough vocal sound for Paul all make for a muddy sound that compares poorly with the recent single tracks 'Hey Jude'/'Revolution'. For this reason it is hard to believe that George Martin played a big role in its production.

'DEAR PRUDENCE'
(Lennon)

John wrote this about Mia Farrow's sister, who was staying with the Beatles in India. As he explained it in 1980: 'She (Prudence) seemed to go slightly barmy, meditating too long and wouldn't come out of the little hut we were living in. They selected me and George to try and bring her out of the house. She'd been locked in for three weeks and was trying to reach God faster than anyone else.'

John's lyrics read as a letter of advice put under Prudence Farrow's door and state the simpler things in life she was missing out on. As on 'Nowhere Man', the simple and universal imagery of the lyrics make this one of his most endearing songs. Likewise it is certain that the message in 'Dear Prudence' also related to John's own feelings on having ended his LSD-induced seclusion of 1966–68. A perfect match of music and lyrics, the childlike imagery is echoed in the dreamy and repetitive arrangement.

Recorded at Trident studios on eight-track the day after 'Back In The USSR' was completed, Ringo was still missing and so Paul played drums.

'GLASS ONION'
(Lennon/McCartney)

The enormous impact of *Sgt. Pepper* encouraged some bizarre interpretations of its songs. In equal measures fed up and amused at this, John strove, as on 'I Am The Walrus' before it, to write lyrics winding up those who read too much into the Beatles' lyrics. The joke was shared with Paul, who contributed to the lyrics and probably wrote the last verse. John wrote Paul into the lyrics (claiming that it was really Paul who was the Walrus) too, as he felt guilty at the split in their partnership that was being caused by his new relationship with Yoko Ono.

John's haphazard imagery here invokes several Beatles songs and a reference to the new *Yellow Submarine* film. In a further twist of the screw on those who misinterpreted his lyrics, two of the images that sound the most improbable were actually true. The 'cast-iron shore' was a place on the Liverpool docks while the mention of tulips referred to the flower arrangements at a restaurant in Knightsbridge, London where the Beatles often went.

The first version of this track now appears on the anthology series of Beatles out-takes. Its novel use of bizarre sound effects is arguably closer to John's intentions – at George Martin's suggestion these were replaced with strings.

'OB-LA-DI, OB-LA-DA'
(McCartney)

This compulsively catchy ska pastiche, while somewhat lightweight for the Beatles, was wasted as an album track in its own right. As such, Paul spent a whole week at Abbey Road making three separate versions in order to create one good enough to be released on single. Any original charm the song had for John and George was lost in this time and two accounts from studio engineer Richard Lush and Pete Shotton attest to John's open irritation with recording it. This bad feeling led both John and George to veto Paul's request to have it released on single, yet within weeks of the release of *The White Album* numerous cover versions had been recorded. Scottish band Marmalade won out and took their version of the song to number one in the UK charts in January 1969.

Paul took inspiration from the ska music that was commonly played live in London in the late '60s. The title came from Jimmy Scott and the Obla-di Obla-da band, who were named after one of Scott's catchphrases, which meant literally 'life goes on' in the language of Yoruba, the Nigerian tribe Scott came from. On the album's release, Scott quite rightly kicked up a fuss about the use of his catchphrase – under pressure Paul acknowledged Scott's input in an unusual way. Scott, sentenced to a three-month stretch in Brixton prison for non-payment of alimony, was released after Beatles' employee Alastair Taylor went to the prison to pay off the outstanding money, apparently £800 in total.

'WILD HONEY PIE'
(McCartney)

In the 'anything goes' spirit of songwriting that pervaded *The White Album*, Paul knocked off this riff and chant alone at the end of a recording session. A similar daft snippet from Paul, 'Can You Take Me Back?', appears as an uncredited filler between 'Cry Baby Cry' and 'Revolution 9'.

'THE CONTINUING STORY OF BUNGALOW BILL'
(Lennon)

This was written at the Maharishi's meditation camp, after John heard of how one of the students, an American, had taken a break from seeking inner tranquillity to go on a tiger hunt with his mother. The song title is a pun on the name of the legendary cowboy showman Buffalo Bill and the living quarters at Rishikesh, which although called ashrams were effectively bungalows. Though John never clearly stated it, the lyrics are allegorical of the Vietnam war, the chorus clearly echoing US anti-war demonstrators' chant 'LBJ, LBJ. How many kids did you kill today?' (LBJ was President Johnson, in office 63–68).

Written on acoustic guitar, the song owes its camp-fire singalong style to the communal life the Beatles were then living in India.

'WHILE MY GUITAR GENTLY WEEPS'
(Harrison)

Listening to the demo version of this tune on the *Anthology* compilation reveals how much of the beauty and intent were lost after it was given this self-consciously epic heavy rock rendition. The demo, using only voice and guitar, has a lightness that befits what are essentially lyrics of little meaning. The histrionics of the finished version, though, beg to be taken seriously.

The blame for this miscalculation must lie in part with Paul and John. Neither expressing much interest in the song, George was forced to take charge and pulled in his friend Eric Clapton for help, but Clapton's blues rock style is misplaced on George's melodic chord descent. Its leaden sound, too, overbears George's wispy vocals.

The united front the Beatles have put up over the years makes it difficult to envisage what little status George's songs were accorded by John and Paul, though a clear account of his treatment can be found in the transcripts of the *Let It Be* rehearsals as documented in *Get Back: the Beatles' Let It Be Disaster* by Doug Sulphy and Ray Schweighardt (1998).

'HAPPINESS IS A WARM GUN'
(Lennon)

Returning where 'I Am The Walrus' left off, this is a similar collage of unconnected lyrical themes. More ambitiously, though, this song leads the Beatles through four different rhythms that required some 70 takes, with the final version with pieced together from two separate takes.

The last and best part, from which the song gets its name, was written in the highly charged atmosphere after the shootings of Martin Luther King in April 1968 and Robert Kennedy in June 1968. As John remembered George Martin showed him a cover of a gun magazine that said 'Happiness Is A Warm Gun'. Appalled John thought the title 'insane'. Never po-faced, though, John's satire is laced with sexual innuendo and in a delicious twist also manages to fit in a satire of the true-love innocence of early rock 'n' roll. The C-Am-F-G chord pattern here and John's octave jump mid-song to falsetto is identical to 'Angel Baby' by Rosie and the Originals (1960), one of John's all-time favourite records. The overall effect is stunning and is yet another case of the Beatles taking rock music to a place that few could follow.

Elsewhere in the lyrics John reveals the lengths he would go to, to save his offcuts and half ideas. Bootleg recordings from this era show that some of the final doo-wop inspired lyrics came from off cuts of an early, lengthier demo version of 'I'm So Tired'.

The clear sound balance on this song suggests it was one of the few recordings that all four Beatles were keen to perfect. Indeed, both Paul and George have been quoted saying that this was their favourite song on the album.

'MARTHA MY DEAR'
(McCartney)

A prototype of the bouncy melody that characterised many of Paul's songs with Wings, this is the first Beatles track to fully capitalise on the potential of eight-track recording. Recorded at the album's close, each instrument is given a clarity that would provide an indication of the sound of *Abbey Road*. Written on guitar in India, the song had the original title 'Silly Girl' – that it was recorded some six months later suggests that significant rewriting must have taken place in between. The new words presumably had little relevance as Martha was also the name of Paul's sheepdog.

'I'M SO TIRED'
(Lennon)

Ever since 'Strawberry Fields Forever' John had been aiming to write songs in a conversational, stream-of-consciousness style. The inspired flow of the lyrics here are his most convincing use of this method and read as if completed in one brief session. The words came to John while suffering a bout of insomnia in India, caused by the long hours he was spending in meditation. As the lyrics suggest, he had been suffering this problem for three weeks. A great lover of sleep and dreams, he had clearly reached the end of his tether.

The performance of the song was as inspired as its writing, John's vocal flowing unbroken over the changes in tempo. The music too conjures up John's insomnia, the descending chord pattern emphasising his growing weariness.

'BLACKBIRD'
(McCartney/Lennon)

'Blackbird' is a wasted opportunity. Inspired by the widespread horror at Martin Luther King's assassination in April 1968, Paul intended 'Blackbird' to be a metaphor for the US black civil rights movement. Beautifully sung and played, this is one of the standout performances from the album and yet while the lyrics are optimistic, the tune is melancholy. Furthermore, where Paul sings the word 'arise' the tune is sleepy. John claimed to have written a line of the lyrics, but his role must have been small as it is difficult to imagine him making such a mix-up between words and melody. Paul said the tune was based on a piece by Bach he had learnt as a teenager.

'PIGGIES'
(Harrison/Lennon)

In the late '60s, the free love, long hair and alternative lifestyle of the hippy movement were met with widespread envy and anger by 'straight' society and the establishment. In response, the forces of law and order were often heavy-handedly used to clamp down on the hippies wherever possible. Clubs were raided, anti-war protests violently broken up and dope smokers fined or imprisoned. For many hippies at the sharp end of this treatment there was a great deal of bitterness and the emotions expressed in George's lyrics must have echoed the sentiments of many. 'Piggies', though, fails in its ugly imagery, as it is every bit as unpleasant as the 'straight society' it attacks. The use of a prissy sounding harpsichord to mock the establishment's snobbery is also laboured and obvious compared to John's brilliant satire on 'Happiness Is A Warm Gun'. It was John who, not surprisingly, added the song's only good line; having piggies 'eating bacon' implies that the establishment eat their own kind.

'ROCKY RACOON'
(McCartney/Lennon/Donovan)

Musically the attention to detail in Paul's country and western pastiche is sublime, from John's hokey harmonica playing (and bass!) to George Martin's saloon-bar style piano. Yet in a foretaste of his solo career, Paul's yarn about a wild-west gunslinger is clumsy and never compelling. Both John and English folk singer Donovan, a close friend of Paul's, added to the lyrics, but it is hard to believe their contributions were anything but minor.

'DON'T PASS ME BY'
(Starkey)

Ringo had been on the verge of completing a song for the Beatles since 1963, having most of his efforts until 1968 laughed down by the other three. The somewhat childlike lyrics, apparently written in India, are hardly a challenge to the Lennon/McCartney school of songwriting, but are appropriately sung for laughs. A ramshackle beat led by a jaunty piano and a lopsided fiddle all bring a faltering charm, matched in

Ringo's earnest but endearing vocal. The song's only weakness is that at nearly four minutes long it outstays its welcome.
'

WHY DON'T WE DO IT IN THE ROAD?'
(McCartney)

Paul's possessed vocal, driving rhythm and suggestive lyrics are a perfect copy of John's forthright style, so much so that years later John recalled with hurt Paul's decision to record this without him. Paul explained that he recorded it with Ringo while John was busy in another studio, in order to complete the album quickly as its deadline approached in October 1968. Paul got the idea for the lyrics in India, after seeing two monkeys having sex in the road.

More convincing than Paul's other 'cock rock' songs, 'I'm Down' and 'She's A Woman', his performance, especially his unusually gruff vocal (a copy of John's vocal for 'Happiness Is A Warm Gun'?) connects to his earthy lifestyle in mid '68. Reports suggest that following his split with Jane Asher he enjoyed a bachelor life to the full, at times having up to three girls living with him in his St John's Wood home.

'I WILL'
(McCartney)

Another wasted opportunity by Paul, who gives one of his strongest tunes on the album a completely unmemorable set of lyrics. By contrast, on the next track, 'Julia', the tune is simpler but the words have an emotive power entirely missing here. In later years John summed up this problem in Paul's songwriting by saying that he often took a lazy approach to writing lyrics and 'could do better' if he tried.

Paul played all guitars on this track, with percussion by John and Ringo.

'JULIA'
(Lennon)

'Julia' was to John what 'Yesterday' had been to Paul, an intensely private song that was recorded solo. Full of personal imagery, Julia was the name of John's mother who died ten years previously, but the lyrics also describe Yoko. The words 'ocean child' are a literal translation of her name from Japanese, 'yo' meaning ocean and 'ko' meaning child. John had known Yoko only tenuously since 1966, but in India he was won over by a stream of beguiling letters from her. In one she wrote that she was a cloud and that if John looked into the sky he would be able to see her. Inspired by this, John suggests his mother's and Yoko's presence in the elements of the clouds, sand, sea, sky and moon.

'Julia' marked for John a rebirth in his songwriting. He had written many love songs to order in the Beatles' early years, but in search of a more honest approach had given these up between late '65 and mid '68. His relationship with Yoko Ono would, however, from this point on provide inspiration for a constant stream of love songs.

Musically, 'Julia' features an unusual arpeggio taught to John by Donovan while in India. Its feature of a constant drone note is in the same style as 'Dear Prudence'; similarly, here it is used to enforce the emotions of these dreamy, comforting lyrics.

'BIRTHDAY'
(McCartney/Lennon)

Paul concocted this in the studio one evening in September 1968, while waiting for the others to arrive. The exciting rhythm track, full of tempo changes, captures the Beatles' united in purpose and was laid down before the lyrics had even been written. Retiring to Paul's house nearby to watch a film on TV, they returned with lyrics that disappointingly suggest they were written in the foggy glow of either alcohol or drugs – John later rightly called them 'garbage'. The track was completed the same night.

'YER BLUES'
(Lennon)

John viewed blues music with mistrust, as its fans in England had long looked down upon rock 'n' roll as a cheap commercialisation of their music. Such feeling naturally led to some resentment and the drawing of sides, not helped by the fact that the blues in England was traditionally championed by the middle classes. In 1968 a flowering in the British blues-rock scene led by bands such as Cream and Fleetwood Mac set the scene for 'Yer Blues', though as John later admitted he felt self-conscious about recording it. His unease shows in that the middle eight here reverts to rock 'n' roll, copying part of the melody and words from Elvis Presley's 'Heartbreak Hotel'. (Tellingly, it was the one Beatles number John played at the rock 'n' roll revival concert in Canada in 1969.) The music is deliberately ugly – notes are missed, timings go astray, the guitars are crudely distorted and the vocals shriek. Similarly crude are the edits mid-song, which make no effort to disguise that this is a mix of two separate performances. The recording was done in an experimental manner, as a live performance in a cramped storage room next to studio two at Abbey Road.

The lyrics reveal the bouts of inner turmoil and self-doubt John was experiencing in India, no doubt exacerbated by the absence of drugs and alcohol, which he normally relied on. John recalled the song as him 'trying to reach God and feeling suicidal'.

'MOTHER NATURE'S SON'
(McCartney)

Written while Paul was under the spell of the Maharishi, in Rishikesh, India, this was inspired by a lecture the Beatles' guru gave on nature. Such was its effect that John also wrote a song called 'Child Of Nature', later re-written with new lyrics as 'Jealous Guy'. Both songs have a melancholy tune that suggests the lecture was more saddening than uplifting. This effect was compounded on 'Mother Nature's Son' by a slow, spartan arrangement and Paul's lonely vocal – none of the other Beatles took part on this recording. Paul used brass to show that the song's setting should be seen as the Lancashire countryside of his youth rather than the hills of Rishikesh.

'EVERYBODY'S GOT SOMETHING TO HIDE EXCEPT FOR ME AND MY MONKEY'
(Lennon)

Most of John's lyrics stand up to a fair deal of analysis, but this was clearly one song where he was singing the first words that came into his head. John himself explained the lyrics as being about the negative reaction people had to his new relationship with Yoko.

A loose rock work-out recorded live, its exciting switches of tempo and rhythm show a dexterity that few within the genre of heavy rock would ever follow – as does the use of a firebell, as rung by George!

'SEXY SADIE'
(Lennon)

Before going to India, the Beatles explained to the press how the Maharishi would help them to a higher spiritual plane. Their renunciation of him weeks later embarrassed John, provoking the bitterness in these lyrics. The cause of the split came after John and George (the last to leave) heard rumours that the Maharishi had made a pass at a woman on the same course – an act that showed him in their eyes to have more mortal intentions than the infallible god they had first seen him as. This, as Paul pointed out in his biography, was a little unfair as the Maharishi had never made himself out to be a god. It has been persuasively suggested too that John, on realising how naive his expectations of the Maharishi were, used this incident as an excuse to leave.

John started making up the words as he was packing to leave the meditation camp and in its original form the song was called 'Maharishi', being a direct attack on the guru, spiced with four-letter words. He later felt he had 'chickened out' by changing the title, but in doing so he was being true to his better songwriting instincts of making the lyrics more universal.

The song's sentiments would appear to have been important to the other Beatles too, who all made a strong input here. The arrangement of the vocals is back to their highest standards, the playing beautifully poised, particularly Paul's arch school-hall style piano which matches John's child-like phrasing. The Beatles gave the song 70 takes until they got the best performance – a level of commitment missing from much of the album.

'HELTER SKELTER'
(McCartney)

The Beatles were nearly always at their best when they had somebody to compete against. Largely amusing themselves alone on *The White Album*, 'Helter Skelter' was one of its few tracks made with the intention of getting one over on their rivals.

Paul, as he recalled, was inspired after reading a newspaper interview with Pete Townsend saying that The Who had made the loudest, rawest and dirtiest song they had ever done. While the exact quote by Townsend has never been traced, what Paul was clearly referring to was 'I Can See For Miles'. Townsend had regularly trumpeted the record as one that he imagined would blow away its rivals and to increase the suspense had held up its release for several months. On release in November 1967 the song fared less well than Townsend had planned and Paul too was disappointed that it did not live up to its hype. Paul, then, tried to recreate a record that could truly match Townsend's original boast.

To achieve the desired sound the guitars were tuned below their normal pitch of E to create the deepest, lowest sound possible and all instruments were distorted and backed with white noise and random sounds. Typical was Paul's instruction to the studio engineers to 'hike up the drum sound and really get it as loud and horrible as it could'. According to studio engineer Brian Gibson, the Beatles also sought inspiration by taking drugs and were completely out of their heads the night it was recorded. Paul's vocal reveals the effects of the drugs – probably cocaine – with his stifled sniggers. Such was the mood that several takes stretched to 20 minutes long. The finished take was edited down to three minutes, with the ending of one of these marathon takes added on, featuring Ringo's complaint about blisters on his fingers.

A finely constructed song, the ingenious riff and the lyrics, which leave room for interpretation, have made this a popular cover version. A helter skelter – a fairground ride found in Britain – is used by Paul as both a sexual and a drug metaphor. The lyrics also show his ambition in outstripping The Who; the reference to 'miles' in the lyrics is a clear challenge to 'I Can See For Miles'.

'LONG LONG LONG'
(Harrison)

Goerge admitted this was inspired by Bob Dylan's mood piece 'Sad Eyed Lady Of The Lowlands', which uses a similar D, Em, A chord pattern. Similarly George's lyrics bring out a different emphasis for each word in the chorus and say more in their mood than in their meaning. George said it was about his search for God, but it is tempting to see a connection between the song's mood and the fading light at the end of the October day this was recorded on.

George also took inspiration from Joe Cocker's 'With A Little Help From My Friends', which had just entered the UK charts. As in that record, the Hammond organ played by Paul here is slowly faded in and out. The use of the organ also caused the peculiar rattling at the song's end, where a bottle resting on it was caused to vibrate by a note with high resonance.

'REVOLUTION 1'
(Lennon)

In the heady mood of the late 1960s a new order of social values was being drawn up. Such was the impatience of some of the hippies, students and radical thinkers pushing for change that a revolution was openly discussed. This seemed a very tangible prospect during May 1968, when students in France brought the country to a temporary standstill.

With rioting still taking place in Paris, John began recording the provocatively titled 'Revolution', hoping to release it as a topical single. John remembered in 1980, 'I wanted it out as a single, as a statement of the Beatles' position on Vietnam and the Beatles' position on revolution.' Using the same sarcastic boogie-woogie of the recent single 'Lady Madonna', John's message was somewhat lamely put across with its slow-motion pace and poorly emphasised vocals. As a single the recording would not have been a big commercial success, but it would have made an excitingly topical and (mostly) wise response to the events in Paris. For commercial reasons Paul and George voted against the single and the group (ironically considering the lyrics) being a democracy, John had to frustratedly accept defeat.

The veto on the single was a mixed blessing, as in the rush to record 'Revolution' not only had John not given his song a decent arrangement, but he had still not decided exactly what his position *was* on revolution. While the key message of the lyrics is one of anti-violence and a plea of calm (the song's key message that everything would turn out alright, might have made a truer title), after asking to be left 'out' he adds confusingly the word 'in'.

Once the heat of the moment had passed John rethought his lyrics and the arrangement. In July he then recorded a much superior version, which became the B-side to 'Hey Jude'. This faster-paced hard rock recording gives the lyrics a more emphatic and tuneful rendition, which unlike the first recording clearly wants to be taken more seriously. Having had time to think about the arrangement, here key words and phrases are given special emphasis by being double tracked. Staying true to the main theme of the lyrics, John here too plainly asks to be counted out of any revolution.

However wise his words have proved in hindsight, they caused criticism from those vocal in the 'struggle' against the establishment. John came to be embarrassed at this, especially as he had some sympathy with such radicals. In his defence he explained in 1970 that the first drafts of 'Revolution' had been written in the calm of the meditation camp in India. By way of redress John recorded the much more aggressive 'Power To The People' the following year, with the message that those seeking a revolution should go ahead and do it. Years later John's wisest words from this song are often overlooked; rather than commit violence against others, he preaches us to instead free our minds.

'HONEY PIE'
(McCartney)

Until hearing rock 'n' roll aged 13, Paul had been brought up in a household that was dominated by the sound of 1930s dance band and showtime music. His father, who played in his own dance band in the 1930s, passed onto Paul a love of this music. In the rock magazine *Mojo* in 2000, Paul quoted 'Cheek To Cheek' as sung by Fred Astaire, and the Hoagy Carmichael song 'Stardust' as two of his top ten favourite songs of all time. 'Honey Pie' is a homage to the sound of the 1930s dance orchestras, with its score of swooping clarinets and saxophones. After going to all the effort of achieving such authenticity, though, Paul chickened out of singing a straightforward lyric, turning the whole affair into a limp joke that ended up tagged on at the album's close.

'SAVOY TRUFFLE'
(Harrison)

To all intents and purposes this is one of the most throwaway tracks on *The White Album*, the lyrics a barely risible joke on the effects of eating too many chocolates – a private joke on his friend Eric Clapton, from whose box of chocolates he took most of the lyrics. What 'Savoy Truffle' demonstrates, though, is that George was at long last comfortable mastering the art of structuring a song. Its mix of verse, chorus, bridge and guitar solo are his most slick to date and a clue to the amazing jump development he was about to make with 'Something' and 'Here Comes The Sun'.

'CRY BABY CRY'
(Lennon)

'Cry Baby Cry' seductively plays with sound textures, rhythms and alliteration in the same way John employed them on 'I Am The Walrus' and 'Sexy Sadie'. Looking back at the song in 1980, though, he dismissed it as 'rubbish', a comment surely based on the fact that the lyrics do not hang together. These read like a failed attempt to recreate the fairy-tale setting of 'Lucy In The Sky With Diamonds', the fault chiefly lying with the chorus which bears no relation to the verses.

'REVOLUTION 9'
(Lennon)

The blame or the credit, depending on your taste, for 'Revolution 9' lies with classical composers John Cage and Stockhausen, both of whom were seeking in the 1960s to redefine the way people listened to music. The radical, confrontational nature of their music appealed to both John and Paul's thirst for pushing back the boundaries of pop.

It was Paul who first attempted such a collection of sound effects and disjointed tapes in January 1967 with the as yet unreleased 'Carnival Of Light', and who arranged the discordant orchestral crescendo on 'A Day In The Life', based on ideas he had taken from Stockhausen. Paul claimed it was he who instructed John on how to create such tapes by manipulating the Brennel tape machine he kept at home. John duly created similar tapes, but initially, like Paul, did not seek to release them.

In the meantime, the first fully blown venture into such musical anarchy issued by a rock group was 'The Chrome Plated Megaphone of Destiny' on Frank Zappa and the Mothers Of Invention's album *We're Only In It For The Money* from March 1968. The album was a parody of *Sgt. Pepper* and the six-and-a-half minutes of cut-up tapes and sound effects with no discernable structure is similarly placed at its close, as 'A Day In The Life' had been.

While John was almost certainly aware of Zappa's track when he made 'Revolution 9', the only inspiration he credited was that of Yoko Ono. Part of New York's avant-garde scene in the late 1950s and early 1960s, Yoko had moved in the same circles as Cage and had used such musical approaches in her art. John saw the creation of 'Revolution 9' as an exercise that cemented his partnership and commitment to Yoko.

Created in the days that followed the recording of 'Revolution 1',

John also saw his sound collage as a further statement on the unrest and excitement generated by the Paris riots. He later explained that it was supposed to signify an 'unconscious picture' of how he envisaged a revolution to be. This picture in sound of a revolution is revealing in its unpleasantness. The disembodied, emotionless voices and anarchic sound effects create an aural nightmare, showing if anything that the idea of revolution filled John with horror. In the same way that John was encouraged by the radical press to recant the lyrics to 'Revolution', he later referred to the mood of 'Revolution 9' as a 'mistake'. To read too much into the track, though, is a mistake too, for John's main intentions seem typically lighthearted, particularly with the placing of a tape loop announcing 'number nine', a reference to his favourite number. That George Martin and the other Beatles sought to persuade John to leave this off the album now seems unfair, as the album is in fact full of such similar jokes.

'GOODNIGHT'
(Lennon)

'Goodnight' was a bedtime lullaby for the four-year-old Julian Lennon and appears to have been written in June 1968 after John had left his wife Cynthia to live with Yoko Ono, in doing so limiting his contact with Julian. In the same way, Paul would write 'Hey Jules' (later 'Hey Jude') for Julian the next month. If guilt about his separation from Julian was the motivation in writing 'Goodnight', then John did not stay true to his intentions. By handing over the vocals to Ringo and the orchestration to George Martin, the song lacks any of the tenderness and sincerity that 'Beautiful Boy' would have when recorded for his other son Sean in 1980. John did sing the words at an earlier stage in the recording process, though. Paul, who heard this version, remembered it as 'great', but thought that John did not sing it to protect his image. George Martin was instructed by John to give 'Goodnight' a 'corny Hollywood' sound, his score ending up sounding similar to the soundtrack music he had been recording for *Yellow Submarine* earlier in the year. Other than Ringo, who renders what he later described as a nervous vocal, no other Beatles were involved in its recording.

12. Let It Be

GET BACK
(McCartney/Lennon) (album and single version) Single
released 11 April 1969

If all the tracks on the *Let It Be* project had succeeded as well as this, it
could have been their best album rather than their worst. On so many of
the songs the group make begrudging, bored contributions, but this was
clearly one song from the project all four of them enjoyed playing.
Evolved from a bass line that Paul introduced into a group jam, the lyrics
and music were pieced together over a 20-day period in January 1969.
The only Beatles single created in such a fashion, arguably it should have
been given a group credit rather than the sole Lennon/McCartney credit
it received.

After numerous rehearsals, the Beatles plus Billy Preston knew the
song inside out and delivered a masterly performance of lean rock 'n' roll
playing that allowed several instruments virtuoso roles. John plays the
dreamy guitar solo and the taut Chuck Berry riff, Billy Preston's
understated organ solo gets a share of the spotlight, while the subtle
playing of both George and Paul merge into one over Ringo's infectious
skipping beat. John's unusual role as lead guitarist on this track was due
to George's walkout from the group in mid-January. Over several days
the song was evolved without George, with John working out the guitar
parts in his absence.

Two versions of 'Get Back' exist, a straight performance used for the
single version and a second edited with chat at the start and applause
from the rooftop concert at its close, to give the impression of being
recorded live. Some confusion exists over whether these are actually the

same or different performances. Close scrutiny reveals little to tell them apart, the only key difference being the addition of a false ending to the single version where John leads the band back with a tougher attack on the Chuck Berry riff, releasing more of the song's pent-up energy. Unlike the confusion over the album and single versions, all sources agree that this extra piece of music was edited from a separate performance recorded on 28 January.

Stylistic inspiration came from the January 1969 chart hit 'Going Up The Country' by Canned Heat, which featured a similar bass line and drum riff, and from which Paul mimicked the clear high-pitched vocals of Bob Hite. Out-takes from the *Let It Be* sessions reveal the Beatles playing a snatch of 'Going Up The Country' only days before 'Get Back' evolved.

The lyrics evolved with the jam, starting as a lame joke on the anti-immigrant hysteria encouraged by British politician Enoch Powell in 1968. This then evolved into a by now typical Beatlesque lyrical tease of barely hidden sexual and drug references alluding to marjuana and a transvestite. One account says that the lyrics in part were based on Chris (Christine) O'Dell, a worker for Apple records in Saville Row from 1968–69, who grew up in Tuscon, Arizona and moved to work in Los Angeles (California), before coming to work in London.

'DON'T LET ME DOWN'
(Lennon) B-side to 'Get Back'

Like 'Get Back', this evolved slowly but surely over the length of the *Let It Be* project, being rehearsed and recorded over nine separate days in January 1969. After 'Get Back' it is the second-best performance from the project and the album is much the poorer for its exclusion. Similarly it allows virtuoso performances from George on lead guitar and from Billy Preston again on organ. It also has an arrangement of three separate tempos that interchange through the song. The real star of the song, though, is John's expressive vocal, which over each tempo change turns from passionate and anguished on the chorus, to gentle on the verses, to uplifting and confident on the middle eight. Like 'Julia', this is John rediscovering and redefining the boundaries of a love song. Paul claimed that the lyrics were not just about his love for Yoko Ono, but his fear over the heroin use that both he and Yoko were indulging in.

The emotions within 'Don't Let Me Down' are all the better for being played in the raw, stripped-down style that the *Let It Be* project dictated;

the glitches of differing sound levels for the vocals in the verses merely add to its charm and immediacy.

LET IT BE
Album released 8 May 1970

Let It Be was the third and final attempt of Paul's to revitalise both John and George's waning enthusiasm for the group. Correctly realising that the Beatles always needed a new goal to keep them motivated, he proposed the bold and original plan that they would rehearse a new album over several weeks for it to be both filmed and recorded live to an invited audience. While the studio had once excited the Beatles, they had grown complacent and bored while recording *The White Album*. Paul's plan was that if they had the prospect of a public performance ahead of them they would be 'scared' into raising their standards, as in their early days.

In light of the project's subsequent failure – only by the Beatles' high standards – both John and George in hindsight damned the project, though both, particularly John, as rehearsal out-takes reveal, were initially intrigued by and committed to it.

John's contribution to the project was his insistence that if they were to play live, then the performances would have to be 'honest' and no special effects or overdubs should be used. The Beatles' debut album had notably been recorded in a similar and successful fashion.

Let It Be, though, proved one challenge too far. While initially enthusiastic, as the deadline for the concert loomed neither John nor George felt any great incentive to go out and prove themselves as a live act again. The bad memories of the Beatles tours were also still fresh and both had been the most vehement about ending touring back in 1966. As John recalled the Beatles at this point no longer believed in themselves and crucially no longer had a common goal. Such was the atmosphere that the Beatles openly discussed splitting up during the rehearsals.

The project had other major problems. Chief among them was the choice of the cavernous Twickenham film studios to rehearse in. None of the Beatles enjoyed being filmed while they were playing and the large open room was not conducive for the intimate atmosphere often crucial to the creative process. Also John, as he later admitted, was on heroin throughout the sessions. Lethargy was his natural state and he only raised himself to contribute one major song to the project, 'Don't Let Me Down'. George by contrast had a surfeit of good songs (including

'Something'), but was so peeved at Paul and John's disinterest in them that he held them back from the project.

The project might have survived this lack of input, as fortunately Paul had a number of strong songs to record. Yet faced with an awkward and argumentative George and a dopey John, he found himself coercing both of them to match his hopes for the project. George, already fed up at John's apathetic behaviour, especially on George's songs, now blew up at Paul's coercion and walked out ten days into the project. Some reports also state that John and George actually came to blows during this time.

George's departure forced a rethink. A compromise was reached where the album would be completed at the Apple studios in Mayfair (the Apple HQ), to be capped with a rooftop performance. By all accounts recording now became far more productive, particularly after George had the masterstroke of bringing in old Hamburg friend Billy Preston on organ. George reasoned rightly that the presence of a respected musician would inhibit inter-band bickering. Indeed, in hindsight this was a much better way of revitalising the Beatles than Paul's idea of a live performance and film. With this new line-up, over the last few days of January most of the songs were given 'best' performances, including the lunchtime rooftop concert on the 30th.

Problematically the Beatles were now faced with up to 24 hours of tapes to turn into an album. Aware of how poor so much of these were, neither John nor Paul could face editing them. Instead the job was entrusted to freelance engineer/producer Glyn Johns, who in the spring of 1969 presented the Beatles with an album on acetate disc. This album, now much bootlegged, was considered too poor to release. Until 1970 it remained unreleased, when at John's suggestion the tapes were handed over to Phil Spector to see if he could work a magic touch on them and produce something decent. The band at this stage had effectively split up and communication between them was strained, explaining John's fait accompli. Paul, on hearing of the decision, boycotted the sessions and would not help out in any way, although both Ringo and George Harrison made new overdubs.

Spector smoothed the cracks over some of the tapes by adding orchestral and choral overdubs and wiping some of the weaker contributions, e.g. John's bass on the title track. While not true to the original intentions of a 'live' album, Spector succeeded in making a commercially viable album. Spector recalled that the Beatles were so ashamed of the album that they let him be the final judge of what was best to do with it. Paul's account differed; he claimed that he had no knowledge of the overdubs to 'Let It Be' and 'The Long And Winding Road' and has been bitter about Spector's input ever since.

Spector's album differed in other ways to the Glyn John version. By the spring of 1970 the film of the *Let It Be* rehearsals had been finished and was ready for release. The finished cut of the film showed the Beatles rehearsing both 'I Me Mine' and 'Across The Universe'. As no decent version existed for either from the *Let It Be* tapes, a new recording of 'I Me Mine' was recorded in early 1970, while the old 1968 recording of 'Across The Universe' was dug out of the vaults.

'TWO OF US'
(McCartney)

This account of Paul's adventures with Linda in the early stages of their romance is a blueprint for John's 'Ballad Of John And Yoko'. The lyric tells of their rides out into the countryside, on which to amuse themselves they would try to get lost. On one such drive Paul began writing 'Two Of Us'. Their intimacy is replicated in the vocals of John and Paul who share a single microphone, a style they consciously copied from the Everly Brothers whose songs they had played live in a similar fashion in their early days in Hamburg and the Cavern. Recorded at Apple studios, the shaky timing (there is no bass) of this live performance is true to the album's ethos, but the song really deserves a better production.

The song opens with a piece of Lennon humour, that contrary to how it appears, was recorded separately. Placing these snippets between songs was an idea that Glyn John had on the first mix of the album in 1969; Phil Spector kept them in for the same purpose of presumably showing that much of the album should not be taken too seriously. Some commentators have claimed that these snippets seem to mock Paul's project, yet their humour is actually in keeping with the Beatles' early live appearances.

'DIG A PONY'
(Lennon)

In part 'Dig A Pony' reveals John's lethargic, couldn't-care-less attitude to the *Let It Be* project with its nonsense imagery and equally pointless ugly, loping guitar riff. John's vocal, though, especially on a very soulful rendition of each chorus, makes this performance hang together surprisingly well. The chorus, which lyrically bears no relation to the verse, shows John again experimenting with the format of writing a love song. The only message he wants to communicate is his desire for Yoko – anything else is pointless. 'I Want You (She's So Heavy)', which was rehearsed but not completed during the *Let It Be* rehearsals, takes this process a step further by dispensing with verses altogether.

As with all John's nonsense verse, some of it does contain the odd line of special significance. Its allusion to the Rolling Stones and imitation was an intentional jibe. John, while close friends with Mick Jagger, was sensitive about the Stones more fashionable status at this time. He resented this particularly as the Stones' had copied many of the Beatles gimmicks such as sitar, strings and album concepts. To add to this list the Rolling Stones had released their *Beggars' Banquet* album with a largely plain white sleeve on 28 December 1968, a month after the Beatles had released their *White Album*.

This performance of 'Dig a Pony' was recorded midway through the rooftop concert – turn up the last few seconds at 3.48-3.50 and you can hear John complain that his hands are too cold to play the guitar.

'ACROSS THE UNIVERSE'
(Lennon)

The Beatles, usually masters at turning weak material into great recordings, here managed the opposite by making a disastrous recording of John's complex and pretty 'Across The Universe'. Shortly before his death John bitterly blamed Paul for encouraging a spirit of 'looseness and casualness and experimentation' on its recording. The truth, though, is that the blame must lie with John, as he himself admitted he was 'psychologically destroyed' at the time, owing to his prolonged LSD use since 1966. John's accusation against Paul also seems unfair in that John benefited far more from Paul's input into his songs than vice versa.

Apart from the unusual metre of the song, one of the main difficulties in arranging it was the lyrics' subject matter. While full of pretty imagery, their meaning and hence their mood are difficult to ascertain, explaining the problems faced in finding an appropriate arrangement. Knowing that the unusual song needed something unique, the first recordings in February 1968 tried out a number of new effects such as a wah-wah pedal on guitar, a harp-like sound on sitar, falsetto harmonies from two girl fans from outside the studio and even humming! When John tried to get the Beatles to re-record the song in January 1969 for *Let It Be*, he again experimented with new arrangements featuring an organ drone and new vocal harmonies. Ironically, the one person who could have found the right arrangement for the song, Phil Spector, would eventually end up trying to salvage something from these recordings.

Three versions of the song now exist. An early, unadulterated take with sitar is on the *Anthology 2* compilation. A second version exists on the *Past Masters* compilation which was remixed by George Martin in October 1969 and a third is on *Let It Be* as rearranged by Phil Spector. The second version, which John donated to a charity compilation album, had sound effects added and was speeded up by George Martin. The intention in speeding it up seems to have been an effort to disguise the fact that John's singing goes out of tune in places.

While no one of these versions is perfect, the second is preferable for highlighting the song's unique rhythm and the third is preferable in emphasising the melody. Phil Spector, presumably acting under John's instructions to do something special with the song, radically wiped much of the instruments from the February 1968 recordings and replaced them with strings and choir, while slowing down the original tape. From a purist's point of view this Spector version may be unpopular, but it is the most listenable of the three.

John wrote 'Across The Universe' in late 1967 after an argument at home with his wife. The first line, as he recalled, was a comment on her 'nagging', though as he explained from there the song turned 'into a sort of a cosmic song, rather than an irritated song'. The 'cosmic' nature of the lyrics, with their mantra chant as the chorus – a reference to the Maharishi's own guru, Deva – read like an anticipation of the spiritual awakening John foresaw from his planned trip to the Maharishi's meditation camp in early 1968. The lyrics, which John rated as among his very best, feature a rare use of onomatopoeia, the rhythm of the words pattering out like rain falling onto paper.

'I ME MINE'
(Harrison)

This is a thinly veiled attack on John and Paul written midway through the *Let It Be* project. As transcripts of the *Let It Be* rehearsals show (see *Get Back: the Beatles' Let It Be Disaster* by Doug Sulphy and Ray Shweighardt), neither John nor Paul were taking any of George's contributions to the project very seriously. Looking to create a more equal role for himself within the band, George was fed up with what he saw as the egotism of John and Paul. Probably sensing the nature of George's lyrics, neither John nor Paul took a liking to 'I Me Mine' either; indeed John was recorded mocking the song's droning melody during the *Let It Be* sessions. Not surprisingly it was never completed satisfactorily during the *Let It Be* sessions and a new recording was made on 3 January 1970 with a group made up of George, Paul, Ringo and Billy Preston. The reason for this unusual recording, long after the Beatles had officially split up, was that the song was edited to appear in the film of *Let It Be*, with John and Yoko memorably dancing a waltz to it. To this new version Phil Spector added strings in April and also extended the song's length by repeating some sections, neither of which George's solemn dirge merited.

'DIG IT'
(Lennon/McCartney/Harrison/Starr)

A witty 51-second snippet of a 12-minute jam, led by John at Apple Studios, that appears to be loosely spoofing Bob Dylan's 'Like A Rolling Stone'. Once a big fan of Dylan, John had grown suspicious of his wordy style and after 'I Am The Walrus' this was his second Dylan spoof (and not his last – listen to 'You've Got To Serve Somebody' from 1980). Paul in his biography claimed that all four Beatles added to the comically disparate images in the lyrics, hence the equal writing credit to all four.

'LET IT BE'
(McCartney)

It is a measure of the misery Paul endured in trying to hold the Beatles together that he sought solace in the religious imagery used in 'Let It Be'. Paul had seen his close partnership with John eroded by Yoko Ono and generally observed the close bond of friendship amongst the Beatles rocked by bickering during 1968 and early 1969. Paul took the strain more than the others, as while John and George were both contemplating careers outside of the Beatles at this stage, he still wanted the band to continue.

In 1997 Paul explained, 'One night during this tense time I had a dream, I saw my mum who had been dead ten years or so. In the dream she said, "It'll be alright." I'm not sure she used the words "Let it be", but that was the gist of her advice.'

While the song has quite deliberate gospel influences – Paul offered it to Aretha Franklin to sing before the Beatles released their version – that

Paul's mother was called Mary gives the song deeply Christian overtones, intentionally or not. Begun in late 1968, Paul seems to have taken inspiration from John's song to his mother, 'Julia', which was recorded in October of that year. As in the dreamlike verses to 'Julia' John imagines his dead mother calling his name, on 'Let It Be' Paul pictures his mother speaking to him.

The simple yet powerful imagery of 'Let It Be' has made it one of the Beatles' most popular songs. Played live it has become a crowd-pleasing favourite when performed by Paul or as a cover version by other artists. It seems quite probable that when Paul wrote it he too realised how well it would work live and was inspired to think up the whole concept of a Beatles live album around it. To his misfortune, though, 'Let It Be' never quite received the recording it deserved.

While the Beatles motivated themselves for songs such as 'Get Back' on the *Let It Be* project, the film of them recording the title song reveals Paul as the only animated Beatle, the others looking bored. John particularly looks stoned, sitting on the floor playing a bass line so poor it was subsequently wiped from the track. John was openly mocking of 'Let It Be' too, which he thought twee (as can be heard in his mocking introduction on the album) and in later years he compared it unfavourably to Simon and Garfunkel.

Three versions of 'Let It Be' now exist. There is the bare version taken from Glyn John's initial mix, a second version remixed by George Martin for release as a single and the album version with added strings and backing vocals put there by Phil Spector. One of Spector's worst productions for the album, his overdubs drown out both Paul's vocals and the intimacy of the lyrics.

'MAGGIE MAE'
(traditional)

This is a candid and comical performance of a warm-up song the Beatles first learnt in the 1950s. Clearly, though, John had difficulty remembering all of the words. The second verse should actually read 'I was paid off at the pool in the port of Liverpool, three pounds ten a week that was my pay, with a bucket full of tin, I was very soon taken in, by a gal with the name of Maggie May'.

Originally a nineteenth-century sea shanty about a mythical prostitute who robbed seamen of their pay and clothes, many versions of the lyrics to 'Maggie May' exist, which variously place the song's setting in Bristol, Glasgow, Liverpool, London and Swansea. The Beatles based their version on that released by the Viper Skiffle Group in 1957. The Viper's version was much more tame; where John sings 'dirty Maggie May', they sang 'Maggie, Maggie May'. John also sings in a comically exaggerated Liverpool accent not hinted at on Viper's version.

The Vipers were one of Britain's best skiffle groups, though often overshadowed by the more gimmicky and commercial Lonnie Donegan. They clearly made an impression on the Beatles, despite having had only one small British hit single. Another track of theirs, 'No Other Baby', was also sung by the Beatles in their early performances and covered on Paul's *Run Devil Run* album in 1999.

'I'VE GOT A FEELING'
(McCartney/Lennon)

One of the last true Lennon/McCartney co-compositions, Paul's first half in its soulful, improvised feel mimics John's style of writing. Indeed, its very lyrics sum up the personal, intuitive style John favoured, e.g. 'Yer Blues' and 'I'm So Tired'. As such, Paul may well have written it to cajole the strung-out John into contributing to the *Let It Be* project. The ploy – if it was one – worked, as John can visibly be seen to be enjoying the song in the film of *Let It Be* and he duly responded to Paul's invitation.

John's lyrics, which date from India in 1968, are a list of bizarre and mundane media images, similar to those used in 'A Day In The Life'. One line appears to refer to Max Romeo's risqué and banned reggae hit 'Wet Dream', then in the UK charts.

This performance was recorded from the Beatles' rooftop concert.

'ONE AFTER 909'
(Lennon/McCartney)

One of the John and Paul's earliest songs, written in 1957–58, this was resurrected for the *Let It Be* project as a symbol of their attempt to 'get back' to their beginnings, but also as something of a joke. Its clumsy structure was both a reminder of how far they had come and also of how foolish they must have looked playing the song in their early days. The melody for 'One After 909' is a thinly disguised copy of Jerry Lee Lewis's songs 'Whole Lotta Shakin' Goin On' and 'Great Balls Of Fire'. Lyrically too it clings closely to the tried and tested early rock 'n' roll and skiffle themes of railway songs (e.g 'Mystery Train' and 'Six Five Special').

The most casual and shambolic of the rooftop concert performances, this is especially ruined by George's pointless and obtrusive blues fills between the verses. The freedom George takes was typical of the role many lead guitarists were assuming in late '60s rock 'n' roll, and Paul's curbing of such excess was one of the reasons for George walking out halfway through the *Let It Be* project.

'THE LONG AND WINDING ROAD'
(McCartney)

The Phil Spector overdubs to the 'Long And Winding Road' annoyed Paul so much that he quoted them in the High Court in 1970 as one of the main reasons for dissolving the Beatles' business partnership. The addition of strings and a female choir – Paul was particularly scathing about the latter – have a sweet and false air about them, unlike Paul's essentially bare and honest rendition.

In truth, the damage to the song had been done long before that. The unadulterated, original live performance recorded at Apple studios is only noteworthy for Paul's vocal and piano. Neither the inept bass playing of John or the pointless wash of acoustic guitar played by George add anything to the recording. Phil Spector's removal of these two instruments from the mix was a blessing. Like 'Let It Be', evidently neither George nor, especially, John were enthusiastic about the song, leaving the impression that Paul would have been better off re-recording the whole thing himself.

Spector's overdubs must have been particularly annoying for Paul as until the release of the *Anthology 3* compilation in 1996 there was no alternative version officially released, unlike that for 'Across The Universe' and 'Let it Be'. Consequently Paul returned to the song several times in his solo career, re-recording it for his *Give My Regards To Broad Street* album and playing it live with Wings.

Paul started the song around the same time as 'Let It Be' in 1968 and its mood and lyrics were likewise inspired by his unhappiness at the loss of his close friendship with John and the bickering within the Beatles. Paul has since stated that he took musical inspiration from Ray Charles. In tempo and delivery it owes much to his 1960 recording, 'Don't Let The Sun Catch You Crying'. Paul had sung this live with the Beatles in their early years and was recorded playing a snatch of it during the *Let It Be* sessions in January 1969, when he was still completing the lyrics to 'The Long And Winding Road'. Notably, as in Charles's song, he uses the word 'door' as a metaphor for openess in a relationship. Ironically the slick recording of 'Don't Let The Sun Catch You Crying', which was obviously a favourite of Paul's, features mainly piano, strings and a female choir.

'FOR YOU BLUE'
(Harrison)

The *Let It Be* rehearsal tapes reveal that George was the project's biggest dissenter; notably he was recorded at one stage saying that he did not want any of his songs used. As a compromise George held back some of his better songs and contributed this modest effort, realising astutely that its blues formula would be enhanced by being recorded live.

The song and style owes much to Dylan's 'Country Pie', which George would have heard before its early 1969 release when staying with Dylan in Woodstock, New York in late 1968.

13. Abbey Road

'THE BALLAD OF JOHN AND YOKO'
(Lennon/McCartney) Single released 30 May 1969

Once John met Yoko he began writing songs to suit the two of them, rather than to fit in with any notion of what would be best for the Beatles. The lengths Paul would go to, to accommodate this waywardness in order to keep him from leaving the group, is at its clearest here. John's lyrics, of course, mythologise the very relationship that was eating away at his partnership with Paul.

Recorded weeks after his marriage to Yoko, John hurriedly sought to release the song so as to capitalise on his ongoing publicity stunts for peace. With George out of the country and Ringo acting in the film *The Magic Christian*, only Paul was available to help. As Paul remembered in 1988: 'He came round to my house, wanting to do it really quick, he said "Let's just you and me run over to the studio." I said "Oh alright, I'll play drums, I'll play bass."'

Starting from John's unpromising E, E7, A, B chord progression on acoustic guitar, over a single day's recording every trick was used to fill out the sound and give it commercial appeal. Paul's bass line (which he openly stole from the intro to Elvis Presley's 'Don't Be Cruel' with an extra note added) is pushed high in the mix for a counter melody, a decorative lead guitar figure is added and piano seeps in to emphasise the chords. For extra presence too Paul's vocal shadows John's, the drums are given echo and after the middle eight, maracas enter at double time, maintaining the listener's attention until the song's end. As a foursome the Beatles could have made more of it, but not by much.

John's title alludes to Georgie Fame's 1968 hit 'The Ballad Of Bonnie

And Clyde'. He clearly drew a parallel with the American bandits who played cat and mouse with the US press and authorities, criss-crossing state lines. John and Yoko were similarly pursued across Europe, as the lyrics explain, as they turned their wedding and honeymoon in March 1969 into a publicity stunt for peace. John also clearly takes inspiration from Paul's 'Two Of Us', recorded in January for the *Let It Be* album, which had, in a more subtle manner, romanticised Paul's relationship with Linda Eastman and their travels in the English countryside.

The flippant mention of Jesus Christ and John's allusion to being treated in the same way in the chorus got the record banned by many radio stations in the USA, where it only reached number eight in the national charts. Commercial considerations, though, were not top priority for John, as had been the case for the planned release of 'Revolution 1' as a single the year before. That John was given the go-ahead for 'The Ballad Of John And Yoko' as a single speaks volumes about Paul's wishes to avoid the tensions his veto of 'Revolution 1' had caused. Indeed, by most accounts John and Paul worked so well on this recording that John seems to have backed off from creating too much conflict on the recording of *Abbey Road*.

'OLD BROWN SHOE'
(Harrison) B-side of 'Ballad Of John And Yoko'

One of the most anonymous of all Beatles songs, the key ingredient missing here is their usually strident and clear vocals. Here by contrast George's voice is buried in the mix, there are no vocal harmonies and any lyrical meaning is thus lost. The surprise though is the playing – full of key and tempo changes, it reveals a band playing together much closer than the reported arguments from this time would suggest.

ABBEY ROAD
Album released 26 September 1969

In hindsight the decline of the Beatles on *The White Album* and *Let It Be* looks terminal and logically *Abbey Road* should not have been a success. Indeed, the tensions and in-fighting that dogged the albums previous to it continued during the recording on *Abbey Road*, Paul going as far as to describe the atmosphere as having a 'serious, paranoid heaviness'. What was different about *Abbey Road* was that the Beatles had a common goal. Their new manager Allen Klein was negotiating a new recording contract that would bring them the millions they rightly should have earned years before. To strengthen his position, the Beatles needed to be seen as a viable going concern. With this in mind they set about recording *Abbey Road* only weeks after the end of the *Let It Be* debacle.

This business-like approach to the album was also reflected in the style of recording. The Beatles gave up on the live performance recording style that had necessitated all four of them to be in the studio at the same time. Instead they returned to the *Sgt. Pepper* style of bit-by-bit layer recording. For this process a first performance by the band might be needed, but the meticulous process of overdubbing could be done on an individual basis. John was not used for the initial performances of 'Here Comes The Sun', 'Golden Slumbers' and 'Carry That Weight' and also appears to have partaken in next to no overdubbing of songs that he had not himself written. Paul later claimed that by the time of *Abbey Road* 'John wasn't much interested in performing anything he hadn't written himself'. It seems likely that John by this time was already seeing his songs largely as solo exercises, with the other Beatles as session musicians. Paul picked up on this vibe so much that he claimed he did not offer to contribute backing vocals to 'Come Together'.

The absence of John from many of the recordings, though, gave more freedom to the production ideas of both Paul and George Martin, and the latter was to play his fullest role on a Beatles record since *Sgt. Pepper*. The end result pleased Paul and particularly George Martin so much that like many others they both rate it today as the Beatles' best album.

John, by contrast, damned the album as having no life in it. This difference of opinion summed up John and Paul's incompatibility and shortly before its release in September 1969 John quit the band. Looking to escape the tag of the Beatles and forge a solo career, he saw *Abbey Road* as adding to the Beatles' fame and thus its legacy for him as an artist. Speaking after he had split from the Beatles he expressed regret that *Let It Be* had not been the last Beatles album, as he felt this would have broken the 'myth' surrounding them. *Abbey Road* in its slickness, he said, had helped preserve the Beatles myth.

After the split Paul voiced the opposite sentiment, saying that he did not want *Let It Be* to be their last album because he felt it was not a true reflection of what the Beatles were capable of. Aware that the Beatles were probably not going to last much longer, Paul made every effort to make sure that *Abbey Road* was good, so that they would bow out on a high note.

For all John's unease over *Abbey Road*, ironically the business deal struck during its recording made him rich enough to be able to forge a solo career without worrying whether it had to be a commercial success or not.

The slick sound of *Abbey Road* was gained through the use of eight-track recording equipment on all tracks. A live performance of drums, bass and guitar and/or piano would be channelled onto three tracks, leaving five tracks free for overdubs and multi-tracking. The opening track, 'Come Together', demonstrates the strengths of this sound best, as it allows great clarity for each of the vocals, guitars, bass, drums and organ. However, over-reliance on separation of sound on some tracks means a loss of the distinctive liveliness and warmth typical of the Beatles sound, 'Oh Darling' and 'Octopus's Garden' suffering the most.

Recording took place intermittently from February to August '69, but George Martin only started his contribution from June and several songs were recorded in his absence. His biggest role came in July and August, when most of the 'medley' was recorded.

While in the USA in December 1968, George bought one of the first commercially available synthesisers. In early 1969 he recorded an album of electronic sounds for release on the Apple label and by default became its expert. Like all new gimmicks the Beatles came across, it initially proved irresistible, overcoming their better instincts, and its use on 'Maxwell's Silver Hammer', 'I Want You' and 'Because' was unwarranted.

Large drum kits had become fashionable in 1969 and Ringo's was duly expanded; this greater breadth of tone is most evident on the drum solo on 'The End'.

'COME TOGETHER'
(Lennon/McCartney)

While *Abbey Road* is largely an album of melodic treats, the thrill of 'Come Together' is in its rhythm and textures of sound. The sexy, teasing interaction between the drums and bass are contrasted by the lead guitar and organ which glide dreamily above. Such fine work was the product of John and Paul's last-ever true co-composition. John brought the song complete to the studio as a Chuck Berry-style strum on acoustic guitar set to the metre of the lyrics (and a few words) of Berry's 'You Can't Catch Me'. As Paul recalled, John asked him for an arrangement that would disguise the Chuck Berry origin of the song (though John was later sued anyway). Paul came up with the contrapuntal bass line and no doubt had a hand in directing Ringo to play the song's peculiar drum pattern. John never mentioned this help, but did however speak favourably of Paul's playing on Hammond organ.

John started 'Come Together' after meeting Timothy Leary in April 1969 in Canada. Leary wanted John to write a campaign song for his bid to become governor of California and suggested the title 'Come Together', which was to be his campaign slogan. John tried to meet Leary's request, but evidently lost interest and ended up writing something quite different. The chorus puns Leary's slogan with that of simultaneous orgasm, a reflection no doubt on John's then highly physical relationship with Yoko Ono. The verses meanwhile are a mix of gobbledegook and drug references.

'Come Together' sets an unusual parallel with John's later solo recording of 'Cold Turkey' in September 1969. Between the two songs John had forced himself through the painful withdrawal from heroin addiction. The beautiful guitar notes that conclude 'Come Together', with accompanying moans, contrast the ugly guitar and terrifying screeches that conclude 'Cold Turkey'. As such they make an unusual pairing, as firstly the evocation of a heroin high and secondly a warning of the horrors of withdrawal from the drug.

'SOMETHING'
(Harrison)

The song title 'Something' sounds like the tongue-tied descriptions George would temporarily give to his early recordings, when he had not settled on a chorus or key phrase. In contrast to those attempts at expressing himself, 'Something' triumphs in its acceptance of the inarticulacy of explaining love in words. George here, inadvertently perhaps, hit upon a sentiment that found recognition all around the world, making it a song that rivals Lennon/McCartney's very best songs for popularity. George's lyrical breakthrough equally seems to have inspired its joyous and serene melody.

George's lyrics about his wife Patti also succeed in the way the verses are personal but the middle eight switches attention directly to the listener. This change of mood and 'voice' is similar to the way John contributed to Paul's songs, e.g. 'We Can Work It Out' and 'Getting Better'. In the hands of such expressive singers as Shirley Bassey and Frank Sinatra this middle eight is open to a great range of interpretation, explaining its popularity as a cover version. George's vocal, though, provides the truest version, avoiding histrionics in favour of vulnerability.

If George had learnt from John in the lyrics, he appears to have learnt too from Paul in the way the tune flows flawlessly between verse, chorus and middle eight. Written in late 1968, George delayed recording 'Something' as, like Paul with 'Yesterday', he was unsure if the melody was taken subconsciously from another tune. (The lyrics were though; George took James Taylor's 1968 song title 'Something In The Way She Moves' as the basis for his lyrics.) Likewise, George too offered it to another singer (Joe Cocker) before the Beatles eventually started recording their version in April 1969. Joe Cocker was unusually slow to record it and released it only on album, shortly before *Abbey Road* 's release.

Recorded over several sessions from April to August '69, this is the most complex of all *Abbey Road* productions. Particularly, Paul's bass works in intricate (some would say fussy) counterpoint to the vocal melody. The only step too far is in the overdub of strings, whose only purpose is to soften the sound, a style the Beatles had previously avoided.

'MAXWELL'S SILVER HAMMER'
(McCartney)

'Maxwell's Silver Hammer' is one of Paul's grandest follies and highlights the often inexplicable side to his songwriting, that of regressing rather than developing over the years. The bewilderment this has caused Beatles fans ever since was echoed first here by John and George's exasperation at the attention to detail Paul put into 'Maxwell's Silver Hammer'. Done in the busked, casual style of *The White Album*, during which it was first created, it might have been more acceptable. The glossy, perfect production of *Abbey Road* only makes its lyrical poor taste and corny melody glaringly obvious. This was not merely a lapse of good taste though, for Paul's persistence in recording a song that John openly hated must in part be attributable to the eventual decision of John to leave the band in September 1969. John claimed that Paul made the Beatles record it a 'hundred million times' in an effort to make it good enough to be released as a single. Records show that the song was rehearsed on four days of the *Let It Be* project and that recordings of it took place over another four days in the summer of 1969.

'OH DARLING'
(McCartney)

'Oh Darling' never quite convinces, as Paul does not make it clear whether the lyrics are a joke or sincere. The music, with its overdriven guitar sound and a structure that owes much to Sam Cooke's 'Bring It On Home To Me', puts it in the same bracket as the Beatles' other ironic rock 'n' roll spoofs 'Lady Madonna' and 'Happiness is a Warm Gun'. The great attention Paul spent on the vocal suggests that he took it more seriously. He came into the studio on five separate days to capture a suitably raw and impassioned vocal, yet in its strain and exertion this again only suggests a spoof on early rock 'n' roll. There was no such confusion for the many glam rock bands of the early 1970s, who recorded much that was similar to 'Oh Darling' (also 10cc's 'Donna'), but who clearly played it for laughs.

'OCTOPUS'S GARDEN'
(Starkey/Harrison)

During a tense moment in the making of *The White Album*, Ringo stormed out on the Beatles and flew off to Sardinia. Contemplating his actions on a sea cruise, he was told of the lives of octopuses and how they built 'gardens' at the bottom of the sea. This struck a chord with Ringo, who later half-jokingly said that this was exactly where he felt like being at the time. As such he began the song, presumably at this stage, for use in a solo career. The fact that he refers in the lyrics to an octopus's garden as somewhere one could be free from being ordered about might be seen as a reference to the reason for Ringo's split from the Beatles – Paul's overbearing instructions on how to play drums.

Rehearsals recorded during the *Let It Be* project in January 1969 show that Ringo had initially only written one verse and sought George's help to complete it. As George later co-wrote and produced many of Ringo's solo records, it seems probable that he should have been afforded a writing credit here too. Sadly this is one of *Abbey Road's* worst productions, the lightweight charm of the song being lost under a sea of overdubbing and compressed sound.

'I WANT YOU (SHE'S SO HEAVY)'
(Lennon)

This may be the Beatles' most derivative track. The multi-tracked guitar arpeggio style is copied from Cream's single 'Badge', released in January 1969, and the riff itself is reminiscent of the one used on 'Because', which John admitted came from Beethoven's 'Moonlight Sonata'. Paul's bass riff owes much to Led Zeppelin's 'Dazed and Confused' from their debut album, released again in January 1969. Led Zeppelin's debut caused shockwaves on its release for its new heavy metal style, which John's title in parenthesis, '(She's So Heavy)', seems to pun. A song of two distinct segments, the 'I Want You' vocal refrain is an almost direct lift in melody and arrangement from Mel Torme's 1962 US hit and lounge music classic 'Comin' Home Baby'. John's lyrics were addressed, naturally, to Yoko Ono.

When the basic track was recorded in February '69, Billy Preston was still working with the Beatles and he makes a classy contribution on organ. Both John and George were happy to have Billy Preston in the group, but his role on keyboards encroached on what was normally Paul's role within the group. Though never formally stated, it was Paul's coolness for Preston's presence that prevented him staying on.

'HERE COMES THE SUN'
(Harrison)

As on 'Something', here George tuned into the same seam of enlightenment that had eluded him for so long. Like 'Dear Prudence', his joy at the simpler pleasures in life are more profound than any of his previous 'message' songs. Much of the credit for the unlocking of George's hidden talents must have come from the calming, restorative powers of meditation. Inspiration for the song came to George after he absconded from a series of Beatles business meetings for a day. In the same way that Paul's 'Getting Better' had originated two years before, George, taking time out in a garden and enjoying one of the first warm days of spring, thought of both the tune and melody. Similarly, his reference to a long, dark and lonely winter in the lyrics would seem to refer to much more than the weather. George had suffered a series of set-backs over the months prior to writing 'Here Comes The Sun'. He had walked out of the Beatles temporarily in January, been hospitalised for eight days with tonsillitis in February and arrested for possession of marijuana in March. On 31 March George had escaped a prison sentence for possession of marijuana, suggesting early April as the time he felt positive enough to write the lyrics for this song. Musically George had also turned a new leaf; in December 1968 he had given up his rigid daily routine of practising sitar and his playing on guitar here shows a joy long missing from his playing.

'BECAUSE'
(Lennon)

An unusually gimmicky song from John. The melody was based around the notes from Beethoven's 'Moonlight Sonata', while the cheap and nasty-sounding moog synthesiser does nothing to add to the harmony vocals from John, George and Paul, which George described as the most complex they had ever done. These vocals too are not left alone, being given a syrupy triple-tracked sound. While the Beatles nearly always recorded the definitive versions of their own songs, the simple sound of the instrumental version recorded by Vanessa Mae on George Martin's *In My Life* compilation makes in many ways for a preferable version.

Recorded several weeks after the first moon landing in July 1969, it seems probable that John, always the most news-conscious Beatle, wrote the line here about the shape of the earth inspired by the pictures of our planet transmitted by Apollo 9. The lyrics from John are otherwise notable for being neither political nor emotionally challenging, or about Yoko.

Barring overdubs, this was the last complete Beatles song ever recorded, on 1 August 1969.

'THE MEDLEY'
B-side to Abbey Road

Paul's ambitious medley is typical of his constant efforts to take the Beatles in new and uncharted directions, even while the group was falling apart around him. Like most of his big projects since *Sgt. Pepper*, he and George Martin ended up doing most of the work, largely failing to get John and George as enthused about it as he was.

Paul's inspiration would appear to have come from two sources. The bringing together of half-finished songs into one continuous piece of music had been first tried by the Beatles on 'Happiness Is A Warm Gun'. Unlike John's song collage, though, Paul's medley does have a theme of sorts, one that bares close resemblance to The Who's 1966 'mini opera' *A Quick One While He's Away*. The themes of strife, security and reconciliation in Pete Townsend's songs 'Ivor The Engine Driver', 'Soon Be Home' and 'You Are Forgiven' are repeated in the same order here on 'You Never Give Me Your Money', 'Golden Slumbers' and 'The End'. The link becomes even more compelling in the knowledge that Paul was a big fan of The Who and would have heard John playing snatches of 'A Quick One While He's Away' during the *Let It Be* rehearsals.

While one of the Beatles' most popular pieces of music, John was quick to dismiss the medley as 'junk', an opinion no doubt influenced by the weakness of the three songs he contributed to it. It seems likely too that he made this lack of enthusiasm known during its recording. With this in mind it seems illogical that Paul should have asked him to contribute, when he already had the main themes of the medley in place. Why not, for instance, ask George, who had produced two such amazing songs already for the album, to contribute new material to the medley? The answer seems likely that Paul, in the face of John's apathy to the Beatles in 1969, was as ever seeking to keep their dying partnership alive.

'YOU NEVER GIVE ME YOUR MONEY'
(McCartney)

Paul's best song on the album, like 'Let It Be' and 'The Long And Winding Road' before it, tells of the problems that beset the Beatles in their final year. The anguish these problems caused Paul similarly inspired its touching melody and performance. Its structure incorporates three other sections, one about being a hard-up student, one about travelling and a children's rhyme about going to heaven. These serve as an overture for Paul's mini-opera, previewing its main themes of strife, homesickness and reconciliation.

The first segment is Paul's lament for the business problems that beset the Beatles in the spring of 1969, the lyrics directly addressing new Beatles business manager Allen Klein. The middle two sections read like a description of Paul's relationship with Linda. The latter section seems another link to The Who's mini-opera, the religious theme matching the angelic tone of 'You Are Forgiven'. This section was sung by John, which suggests it was his idea.

The main guitar riff played by George copies the gorgeous sound first used on 'Badge', the recent single by Cream. George had played rhythm guitar on that single and ironically may have suggested the effect to Eric Clapton in the first place. The chiming effect was achieved by putting George's Gibson Les Paul through a Leslie amp, which rotates the sound of the guitar.

'SUN KING'/'MEAN MR MUSTARD' (Both Lennon)
(Recorded as one performance)

These two song doodles that John had lying around barely deserved to be included in Paul's medley. Only the glossy eight-track production of *Abbey Road* make them presentable, 'Sun King' especially benefiting from a convincing stylisation of Fleetwood Mac's 'Albatross', a massive chart hit in early 1969. The lyrics on this segment are a curious and nonsensical mix of Portuguese, Italian and Spanish.

'Mean Mr Mustard', written in India, was so poor it was rejected from both *The White Album* and *Let It Be.* John based the lyrics on the story of a tight-fisted man he read about in a tabloid newspaper. When it was rehearsed during the *Let It Be* sessions, the lyrics called Mr Mustard's sister Shirley, but this was changed to Pam to fit into the next track.

'POLYTHENE PAM' (Lennon)/'SHE CAME IN THROUGH THE BATHROOM WINDOW' (McCartney)
Recorded as one performance

'Polythene Pam' was another cast-off written in India, no doubt as light relief for John and the other students at the Maharishi's meditation camp. A typically coy tale of both hidden and open sexual connotations, the lyrics tell of a woman John once slept with who wore plastic bags as a sexual fetish. The character was also a combined description, in John's words, of a 'mythical Liverpool scrubber' and so is sung in an exaggerated Liverpool accent. The phrase 'killer diller' comes from Bo Diddley's song 'The Story Of Bo Diddley' from 1959, where it is used as a term of sexual prowess.

'She Came In Through The Bathroom Window' is another improbable but true tale of a girl fan who broke into Paul's house in St John's Wood, London and stole some of his family photos. The mention of a job in the police is a reference to Paul's detective work in getting the girls outside his house to get back his photos.

'GOLDEN SLUMBERS'/'CARRY THAT WEIGHT'(McCartney/Dekker)
Recorded as one performance

'Golden Slumbers' introduces the themes of home, rest and safety after the themes of strife in the opening songs. Returning home was a common theme in Paul's songs in this period, notably used on 'Two Of Us' and 'The Long And Winding Road'. After these opening lines about returning home, the lyrics switch directly to the words of a 400-year-old English song by Thomas Dekker, also called 'Golden Slumbers'. Paul found the words in a book at his father's home.

'Carry That Weight' with its group chorus announces the grand ending, before reviewing 'You Never Give Me Your Money' which shares the same lyrical themes here of the Beatles' business problems and the burdens they placed upon Paul.

'THE END'
(McCartney)

'The End' is an acknowledgement of the late-'60s trend for rock musicians to show off their musical virtuosity in long and often boring instrumental passages. To their credit and good taste the Beatles show how this should be done, providing only teasing snippets of each band member in the spotlight. Ringo, who obviously had a horror of such solos, at first point blank refused to play until he was persuaded that nothing overblown was required of him. His solo should be the standard for all rock drummers, being both brief and logical to the song in question. It builds up an entrance to the exciting duel of guitar solos from Paul, George and John in turn, with George arguably coming out best.

The only disappointment here is that after its eloquent and sincere start Paul finishes the medley with the empty and questionable comment that we get as much love as we give.

'HER MAJESTY'
(McCartney)

A 23-second ditty that was originally placed between 'Mean Mr Mustard' and 'Polythene Pam'. Paul, seeing it as surplus to requirements, had it edited from the final mix, but engineer John Kurlander rather than throw it out stuck it on the run-out tape for the album's final mix where it stayed. Paul wrote the song shortly after seeing the very first TV documentary about the British royal family that allowed cameras into their private lives.

'YOU KNOW MY NAME (LOOK UP THE NUMBER)'
(Lennon/McCartney) B-side to 'Let It Be', released 6 March 1970

During the Beatles' experimental phase from June–July 1967, John saw the phrase 'You know my name look up the number' written on the telephone directory at Paul's house and wrote a song consisting of just those words. Its hotchpotch of camp musical styles – parts of which owe something to Nina Simone's 'My Baby Just Cares For Me' from 1958 – is similar to that of the Bonzo Dog Doo Dah Band who were then a popular club act and were signed to the Beatles' label Parlophone. The off-key saxophone as played here by Brian Jones of the Rolling Stones was also typical of the Bonzo's style.

This daft, throwaway performance would seem in part to be dictated by the mood in which the Beatles were then completing songs for inclusion on the *Yellow Submarine* film. Rejected by the film's producers, the track remained untouched until April 1969 when John and Paul overdubbed new vocals and sound effects. While untypical of the Beatles' musical output, the song is a good indication of the Beatles' love of humour, which in itself was often hidden beneath the surface of many of their songs.

14. Anthology 1 and 2

ANTHOLOGY 1
Disc 1 released December 1995

'FREE AS A BIRD'
(Lennon/McCartney/Harrison/Starkey) Single released
4 December 1995

'Free As A Bird' is a few verses of a song John recorded at home in New York some time in 1977. At the time of his death, this promising sketch remained unfinished and survived only on a home tape recording. It is unlikely that it would have stayed that way for long, as John often returned to ideas he had developed years before, so the decision of Paul, George and Ringo to 'complete' the song at Yoko Ono's behest seems reasonable. However all the technology available in 1995 could not rescue the poor quality of the original recording. Unlike Buddy Holly's posthumously reworked home recordings, 'Wishin', Hopin', Cryin'' and 'Peggy Sue Got Married', the joins between old and new recordings here are painfully obvious. George's neat slide guitar is of merit, but the questionable lyrics, added to the middle eight, and Jeff Lyne's horrendous ELO-like drum sound, sit queasily with John's original, light but somewhat touching refrain.

While a hit in many countries when it was released, this single has already aged badly and lost any novelty value it had in its first few weeks of release, and indeed now it sits uneasily on the *Anthology* compilation.

Beatles
For Sale

'THAT'LL BE THE DAY' (Allison/Holly/Petty)/'IN SPITE OF ALL THE DANGER' (McCartney)

While a shaky recording of the Quarrymen, John's first group, playing live in 1957 apparently exists, these are the best early recordings available. Featuring John, Paul and George on guitars, occasional member Duff Lowe on piano (though barely audible) and soon to be departing drummer Colin Hanton, they were recorded on a portable tape recorder rigged up in a house in Liverpool, where for a small fee they had the excitement of transferring one of their performances onto disc.

This line-up existed in 1958–59, not because the public demanded it but simply because John, Paul and George loved what they were doing. At some point in those years their live bookings dried up altogether; in part this was due to the decline in the skiffle boom in the UK, but it also must have been in part a result of the shaky musicianship evident on these recordings.

The Quarrymen, though, obviously spent some time rehearsing 'That'll Be The Day' and John's lead vocal shows promise, yet ultimately the recording must have been a disappointment for its amateurish performance and sound. Unlike their later, usually judicious choice of cover versions, the nascent Beatles here chose a number they were incapable of improving on. The song appears to have been chosen simply because they wanted to hear how close they could get to sounding like the genuine rock 'n' roll group they are so obviously struggling to be.

John's authoritative, clear voice is again the saving grace on 'In Spite Of All The Danger', his vocal lending an unmerited professionalism to Paul's words. That John took lead vocals on Paul's lyrically dire and somewhat camp piece of juvenilia is revealing of their early partnership, Paul seemingly being recruited to back up John's weak musical skills, not for his singing.

George was credited here on the original label as co-writer for 'In Spite Of All The Danger', though Paul has subsequently claimed that this was simply for writing the guitar solo. Presumably neither of them knew in 1958 that such solos did not usually get a credit.

Beatles
For Sale

'HALLELUJAH I LOVE HER SO' (Ray Charles)/'YOU'LL BE MINE' (McCartney/Lennon)/'CAYENNE' (McCartney)

Early 1960 was one of the bleakest times for the Beatles; still without regular live gigs, they also lacked a drummer. Yet what is revealing from this home recording is the growth in quality of the Beatles sound from their 1958 recordings. Beneath the horribly distorted guitars on 'Hallelujah I Love Her So', Paul's vocals do a very passable impersonation of Eddie Cochran's Oklahoma drawl. The joke ditty 'You'll Be Mine' is treated as a frivolous diversion from the business of attempting note-perfect impersonations of US rock 'n' roll records and yet as good as the humour of their later recordings. 'Cayenne', a modest and largely tuneless guitar workout, displays Paul's fascination with Latin acoustic guitar styles that he would pursue throughout the Beatles' recording career. This latter recording is notable for one of the rare recordings of Stuart Sutcliffe's basic and somewhat heavy-handed bass playing.

'MY BONNIE' (Traditional arranged by Tony Sheridan) single released in Germany in August 1961/'AIN'T SHE SWEET' (Ager/Yellen)/'CRY FOR A SHADOW' (Harrison) B-side to 'My Bonnie'

The Beatles, on their second jaunt to Hamburg from May–August 1961, regularly backed the popular Tony Sheridan and as such were spotted by German producer Bert Kaempfert. Sheridan and the Beatles were invited by him to record a number of songs, a few of which were released in Germany on the Polydor record label. To the Beatles' disappointment Kaempfert had total control over which songs were chosen – the Beatles in particular disliked 'My Bonnie', John later calling it 'terrible'.

The sheer awfulness of 'My Bonnie' might logically be put down to the Beatles' early inexperience, yet this mismatch of sea shanty with rock 'n' roll is actually intended as a joke by Tony Sheridan on the large number of sailors who visited the rock clubs of Hamburg requesting the song.

Kaempfert allowed the Beatles two of their own recordings without Sheridan. 'Ain't She Sweet' was a cover of a song recorded by Gene Vincent in 1957. Vincent gave the song a slow, languorous tone, but the German audiences and Kaempfert demanded a more raucous style. This changes the lyrics' tone, creating a leering, menacing air at odds with Vincent's recording. Such changes of tone and pace are typical of nearly all cover versions that John sang with the Beatles.

'Cry For A Shadow' appeared as the B-side to 'My Bonnie' and makes a good pairing as another spoof recording. George created it as an attempt to fool fellow Liverpudlian band Rory Storm and The Hurricans (who were playing with the Beatles in Hamburg at the same time that the instrumental was in fact a cover of the latest Shadows record. The Shadows were at the time enjoying a run of massive chart success in the UK, which must have been a source of some bemusement to the Beatles. While professional and accomplished they lacked the Beatles' rock 'n' roll earthiness and were essentially peddling watered-down rock 'n' roll. While the Beatles admired the Shadows' first hit 'Apache' enough to play it live, their next records such as 'Man Of Mystery' and 'FBI' had a contrived feel that was parodied here.

'SEARCHIN'' (Leiber/Stoller)/**'THREE COOL CATS'** (Leiber/Stoller)/**'THE SHEIK OF ARABY'** (Smith/Wheeler/Snyder)

The Beatles' early fan and friend Klaus Voormann recalled that the first time he saw them play in Hamburg, it was George's voice that excited him the most. The raw if untutored attack of his voice stood out from the Beatles' audition for the Decca record label on New Year's Day in 1962. Except for the rousing 'Searchin'', John and Paul it would seem were largely suffering from the nerves of the occasion.

Both 'Searchin'' and 'Three Cool Cats' were songs covered from the Coasters, a five-man vocal group who specialised in humorous songs using a wide range of vocal styles. The Beatles covered at least six of their songs live.

'The Sheik Of Araby' was a cover of a recording by cockney cabaret-style rocker Joe Brown from 1961. George sang five other Joe Brown songs live; all of them, with the exception of 'A Picture Of You', were joke songs including the dire 'I'm Henry VIII I Am'.

'LIKE DREAMERS DO' (McCartney/Lennon)/**'HELLO LITTLE GIRL'** (Lennon/McCartney)

Between 1962, when these were recorded at the Decca auditions and 1958, very little rock 'n' roll had made the US or UK charts. In its place were insipid, soulless ballads sung by pretty, neatly packaged singers – '60s pop commentator Nik Cohn went as far as to claim 1960 as the worst ever year for pop music. In such an environment it is easy to see why the Beatles believed the contrived, limp insincerity of 'Like Dreamers Do' would impress record companies. Paul, who wrote most of it as far back as 1958, said it was the first song of their own that they played live. From the same era, and only marginally better, was 'Hello Little Girl', a song written by John apparently after he found that Paul had written the latter song. Feeling his authority challenged by this coup, he pretended to have already written a song and promptly made up most of 'Hello Little Girl' on the spot. Some sources trace both songs back to 1957; whether they were actually written this early is open to question, but undoubtedly their structure was worked on between then and 1962.

'BESAME MUCHO'
(Velasquez)

Paul learnt 'Besame Mucho' from the Coasters' 1960 cover version, but avoids their high-camp mix of baritone lead vocals with falsetto backing vocals to sing the song straight. The performance here from the 6 June 1962 recording test at Abbey Road shows that he relished performing the song, something that was again evident when he was filmed revisiting it in the *Let It Be* film. Paul later said he was fascinated by the chord changes in the song, which while holding the same key switches from a minor chord in the verse to a major chord in the chorus. He would later employ the same chord changes for 'Things We Said Today'.

'Love Me Do' (see entry in chapter one)
'How Do You Do It' (see entry in chapter one)

'PLEASE PLEASE ME'
(Lennon/McCartney)

The *Anthology* sleeve notes claim this as the long-lost 11 September version of 'Please Please Me', which George Martin instructed the Beatles to rearrange at a faster tempo. This surely cannot be the case, as the speed with which it is played matches that of the final version recorded on 26 November. John was also recorded saying in February 1963 that the lyrics had been changed between both recording dates – the lyrics on this performance are identical to the final version. Logically then this performance suggests itself as an early take from the November recording session.

'ONE AFTER 909'
(Lennon/McCartney)

For sentimental reasons the Beatles remained inordinately fond of this song, of little merit, which they had written as far back as 1957–58. The act of giving it a slick new arrangement and recording it in 1963 was perhaps a way of validating their early, struggling songwriting efforts. None of the slick guitar passages that George inserts in the song, though, can disguise that this is an embarrassing piece of juvenilia and no doubt on hearing the tape played back to them, they decided against releasing it (presumably as the B-side to 'From Me To You'). Even then the Beatles did not give up on the song, John apparently offering it to the Rolling Stones in September 1963, at the meeting where they also offered the more appetising 'I Wanna Be Your Man'.

'LEND ME YOUR COMB'
(Twomey/Wise/Weisman)

One of the many live performances the Beatles recorded for BBC radio between 1962–1965, this is a straightforward cover of a Carl Perkins song recorded on 2 July 1963. Like most of their Perkins covers, this lacks any of the authority or earthiness of the original.

'I'LL GET YOU'
(Lennon/McCartney)

The Beatles' live recordings from 1963–66 are largely a dead loss, owing to either poor performances, poor sound quality or the screams of the audience. What makes this performance of 'I'll Get You' for a live TV performance at the London Palladium on 13 October 1963 remarkable is that not only is the sound clear, but it reveals a much more soulful rendition than the one they gave at the original, rushed *Abbey Road* recording session from 1 July.

'I SAW HER STANDING THERE' (McCartney/Lennon)/
'FROM ME TO YOU' (McCartney/Lennon)/'MONEY'(That's
What I Want) (Bradford-Gordy)/'YOU REALLY GOT A HOLD
ON ME'(Robinson)/'ROLL OVER BEETHOVEN' (Berry)

These recordings in Sweden from October 1963 are yet more rare, but
good quality live performances. They serve to show, if nothing else, that
the sound they were recording on disc in 1963 was essentially the same
as they were playing live.

DISC 2
'SHE LOVES YOU' (McCartney/Lennon)/'TILL THERE WAS
YOU' (Wilson)/'TWIST AND SHOUT' (Medley/Russell)

Until the Beatles performed on the Ed Sullivan show in February 1964,
these three immaculate performances counted as the Beatles' most
important. Recorded at the Prince of Wales theatre, close to Leicester
Square in London, for an audience including the Queen Mother and
shown to the British public on TV, the high profile of the occasion was
not lost on the Beatles. In contrast to some of their other live
performances they sound here to be trying extra hard, especially on 'She
Loves You'. The effort was worthwhile as the show, recorded on 4
November 1963, imprinted the Beatles fully on the national
consciousness of the UK for the first time.

'THIS BOY' (Lennon/McCartney)/'I WANT TO HOLD YOUR
HAND' (Lennon/McCartney)

These live recordings, made for a UK TV show in December 1963, are
only remarkable for their quality and lack of screaming and that the
version of 'I Want To Hold Your Hand' features slightly different lyrics
to the studio version.

'CAN'T BUY ME LOVE'
(McCartney/Lennon)

An early recording of 'Can't Buy Me Love' in Paris, January 1964, this
features a knock-out vocal from Paul but some rather duff harmonies
from John and George. The harmonies were dropped, presumably due to
the strength of Paul's singing here.

'ALL MY LOVING'
(McCartney/Lennon)

The enormity of appearing on US television and being in the land that created rock 'n' roll appeared to catch up with the Beatles here, as this performance on 9 February 1964 has none of the confidence of their later UK live shows.

'YOU CAN'T DO THAT' (Lennon/McCartney)/'AND I LOVE HER' (McCartney/Lennon)

This early take of 'You Can't Do That' reveals that its arrangement only needed some tightening up over the day before it was ready. Within the bounds of the Beatles' three-guitar, drums line-up this would have been straightforward. However, the growing ambitions of Paul's songs required more work. This early take of 'And I Love Her' reveals how it started out as a conventional Beatles arrangement – even if Paul had first envisaged this song as lacking drums, his loyalty was to the group and he must have felt bound to try it like this first. It seems likely that once this try-out had proved too heavy handed, George Martin's prompting would have given Paul the go ahead to try the arrangement he had probably envisaged all along.

'A HARD DAY'S NIGHT'
(Lennon/McCartney)

This early run-through of 'A Hard Day's Night' reveals Paul singing a slightly different lyric to the one that was finally recorded. The changes were not surprising in that John had only written the song the night before.

'I WANNA BE YOUR MAN' (Lennon/McCartney)/'LONG TALL SALLY' (Johnson/Penniman/Blackwell)/'BOYS' (Dixon/Farrell)/'SHOUT' (Isley/Isley/Isley)

While the Beatles retained a respect for their audiences, once the UK had been won over they rarely broke sweat to impress them again. These somewhat sloppy performances from a UK TV show in April 1964 are only notable for the recording of the Isley Brother's 'Shout', a song whose arrangement the Beatles were enormously influenced by. Here the Beatles all take lead vocals, starting off with Paul, followed by John, George and Ringo.

'I'LL BE BACK'
(Lennon/McCartney)

The first take here reveals an attempt to record 'I'll Be Back' in 3/4 waltz time. The problems this caused are evident in John's vocal and the next take shows a reversion to the regular 4/4 beat used on the final recording. John and Paul, though, overcame their problems with this time signature on the next album with 'Baby's In Black'.

'YOU KNOW WHAT TO DO' (Harrison)/'NO REPLY'
(Lennon/McCartney)

These two songs were demoed at the end of the recording for the *Hard Day's Night* sessions on 3 June 1964, without Ringo after he had fallen ill that morning. The presence of drums and only one six-string guitar suggests that George is playing the rudimentary beat here, perhaps explaining the hilarity in John's voice.

While 'No Reply' emerged much improved when recorded in September, George's song was not returned to. One can only speculate that during the gruelling world tour that followed over the summer of 1964, George did not find the time or inclination to return to his song. Furthermore, shut out of the Lennon/McCartney songwriting partnership he lacked anyone to encourage him. Alternatively George may not have had the stomach to continue writing the commercial pop that John and Paul were churning out.

'MR MOONLIGHT' (Johnson)/'LEAVE MY KITTEN ALONE' (John/Turner/McDougall)

'Leave My Kitten Alone' is generally accepted as the best-ever Beatles out-take. Its omission today looks surprising considering some of the lacklustre cover versions on *Beatles For Sale*, particularly the early take of 'Mr Moonlight', revealed here, which was recorded on the same day in August 1964. What little is known about the reasons behind its exclusion was that John, notoriously shy of his own voice, was unhappy with his vocal performance.

'Leave My Kitten Alone' was originally recorded by Johnny Preston in

1960. His version has the same pace as the Beatles, but like Preston's other big hit, 'Running Bear', the arrangement was done for laughs and his voice lacks the menace that John brings to the song. A notable omission from the Beatles arrangement are the female backing vocals on Preston's record, which sing 'miaow' throughout.

'NO REPLY'
(Lennon/McCartney)

An early take of 'No Reply' which in part reveals more of the Latin influences used in its arrangement.

'EIGHT DAYS A WEEK'
(McCartney/Lennon)

The experimentation Paul wanted on this track required more time than the Beatles could afford and the tension this caused is evident in the barely polite exchanges recorded here between John and Paul.

'KANSAS CITY'/'HEY, HEY, HEY, HEY'
(Leiber/Stoller/Penniman)

The Beatles made two attempts at this on the 18 October 1964, the first version appearing on *Beatles For Sale*. That this second version was recorded shows the Beatles recognised that the first could be improved upon. This version though also lacks conviction and with little time to record, the Beatles moved on to another track.

ANTHOLOGY 2
Album released March 1996

'REAL LOVE'
(Lennon/McCartney/Harrison/Starr) Single released 4 March 1996

Although the second single, released to promote the *Anthology* series, 'Real Love' is stronger. Unlike 'Free As A Bird', John had given it a fully worked out verse/chorus structure and coda in 1979 and here by contrast the musical backing that Paul, George and Ringo provide actually sounds like they are doing John a favour. Lyrically, John's musing on life is echoed by many of the lines from 'Beautiful Boy', released in 1980.

'YES IT IS' (Lennon/McCartney)/'I'M DOWN'
(McCartney/Lennon)/'YOU'VE GOT TO HIDE YOUR LOVE
AWAY' (Lennon/McCartney)/'IF YOU'VE GOT TROUBLE'
(Lennon/McCartney)/'THAT MEANS A LOT'
(McCartney)/'YESTERDAY' (McCartney)/'IT'S ONLY
LOVE' (Lennon/McCartney)
Recorded February and June 1965

These out-takes and first run-throughs of songs destined for the *Help!* album or B-sides in early 1965 reveal the growing disdain which the Beatles held for the cliche ridden tin pan alley lyrics they were still churning out for their teen girl fans. Ringo sounds thoroughly ill at ease with the lyrics Paul had crafted for him on 'If You've Got Trouble'. Paul is openly mocking of his own lyrics on 'I'm Down' and bored on 'That Means A Lot', as John is likewise on 'Yes It Is' and 'It's Only Love'.

The very worst of these songs 'That Means A Lot' and 'If You've Got Trouble' were dropped from the *Help!* album in place of the cover versions 'Act Naturally' and 'Dizzy Miss Lizzie'. The inclusion of daft lyrics (e.g. 'She Loves You') had not troubled the Beatles before, but the presence of the serious and personal lyrics for 'You've Got To Hide Your Love Away' and 'Yesterday' had raised their standards, while the growing success of Dylan was making them think twice about what they sang.

These early run-throughs are also revealing of the development in the studio of the lyrics to 'You've Got To Hide Your Love Away' whose 'Hey' chant is absent and for Paul's ad hoc lyrics on 'I'm Down'.

'I FEEL FINE'(Lennon/McCartney)/'TICKET TO RIDE'
(Lennon/McCartney)/'YESTERDAY'
(Lennon/McCartney)/'HELP!' (Lennon/McCartney)

These performances from a TV show recorded in Blackpool, England in August 1965 are notable firstly for the low level of screaming and also for the quality of the performances. While on some of their live performances the Beatles barely tried to play in time or in tune owing to deafening screams, here knowing that they were being recorded for posterity, they turn in performances almost as good as on vinyl.

'EVERYBODY'S TRYING TO BE MY BABY'
(Perkins)

A spirited but otherwise unexceptional performance that came to be edited from the famous TV recording of the Beatles at the Shea baseball stadium in New York on 15 August 1965.

'NORWEGIAN WOOD (THIS BIRD HAS FLOWN)'
(Lennon/McCartney)/'I'M LOOKING THROUGH YOU'
(McCartney/Lennon)

These out-takes from *Rubber Soul* reveal the more experimental process each song now underwent, with the initial run-through often differing widely to the finished take. This early take of 'Norwegian Wood' is especially revealing in the plainness with which John sings of the girl he once 'had'; the final recording nine days later used both 'had' and 'met' on each of the vocal tracks.

'12-BAR ORIGINAL'
(Lennon/McCartney/Harrison/Starr)

All the Beatles albums between 1963–65 faced time constraints, particularly *Rubber Soul*. For the first time there was serious concern that a new Beatles album might not be completed in time for its planned pre-Christmas release date. In the rush to write songs, the idea of churning out a 12-bar blues jam in an hour or so for the album must have seemed a very tempting idea. The practice was common among the Beatles' British contemporaries, particularly the Rolling Stones whose B-sides 'Stoned' and 'Under Assistant West Coast Promotion Man' were little more than idle blues progressions with the barest of lyrics added. Unfortunately for such a simple idea the Beatles, while masters at complex melodies and harmonies, were ill-practised at blues jams. Their lack of experience is evident in the main riff here, which leans heavily on that used for Booker T & The MG's 'Green Onions' and the Rolling Stones' 'Stoned'. The Beatles, not used to coming second best to anyone else, wisely decided to scrap the results.

'TOMORROW NEVER KNOWS' (Lennon/McCartney)/'GOT TO GET YOU INTO MY LIFE' (McCartney/Lennon)/'AND YOUR BIRD CAN SING' (Lennon/McCartney)/'TAXMAN'

(Harrison/Lennon)/'ELEANOR RIGBY' (McCartney)/'I'M ONLY SLEEPING' (Lennon/McCartney)

The success of the experimental approach to each song taken on *Rubber Soul* emboldened the Beatles to push the limits of their imagination. While lyrically the approach favoured John, musically it was far more suited to Paul as the group's most accomplished musician. The ability of Paul to translate his ideas effectively to others was also to his advantage when working on such experimental arrangements with George Martin. This explains Paul's ability to completely turn around the early arrangement here for 'Got To Get You Into My Life' and the brilliance of George Martin's score from Paul's original piano arrangement on 'Eleanor Rigby'. As John later admitted, he never got the arrangement for 'Tomorrow Never Knows' that he wished for. The finished take did little to improve on this early run through of sea-sick sounding special effects. This was John's first song recorded for *Revolver* and that he resorted to the more traditional guitar, bass, drums format on his other songs shows one of his first major defeats in his competitive battles with Paul.

The early take here of 'Taxman' is remarkable only for the absence of the backing vocals referring to British politicians Edward Heath and Harold Wilson that were suggested by John in the studio.

'ROCK AND ROLL MUSIC' (Berry)/'SHE'S A WOMAN' (McCartney)

In the *Anthology* video series George claimed the Beatles arrived in Tokyo for their five concerts at the Budokan arena ill-rehearsed. To their surprise, in their first show on 30 June 1966 they found that the Japanese fans did not scream through their music in the way that other audiences did. To their embarrassment, this lack of noise exposed the Beatles' poor level of performance and they subsequently worked harder to make the next shows better. These recordings from the first show appear to refute George's story in their competency; either that or these recordings were not made on 30 June, or else were very judiciously chosen.

'STRAWBERRY FIELDS FOREVER' (Lennon)/'PENNY LANE' (McCartney/Lennon)/'A DAY IN THE LIFE' (Lennon/McCartney)/'GOOD MORNING GOOD MORNING' (Lennon)/'ONLY A NORTHERN SONG' (Harrison)/'BEING FOR THE BENEFIT OF MR KITE!'

(Lennon/McCartney)/'LUCY IN THE SKY WITH DIAMONDS' (Lennon/McCartney)/'WITHIN YOU WITHOUT YOU' (Harrison)/'SGT. PEPPER'S LONELY HEARTS CLUB BAND (REPRISE)' (Lennon)

These Sgt. Pepper's out-takes and demos reveal the long evolution that was now taking place on Beatles songs. John and Paul were still writing conventionally on acoustic guitar or piano, but from this point the songs would evolve into something that bore little resemblance to its first draft e.g. 'Strawberry Fields Forever'. This new process would often take several days studio time for each song. The format now was that after the first session a demo recording would be placed on to an acetate disc for the Beatles to listen to at home. They would then return days later with new ideas on developing the song.

For songs as ambitious as 'A Day In The Life', 'Penny Lane' and 'Strawberry Fields Forever' this was clearly worth the extra time and effort, though songs like 'Good Morning Good Morning' and 'Sgt. Pepper's Lonely Hearts Club Band (reprise)' clearly already work well as stripped-down rock songs and arguably did not require extra production. Some songs, like 'Lucy In The Sky With Diamonds' and 'Being For The Benefit Of Mr Kite!', appear to have been written especially so they could justify a large and intricate production. John soon fell out of love with this style of writing, while George already was clearly wary of it; his lyrics to 'Only A Northern Song' – which was rejected from the album – mock the new style of songs being recorded for *Sgt. Pepper* .

'YOU KNOW MY NAME (LOOK UP THE NUMBER)' (Lennon/McCartney)

The original full-length version of this comedy track contains a long ska section omitted from the final take and also more of the unusual saxophone contribution from Rolling Stone Brian Jones.

'I AM THE WALRUS' (Lennon)/'THE FOOL ON THE HILL' (McCartney)/'YOUR MOTHER SHOULD KNOW' (McCartney)/'HELLO GOODBYE' (McCartney/Lennon)

Tension over the increased role of George Martin in the creative process of *Sgt. Pepper* saw the Beatles rely on him less for the *Magical Mystery Tour* EP and single. This, coupled with an over-reliance on production, shows mixed results here. The early demo versions of 'The Fool On The Hill' and 'Your Mother Should Know' reveal that the finished versions made little improvement on them, in spite of all the time and production work spent. Only the semi-finished forms of 'I Am The Walrus' and 'Hello Goodbye' reveal themselves as having been improved by further orchestration.

'LADY MADONNA' (McCartney)/'ACROSS THE UNIVERSE' (Lennon)

'Across The Universe' is undoubtedly a more beautiful and worthy song than 'Lady Madonna' and John was understandably bitter that it was never recorded well enough for it to be released on single. These raw versions of the two songs, though, reveal why Paul won out. All the work 'Lady Madonna' requires on this early take is for an arrangement of saxophones to be added, where on 'Across The Universe' no satisfactory way of orchestrating the song had emerged. This early take of 'Across The Universe' is remarkable as the first that has been released showing the song at its proper speed.

ANTHOLOGY 3
Album released June 1988

'A BEGINNING'
(George Martin)

George Martin's lush orchestral score for the *Yellow Submarine* soundtrack impressed John Lennon enough for him to allow Martin to orchestrate 'Good Night' in a similar fashion. Ringo, presumably equally impressed, requested this orchestral addition to the intro of 'Don't Pass Me By'. At some point between recording in July 1968 and the album's final editing in October it was dropped from the song.

'HAPPINESS IS A WARM GUN'
(Lennon)

This is a home recording from May 1968 and a sketch of the disparate parts of John's song collage long before they were welded together after great effort by the Beatles in Abbey Road.

'HELTER SKELTER'
(McCartney)

This first studio draft of 'Helter Skelter' is revealing in its lightness of touch. Paul said long after its release that he had been inspired by a Pete Townsend quote in a paper, where he claimed to have recorded the 'loudest, dirtiest record ever'. There is little evidence of such noise on this early run-through, suggesting that Townsend's quote only came to mind some time between this recording from July and the song's eventual final recording in September.

'MEAN MR MUSTARD' (Lennon)/'POLYTHENE PAM' (Lennon)/'GLASS ONION' (Lennon/McCartney)/'JUNK' (McCartney)/'PIGGIES' (Harrison)/'HONEY PIE' (McCartney)

Legend has it that the Beatles all met up in May 1968 at George's house in Esher, Surrey to record these run-throughs of songs they were considering for their next album, though the double tracking that takes place on some of these tracks suggests that each Beatle actually recorded many of these songs at their own home first. Presumably at the meeting in May preferences were stated for songs, which would explain the absence of some here from *The White Album*. Otherwise these recordings are notable for their variance in lyrics and form to their finished versions; particularly some like 'Glass Onion' and 'Piggies' had yet to benefit from the added lyrical input of Paul and John respectively.

'DON'T PASS ME BY'
(Starr)

For all those who disliked the fiddle-playing on 'Don't Pass Me By', here is the finished version minus the offending overdub.

'OB-LA-DI, OB-LA-DA'
(McCartney)

John complained that Paul made the Beatles record this song endlessly in order to perfect it. His frustration becomes clear from this fresh but early performance with a lead vocal that is arguably stronger than the finished version.

'GOOD NIGHT'
(Lennon)

There was a long tradition of John and Paul getting Ringo to sing their weaker or more embarrassing material. John felt unable to sing this twee song, heard here in an even more syrupy run-through than the finished version.

'CRY BABY CRY'
(Lennon)

This early run-through of a song John eventually damned as 'rubbish' is revealing for some strong musical ideas on bass and drums that were oddly dropped from the final version.

'BLACKBIRD'
(McCartney)

A rather unremarkable alternate take of 'Blackbird'.

'SEXY SADIE'
(Lennon)

'Sexy Sadie' received some of the greatest work of any song on *The White Album*, with numerous remakes. This early run-through is notable for using guitar instead of piano as the main instrument.

'WHILE MY GUITAR GENTLY WEEPS'
(Harrison) Recorded 25 July 1968

There is a delicacy and beauty to this demo version of 'While My Guitar Gently Weeps' that was lost on the final version recorded for *The White Album*. While the final version has become known as a rock classic, this demo suggests that it was actually poorly realised.

'HEY JUDE'
(McCartney)

When this run-through of 'Hey Jude' was recorded four days before the final single version, the quality of the song was clear. All there was left to do was work out the embellishments and production tricks that would make this one of the Beatles' biggest classics.

'NOT GUILTY'
(Harrison)

The tension during the making of *The White Album* was not just that between John and Paul. George too came in for some bad feeling from John and Paul owing to his role as the prime mover in the Beatles' aborted trip to Rishikesh in India and the embarrassment it had caused them in the press. George's lyrics here are a defence of his role in the trip. How John and Paul felt about recording around 100 takes of this song remains unrecorded, but bad feeling about the lyrics seems the likeliest cause of it being dropped from the album. This is a loss as its intricate arrangement makes it far superior to either 'Savoy Truffle' or 'Piggies'.

'MOTHER NATURE'S SON'
(McCartney)

The sad, solitary mood of this early run-through of 'Mother Nature's Son' was little altered by the grand orchestration it finally received. This early arrangement reveals how it first sounded when written in India.

'GLASS ONION'
(Lennon/McCartney)

The disjointed sound effects and tapes used on this first run-through of 'Glass Onion' are closer to the humour of John's lyrics than the final version. George Martin's string arrangement, which replaced them, gives the song added harmonic interest, but makes its satire less obvious.

'ROCKY RACOON'
(McCartney)

This early take of 'Rocky Racoon' is in some ways preferable to the final take, in that it makes clear that Paul's song should not be taken very seriously.

'WHAT'S THE NEW MARY JANE'
(Lennon)

John remained inordinately fond of this humourless, nonsense dirge recorded in August 1968; as late as November 1969 he was trying to get it released on the Apple label as the B-side of a single with 'You Know My Name Look Up The Number'. Although little is recorded about John's opinion on this song, his intention, like that for recording a one-chord song ('Tomorrow Never Knows') or a tuneless song ('Revolution 9') would seem to be to challenge the safe, polished image the Beatles had constructed. That he sought to release this single after the release of *Abbey Road* – an album he accused of perpetuating the Beatles myth – only backs this up.

'STEP INSIDE LOVE'
(McCartney)

Where it had been common for John and Paul to write songs for other artists between 1963–65, this practice mostly stopped when they moved away from formula songs that could be easily interpreted by other artists. It was unusual then that Paul should write this piece of fluff as a signature tune for Cilla Black's first TV series. Paul probably felt a sense of loyalty to Cilla, owing to the fact that he had written her first hit 'Love of The Loved', and to Brian Epstein also, who as Cilla's manager, had in one of his last actions before he died in August 1967 secured her the TV series.

'I'M SO TIRED'
(Lennon)

This was one of the best performances on *The White Album*, this collection of early takes from 8 October 1968 show that the final version was no fluke.

'I WILL'
(McCartney)

Paul would appear to be still improving on this song, first written in India, at this run-through in September – the final take, recorded the same day, has slightly different lyrics. Discussions recorded from the *Let It Be* rehearsals suggest that John helped on these final changes, although the style of the song make it seem likely that it would be of little interest to him.

'WHY DON'T WE DO IT IN THE ROAD?'
(McCartney)

This run-though of a song first written in India still has the acoustic arrangement Paul had given it then. That Paul was able to fashion its final dynamic rock work-out without John or George's assistance hurt John especially.

'JULIA'
(Lennon)

John was not proficient at playing intricate guitar parts like the arpeggio used here and the difficulty he had is evident from this early outtake.

'I'VE GOT A FEELING' (McCartney/Lennon)/'SHE CAME IN THROUGH THE BATHROOM WINDOW' (McCartney)/'DIG A PONY' (Lennon)/'TWO OF US' (McCartney)/'FOR YOU BLUE' (Harrison)/'TEDDY BOY' (McCartney)/'RIP IT UP' (Blackwell/Marascalco)/'SHAKE, RATTLE AND ROLL' (Calhaun)/'BLUE SUEDE SHOES' (Perkins)/'THE LONG AND WINDING ROAD' (McCartney)/'OH! DARLING' (McCartney)/'ALL THINGS MUST PASS' (Harrison)/'MAILMAN BRING ME NO MORE BLUES' (Roberts, Katz, Clayton)/'GET BACK' (McCartney)/'LET IT BE' (McCartney)
Recorded January 1969

The Beatles' long, miserable *Get Back/Let It Be* sessions are some of the most bootlegged in all of rock history. The bad vibes, poor playing, poor sound (presumably made from second-generation tapes) and half-finished lyrics of these sessions have in the process done much to tarnish the reputation of those who sell such artefacts. One of the big surprises of the *Anthology* series is that it reveals there were in fact some decent out-takes available, suggesting that those compiling the series had access to tapes never made publicly available before. What is also revealing about these recordings is the number of songs recorded for the *Let It Be* sessions, but saved for *Abbey Road* or later solo albums.

'OLD BROWN SHOE'
(Harrison)

This early demo is revealing mainly for the clearness of George's vocal, which is all but buried on the finished version recorded a month later.

'OCTOPUS'S GARDEN' (Starr/Harrison)/'MAXWELL'S SILVER HAMMER' (McCartney)/'SOMETHING' (Harrison)/'COME TOGETHER' (Lennon/McCartney)/'BECAUSE' (Lennon)/'THE END' (McCartney)
Recorded February–August 1969

These *Abbey Road* out-takes uniformly reveal the early developmental stages of songs later perfected, perhaps the best being the first stripped-down run-through of 'Come Together', with its first draft lyrics.

'COME AND GET IT'
(McCartney)

This is arguably a better song than any Paul contributed to *Abbey Road*. Paul donated it to Apple label new signings Badfinger and produced the single that would reach the top ten in both USA and the UK. Notably, his main direction to Badfinger was to stick to the arrangement that he recorded in a demo version here. By the time it was recorded in July 1969 Paul may have faced difficulties persuading the Beatles to accept such a fait accompli.

'AIN'T SHE SWEET'
(Ager/Yellen)

What the Beatles were doing recording a trio of Gene Vincent covers in the middle of the *Abbey Road* sessions is not clear. Taking a break from recording 'Sun King', they ran through 'Ain't She Sweet', 'Who Slapped John' and 'Be-Bop A Lula'. Other than the chaotic *Let It Be* sessions, where jamming was part of the process of recording, such a recourse to playing cover versions for fun had never been a part of the Beatles' normal recording practice. The purpose of the songs was perhaps to warm up the Beatles with familiar material before they attempted more takes of 'Sun King'.

'I ME MINE'
(Harrison)

This is the original one-minute-and-a-half version of 'I Me Mine', recorded on 3 January 1970, before Phil Spector got his hands on it and unwisely increased its length by repeating some of its passages.

THE BEATLES LIVE AT THE BBC
Album released 30 November 1994

Out of the 55 performances released here that were recorded at BBC studios between 1963–65 only four ('I'll Be On My Way', 'Keep Your Hands Off My Baby', 'Some Other Guy' and 'Soldier Of Love') stand out as ones that would have been worthy of a formal Abbey Road recording.

To be fair to the Beatles, their BBC radio shows were at the time made in the knowledge that they would only ever be heard once. It seems likely that the happy-go-lucky attitude evident on the dialogue interspersing the music here would have been different had they known that these performances would be officially released on record or CD.

The strength of 'Keep Your Hands Off My Baby', 'Some Other Guy' and 'Soldier Of Love' are due to the classic vocal performances delivered by John. Unlike the disinterested vocal performances John gives on much of the rest of this compilation, the lyrics here seem to genuinely matter to him. Tellingly, both 'Keep Your Hands Off My Baby' and 'Some Other Guy' speak of insecurity and jealousy in love, themes that he would return to time and again with the Beatles and in his solo career, while 'Soldier Of Love' in a roundabout way can be seen to preface John's later campaign for peace. All three songs were at various stages in 1963 considered for release with the albums 'Please Please Me' or 'With the Beatles', and it would appear that only the competition from Paul, George and Ringo's songs kept these out.

The only other performance of real merit on this album is that of Paul's composition 'I'll Be On My Way'. While lyrically clichéd and awkward, the harmonies are typically Beatlesque and this deserved more than ending up as a Billy J. Kramer B-side in 1963. The song, as one of Paul's early songwriting efforts from 1961, appears to be an effort to lyrically continue the themes he first introduced on 'I'll Follow The Sun' the year before.

Elsewhere, the BBC performances are revealing of the Beatles' strengths and weaknesses. Notably there is a breadth of styles tackled by few pop artists before or since; both blues and country-based rock 'n' roll, old-fashioned ballads, mainstream pop and soul. Musically, though, the Beatles' ability to play all these styles adeptly is exposed. George is exemplary on the two-string finger-picking country-and-western-style guitar solo such as those on 'I Forgot To Remember To Forget', 'Lonesome Tears In My Eyes', 'I'll Be On My Way', 'That's All Right Mama' and 'The Honeymoon Song', though on many of the more straightforward rock 'n' roll tunes his solos vary between being competent and flaccid. Ringo too rarely asserts himself on the rock 'n' roll songs; his playing on 'Slow Down', 'Dizzy Miss Lizzie' and 'Rock And Roll Music' is gutless and he never provides the sharp attack these songs need. On many tracks the whole band is at fault, suggesting that exhaustion at their heavy schedule in 1963–64 was to blame. 'Carol' 'Johnny B. Goode', 'Rock And Roll Music', 'Dizzy Miss Lizzie', 'Oh My Soul' and 'Slow Down' all fall well below the Beatles' high standards.

The Beatles were clearly more comfortable on melodic songs requiring harmonies such as the Goffin/King-written 'Don't Ever Change' and 'Keep Your Hands Off My Baby'. Although obviously big fans of Chuck Berry (tackling seven of his songs), in hindsight we know that many other bands, particularly the Rolling Stones (whose first LP was released after six of these Chuck Berry numbers were recorded), were much better at interpreting Berry's songs. Particularly, the Stones brought a swagger and attack to 'Carol' never hinted at in the Beatles' performance here. Although fans of such full-on rock 'n' roll, the Beatles, it would seem, recognised their limitations in this field and concentrated from 1964 onwards on what they did best – melodic pop with a rock 'n' roll edge.

Appendix 1

THE CHRONOLOGICAL ORDER IN WHICH THE
BEATLES SONGS WERE WRITTEN

The following list is made up of known dates of songwriting, probability and guesswork. The date 'Michelle' was written is a good example of the guesswork involved: Paul wrote the tune for a party he attended which was thrown by one of John's art school teachers; John was at art school between 1957–60, yet the tune from which Paul took inspiration, 'Trambone' by Chet Atkins, was not released until 1959, which makes it the likeliest date. Later on where no known date exists I have listed the song in the weeks preceeding its recording. The Beatles, especially John, often spoke of only getting down to writing songs, once they knew a recording session was imminent.

From 1962 onwards the following list is representative of the output of songs the Beatles recorded and not of the many songs they gave away between 1963–65. The years before are not representative as many other songs were written in these years that the Beatles subsequently felt were not good enough to be recorded.

1957–58
'I Call Your Name', 'One After 909', 'Hello Little Girl'
'Love Me Do', 'What Goes On', 'When I'm 64', 'In Spite Of All The
    Danger', 'Like Dreamers Do'

1959
'Michelle' (tune only)

1960
'I'll Follow The Sun', 'You'll Be Mine', 'Cayenne'

Beatles
For Sale

1961

'Hold Me Tight', 'I'll Be On My Way', 'Cry For A Shadow'

1962

May: 'Ask Me Why', 'PS I Love You'
August: 'Please Please Me'
September: 'I Saw Her Standing There', 'I Wanna Be Your Man'
October–December: 'Do You Want To Know A Secret?', 'There's A Place'

1963

January: 'Misery'
February: 'Thank You Girl', 'From Me To You'
May: 'All My Loving'
June: 'It Won't Be Long', 'I'll Get You', 'She Loves You'
July–August: 'All I've Got To Do', 'Don't Bother Me', 'Not A Second Time'
September: 'Little Child'
October: 'I Want To Hold Your Hand', 'This Boy'

1964

January: 'Can't Buy Me Love'
February: 'You Can't Do That', 'If I Fell', 'I'll Cry Instead', 'And I Love Her', 'I Should Have Known Better', 'Tell Me Why', 'I'm Happy Just To Dance With You'
April: 'A Hard Day's Night', 'When I Get Home'
May: 'Things We Said Today', 'Any Time At All', 'No Reply', 'I'll Be Back', 'You Know What To Do'
June: 'Baby's In Black'
July: 'I'm A Loser'
August–September: 'What You're Doing', 'Every Little Thing', 'I Don't Want To Spoil The Party'
October: 'Eight Days A Week', 'I Feel Fine', 'She's A Woman'

1965

January–February: 'Another Girl', 'The Night Before', 'You've Got To Hide Your Love Away', 'Yes It Is', 'I Need You', 'Ticket To Ride', 'You Like Me Too Much', 'Tell Me What You See', 'Norwegian Wood', 'If You've Got Trouble', 'That Means A Lot'
May: 'Yesterday' (lyrics only, tune probably written late 1964–early 1965), 'I've Just Seen A Face'

June: 'I'm Down', 'It's Only Love', 'Wait'

September–October: 'Day Tripper', 'We Can Work It Out', 'Drive My Car', 'Nowhere Man', 'Think For Yourself', 'Michelle'(lyrics), 'In My Life', 'I'm Looking Through You', 'If I Needed Someone', 'Run For Your Life', 'She Said She Said'

November: 'The Word', 'You Won't See Me', 'Girl', '12-Bar Original'

December: 'Eleanor Rigby'

1966

January–April: 'Tomorrow Never Knows', 'Love You To', 'And Your Bird Can Sing', 'Rain', 'Paperback Writer', 'Dr Robert', 'Got To Get You Into My Life', 'Taxman', 'For No One' (March), 'I'm Only Sleeping' (March)

May: 'Yellow Submarine', 'Good Day Sunshine', 'I Want To Tell You'

June: 'Here There And Everywhere'

September–October: 'Strawberry Fields Forever'

November–December: 'Penny Lane', 'Sgt. Pepper's Lonely Hearts Club Band'

1967

January: 'A Day In The Life', 'Fixing A Hole', 'Lovely Rita', 'Good Morning, Good Morning', 'It's Only A Northern Song'

February: 'Being For The Benefit Of Mr Kite!', 'Lucy In The Sky With Diamonds', 'She's Leaving Home', 'Within You Without You'

March: 'With A Little Help From My Friends', 'Getting Better', 'Sgt. Pepper's Lonely Hearts Club Band (Reprise)', 'The Fool On The Hill'

April: 'Magical Mystery Tour', 'Baby You're A Rich Man'

May: 'You Know My Name Look Up The Number', 'It's All Too Much', 'All Together Now', 'All You Need Is Love', 'Your Mother Should Know'

July: 'I Am The Walrus'

August: 'Blue Jay Way'

September: 'Flying', 'Hello Goodbye'

December: 'Across The Universe', 'Step Inside Love'

1968

January: 'Inner Light', 'Lady Madonna', 'Hey Bulldog'

February–early April (India): 'The Continuing Story Of Bungalow Bill', 'I'm So Tired', 'Dear Prudence', 'Julia', 'Rocky Racoon', 'Mother Nature's Son', 'Back In The USSR', 'Ob-La-Di, Ob-La-Da', 'Junk',

'Yer Blues', 'Revolution', 'Sexy Sadie', 'Don't Pass Me By', 'Mean Mr Mustard', 'Polythene Pam', 'Teddy Boy', 'What's The New Mary Jane'

Mid-April–May: 'Blackbird', 'While My Guitar Gently Weeps', 'Piggies', 'Not Guilty', 'She Came In Through The Bathroom Window', 'Cry Baby Cry', 'Happiness Is A Warm Gun', 'Revolution 9'

June: 'Everybody's Got Something To Hide Except For Me And My Monkey', 'Helter Skelter', 'Good Night'

July: 'Hey Jude'

August: 'Wild Honey Pie'

September: 'Glass Onion', 'Martha My Dear', 'I Will', 'Birthday', 'Long, Long, Long', 'Honey Pie'

October: 'Why Don't We Do It In The Road?', 'Savoy Truffle', 'Something', 'Los Paranoias'

November–December: 'Let It Be', 'Long And Winding Road', 'Don't Let Me Down', 'All Things Must Pass', 'Two Of Us', 'I've Got A Feeling', 'For You Blue', 'Maxwell's Silver Hammer', 'Oh! Darling'

1969

January: 'Dig A Pony', 'Get Back', 'I Me Mine', 'Dig It', 'I Want You (She's So Heavy)', 'Octopus's Garden', 'Her Majesty'

February: 'Old Brown Shoe'

April: 'Here Comes The Sun', 'The Ballad Of John And Yoko', 'You Never Give Me Your Money'

June: 'Golden Slumbers', 'Carry That Weight'

July: 'Come Together', 'Because', 'Sun King', 'The End', 'Come And Get It'

Appendix 2

THE FUTURE? REPROGRAMMING
THE BEATLES ALBUM

New technologies look like liberating us from the pre-programmed album and the dud tracks that force us to leap up out of our seats to press the skip button. Music stored on databases that can be accessed via the internet or through high street stores should – record companies permitting – allow us to compile our own CDs, with our own favourite tracks.

For the Beatles albums this would offer the potential for us to omit our least favourite tracks and in many cases replace them with singles recorded concurrently. This would overcome George Martin's anguish over omitting 'Strawberry Fields Forever' and 'Penny Lane' from *Sgt. Pepper*. Elsewhere, consider the improved quality of *Beatles For Sale* with the omission of 'Honey Don't' and the addition of 'Leave My Kitten Alone'. *Help!* minus 'You Like Me Too Much' and 'Tell Me What You See' but with 'Yes It Is' and 'I'm Down' added would become a much more unsettling and interesting experience too. The opening four songs from *Rubber Soul* make the best introduction to any Beatles album before they are rudely interrupted by the graceless 'Think For Yourself' and the banal 'Act Naturally'; put 'Day Tripper' and 'We Can Work It Out' in their place and you have the arguably the best-ever Beatles album. Many like *Revolver* as it is, but both 'Paperback Writer' and 'Rain' fit in perfectly with the songs on it and here 'Dr Robert' and 'I Want To Tell You' would make good omissions. *The White Album* would be better as a single album, not just for its depth of quality but for the added potential this would give to programme it better, while 'Don't Let Me Down' would improve *Let It Be*.

What also of the Beatles compilation albums? For true aficionados the Beatles singles do not always represent their best songs. What also of a fantasy Beatles album, made up of the best songs the Beatles recorded solo in the two years following their split? Paul's 'Every Night', 'Maybe I'm Amazed', 'Another Day' and 'The Back Seat Of My Car' would all be strong contenders, not least because most were actually played to the other Beatles during the *Let It Be* sessions. Likewise John's 'Gimme Some Truth', 'Remember', 'Love' and 'Jealous Guy' were all started with the Beatles and 'Cold Turkey' was also originally offered to the Beatles too. From George you could add 'My Sweet Lord' plus songs again introduced to the Beatles, 'Isn't It A Pity?' and 'All Things Must Pass'. For good measure add Ringo's solo hit 'It Don't Come Easy', a co-composition with George.

Bibliography

Since 1990 I have dipped into countless books looking for Beatles references and anecdotes while researching *Beatles For Sale* (or *Story Of the Beatles Songs*, as it was once called). All the important texts are laid out below, but there are countless others I have dipped into.

KEY SOURCES

All You Need Is Ears George Martin with Jeremy Hornsby (Macmillan, 1979)

The Beatles Hunter Davies (Jonathan Cape, 1985)

The Beatles: 25 Years In The Life Sidgwick & Jackson (Mark Lewisohn, 1987)

The Beatles Anthology the Beatles (Cassell & Co, 2000)

The Beatles Lyrics (MacDonald, 1969)

The Beatles Recording Sessions Mark Lewisohn (Hamlyn, 1988)

The Complete Beatles Chronicle Mark Lewisohn (Pyramid Books, 1992)

Get Back: The Beatles' Let It Be Disaster Doug Sulphy & Ray Schweighardt (Helter Skelter Publishing, 1998)

Last Interview – All We Are Saying David Sheff (Sidgwick & Jackson, 2000)

Lennon Remembers Jann S. Wenner (Verso, 2000)

Mersey Beat: The Beginnings Of the Beatles Bill Harry (Omnibus Press, 1977)

Paul McCartney: Many Years From Now Barry Miles (Secker & Warburg, 1997)

Summer Of Love: The Making Of Sgt. Pepper George Martin (Macmillan, 1994)

SECONDARY SOURCES

AWopBopaLooBopALopBamBoom Nik Cohn (Paladin, 1970)

Apple To The Core: The Unmaking Of the Beatles Peter McCabe and Robert D. Schonfield (Brian & O'Keefe, 1972)

Beatlesongs William J. Dowlding (Fireside, 1989)

The Beatles Off The Record Keith Badman (Omnibus Press, 2000)

Be My Baby Ronnie Spector and Vince Waldron (Harmony Books, 1989)

Call Up The Groups: The Golden Age of British Beat 1962–67 Alan Clayson (Blandford, 1985)

A Cellarful Of Noise Brian Epstein (Souvenir Press, 1964)

Come Together: John Lennon In His Time Jon Wiener (Faber and Faber, 1984)

Days In The Life Jonathan Green (Minerva, 1989)

Drummer Out! Spencer Leigh (Northdown Publishing, 1998)

Guinness Book Of Rock Stars, Dafydd Rees & Luke Crampton (Guinness Publishing, 1991)

A Hard Day's Write Steve Turner (Carlton, 1999)

I Me Mine George Harrison (W.H. Allen, 1980)

I'll Never Walk Alone Gerry Marsden and Ray Coleman (Bloomsbury, 1993)

It Was Twenty Years Ago Today Derek Taylor (Bantam Press, 1987)

Jimi Hendrix Concert File Tony Brown (Omnibus Press, 1999)

John Lennon In His Own Words Barry Miles (Omnibus Press, 1980)

John Lennon In My Life Pete Shotton and Nicholas Schaffner (Coronet, 1983)

John Winston Lennon Volume 1: 1940–66 and *John Ono Lennon Volume 2: 1967–80* Ray Coleman (Sidgwick and Jackson, 1984)

The Lennon Tapes Andy Peebles (BBC Publications, 1981)

Let's Go Down The Cavern Spencer Leigh (Vermilion & Co, 1984)

The Lives Of John Lennon Albert Goldman (Bantam Press, 1988)

Love Me Do: The Beatles Progress Michael Braun (Penguin Books, 1964)

The Love You Make: An Insider's Story Of the Beatles Peter Brown and Steven Gaines (Macmillan, 1983)

The Man Who Gave the Beatles Away Allan Williams and William Marshall (Elm Tree Books, 1975)

McCartney Chris Salewicz (St Martins Press, 1986)

The Phil Spector Story Rob Finnis (Rockon, 1975)

The Quarrymen Hunter Davies (Omnibus Press, 2001)

The Quiet One – A Life Of George Harrison Alan Clayson (Sidgwick & Jackson, 1990)

Revolution In The Head Ian MacDonald (Pimlico, 1998)
Shout! Philip Norman (Elm Tree Books, 1981)
Skywriting By Word Of Mouth John Lennon (Pan Books, 1986)
A Twist Of Lennon Cynthia Lennon (Star, 1978)
Yesterday: The Beatles Remembered (Sidgwick and Jackson, 1988)

MAGAZINE ARTICLES
Guitar Player Magazine November 1987
Jamming! Interview by Tony Fletcher 1982

WEBSITES
www.pootle.demon.co.uk The What Goes On website – this is an amazing collection of recording anomalies on the Beatles recordings.
www.about.com/beatles Until it disappeared recently this site had every worthwhile Beatles site on the net listed.

NEWSPAPERS
I have used brief quotes from articles in the *New Musical Express, London Evening Standard* and *Daily Mirror*.